IN
THE HOUSE
OF
STONE
AND LIGHT

Introduction to
the Human History
of Grand Canyon

By
J. Donald Hughes
University of Denver

Copyright © 1978 Grand Canyon Natural History Association
ISBN 0-938216-00-7   LCN 77-93502
Reprinted 1985, 1988, 1991, 1997
Printed in the U.S.A. on recycled paper.

Editor/Project Coordinator: Timothy J. Priehs
Book designer: Christina Watkins
Cover designer: Kim Buchheit

Cover photo (center): Wotan's Throne and Vishnu Temple succumb to afternoon shadows.
Photo by Mike Buchheit
Cover photo (upper right): Hopi children of Walpi c. 1900. GCNP Museum Collection image #9064
Back cover photo: Cheops Pyramid looms above Plateau Point Trail. Photo by Mike Buchheit

CONTENTS

Foreword 1

1 Human History in the Natural Scene 4

2 American Indians 8

3 Spanish Explorations 16

4 American Explorations 24

5 The American Frontier Reaches the Grand Canyon 42

6 Forest Reserve and National Monument 64

7 Grand Canyon National Park:
　　Period of Establishment 84

8 Grand Canyon National Park:
　　Period of Expansion 102

EXPEDITION OF 1872.

1ST LIEUT. GEO. M. WHEELER.
Corps of Engineers, Commanding

This book is a fully revised, rewritten, and updated version of *The Story of Man at Grand Canyon* (Grand Canyon Natural History Association, 1967). Grand Canyon National Park has been expanded to almost double its former area since the earlier book was written, expanding the geographical and cultural frame of the human history included in this book. Ten eventful years have been added to history as well, years during which ecology and environmentalism became widely known words in America. Readers will find more emphasis on American Indians in this book.

The author would like to thank the Grand Canyon National History Association for the invitation to write this new book. The text was reviewed in whole or part by P. T. Reilly, Robert C. Euler, and Louise M. Hinchliffe, as well as the editor, Tim Priehs. These good people helped the author avoid numerous errors; any that remain are not their responsibility, but his. The author also appreciates the work of C. Gregory Crampton, whose *Land of Living Rock* (New York: Alfred A. Knopf, 1972) is an important contribution to Grand Canyon history. In conclusion, I wish to dedicate this book to my beloved parents, Johnson Hughes and Vannelia Blanchfield Hughes.

J. Donald Hughes
Denver, Colorado,
1977

1

HUMAN HISTORY IN THE NATURAL SCENE

The drama of human history in the Grand Canyon region has been enacted on an incomparable stage. But in this drama, the Canyon itself is not just the background scenery for human events; it is an active participant that shapes and colors those events.

The Grand Canyon has been known to human beings for thousands of years. Indians discovered, explored and may have lived inside it as long as 10,000 years ago, and the Spanish conquistadors stood baffled on its rim eighty years before the Pilgrims landed at Plymouth Rock. But in the history of the United States, excluding Alaska, it was one of the last areas to be explored thoroughly, and one of the last to be entered by the westward-moving frontier. These facts can be explained partly by the Grand Canyon's particular location within what has come to be called the American Southwest, and also by what the Canyon is—an intimidating, impressive stretch of topography that has interrupted the ordinary course of human history in this region, and caused its currents to flow in remarkable channels.

The Grand Canyon is far from an ordinary environment, so that its influences on and interactions with people have been exceptional. It is mostly uninhabited, yet the Havasupai Indians have called it home for many centuries. Its first official American explorers came by boat through a desert on a perilous river. It is visited each year by three million people, most of whom come in automobiles, but from one end of it to the other there is no highway bridge across the Colorado River. One can stand on a crowded hotel terrace and gaze across vast segments of wilderness.[1]

The Grand Canyon is the major chasm of the Colorado River and its tributaries, extending from below Lee's Ferry near the northern boundary of Arizona southward and then westward to the Grand Wash Cliffs near Arizona's western boundary, a distance of 277 miles (445 km.). This includes Marble Canyon, which is, topographically speaking, the first subsection of Grand Canyon entered by the river, and which is within the national park.[2] The Grand Canyon is about one mile (1600 m.) deep in its central section, and the rim at Point Imperial rises more than 6600 feet (2000 m.) above the river. The width is variable, but averages about 10 miles (16 km.) from rim to rim. The space between the rims is filled with a series of long, curving cliffs that descend in gigantic, step-like terraces to the river, and rise in towers, buttes and mesas of mountainous size. Historically, the Grand Canyon has been a geographical barrier for human beings. Travelers through the region on foot, on horseback, in boats, or by automobile have found it a formidable obstacle. Because it is easier to get into it than to get out, some have found it a trap, a prison, or even a grave.

The Grand Canyon was formed by the erosive work of the Colorado River and its tributaries, cutting downward through the slowly rising plateaus of northern Arizona over a period of perhaps 10,000,000 years. But the rocks through which it has been cut contain the stratified record of their own formation, as long ago as almost 2,000,000,000 years. In many layers, the fossil record of ancient life forms is preserved. The Canyon is an unmatched geological textbook whose rocky pages lie open to be read, and therefore have been of great value to science. Its mineral deposits are fewer than one might expect, but salt, copper, asbestos, vanadium, and uranium have been mined here at times in the past.

This river that has formed the topography of the region is still at work. One of the major rivers of North America, it flows 1800 miles (2900 km.) to the Gulf of California in Mexico. It drains a generally arid basin of 242,000 square miles (627,000 sq. km.), where undependable precipitation results in a runoff that is extremely variable from year to year. Since records began, the annual natural flow at Lee's Ferry has varied from 5.6 to 24 million acre feet (6800 to 29,300 cu. km.).[3] As a wild river it was heavily silt-laden, carrying about 500,000 tons of sand and mud past a given point in an average day, along with large amounts of dissolved limestone and other minerals. Thus the water of the Colorado River in the Grand Canyon, though potable before its pollution by human beings in the last few decades, is hard, somewhat unpalatable, and difficult of access. Through most of history it has not been used to a great extent in this very region whose dryness makes water a crucial need for all living things.

Nor is the Colorado River a navigable stream in the usual sense. Within the Canyon it drops 2215 feet (675 meters), passing over many dangerous rapids in the course of its fall at a speed as high as 20-25 miles per hour (32-40 kph.).[4] The river bed is filled with enormous boulders. During floods, the sound of moving rocks can be almost deafening. Such a river could never be used for dependable transportation, and some early attempts to boat it met disasters. Even the modern river trips that take passengers through for recreation in light craft with experienced guides have not completely removed the dangers and sense of adventure.

The use of the latent power of the river's falling water forms a late and controversial chapter in the story of human impact upon the Canyon. Major projects to generate power and divert water for agricultural, industrial, and domestic use have been located below and above the Grand Canyon.

The Grand Canyon region is a mosaic of climates that vary mainly with elevation. Although it is generally arid,

The Colorado River near the mouth of Bright Angel Creek. Photo by David C. Ochsner

and its lowest depths lie in the zone of hot deserts, it is not all desert. The Kaibab Plateau, whose edge forms part of Grand Canyon's North Rim, lies at an elevation of 8000 to 9000 feet (2400 to 2800 meters). It receives on an average 27 inches (69 cm.) of precipitation often including over 200 inches (500 cm.) of snow each year. Summers are mild and winters severe, and human occupation on the North Rim has been limited generally to the summer months. The Coconino Plateau, the southern extension of the Kaibab, is lower, at 6000 to 7000 feet (1800 to 2200 meters), and receives almost 15 inches (38 cm.) of precipitation, with about 60 inches (150 cm.) of snow annually. Temperatures are warm in the summer and cold in the winter, while general dryness and altitude combine to produce considerable daily variation of temperature. Climates on the lower plateaus bordering the Canyon, and within the Canyon itself, become warmer and dryer as one descends. At the bottom, one is inside the Inner Gorge at river level, from 900 to 3000 feet (300 to 900 meters) above sea level. Here rainfall averages 7 inches (17 cm.), and in an average year there is no snow. The Inner Gorge presents the climatic conditions of a true desert, and these conditions are magnified by the reflecting and confining canyon walls.

Patterns of vegetation and animal life also tend to follow contour lines of elevation. Early ecologists described the Southwest as a series of "life zones," each with its own typical communities of plants and animals, in broad horizontal bands stacked one above the other according to the elevation of the land. Such life zones are clearly visible in many places as belts of differing vegetation, although the picture is complicated by many forces other than elevation, such as soil, exposure, local sources of water, and prevailing currents of air.[5]

The Kaibab Plateau is covered by a tall forest of conifers and aspen, interrupted by broad meadows. The Coconino Plateau has a typical pinyon-juniper forest, with some groves of ponderosa pine. These forests, especially those on the Kaibab, have been exploited for timber. Both the North and South rims are formed of Kaibab limestone, a permeable rock in which the few permanent springs that may occur are small.[6] Water is found in intermittent tanks or pools. Soil is thin and poor. All

these factors combined to make human agriculture on the plateaus marginal at best, although early inhabitants built check dams and ditches to control erosion and spread floodwaters across their cornfields. Cattle and sheep were brought in later to graze in season on the plateaus. Some of the lower plateaus, and such relatively flat areas within the Canyon as the Tonto Platform, a shelf above the Inner Gorge,

are covered by typical high desert vegetation. Here, as in the lower desert life zone of the Inner Gorge, water is the limiting factor. Cottonwood trees grow near widely spaced springs and along watercourses. Where relatively level soil occurs near a dependable source of water, as at Indian Gardens, on creek deltas along the Colorado River, or on the flat alluvial floor of Havasu Canyon, intensive irrigation agriculture has been practiced.[7]

Along with plants, animals are active members of the living communities in the Canyon region. In times past, the human inhabitants regularly hunted wildlife such as deer, bighorn sheep, and rabbits. Beavers, inhabiting river and stream banks, were sought by white trappers. Birds are abundant at the Canyon. Indians used the meat and feathers of

Vishnu Temple by W. H. Holmes

5

many species, and may have domesticated the turkey. They caught and ate some lizards, including the chuckwalla. Although a few native fishes occur in the Colorado, Indians of the region generally did not eat fish.

The early Indians who settled in the Grand Canyon region, raising crops, gathering wild plants, and hunting, found that their needs were met, and called the Canyon their home. But when other people moved into the Grand Canyon region, they affected the interacting animal and plant communities they found there. While Indians, for the most part, were careful of their natural environment and fit into the "web of life" without breaking its strands, later arrivals were not so careful. As is described in a later chapter, one of the most famous cases of an upset of the balance of nature, involving the Kaibab deer herd, was recorded at Grand Canyon. Other interferences with nature have occurred. Foreign species, notoriously the destructive burro and a host of weed plants, have been introduced. An upstream dam has changed the temperature and patterns of flow of the river, with impacts on life forms. But for the last several decades, large sections of the region have been designated as natural areas and protected against many destructive uses. Thus the living communities of Grand Canyon may be seen today in something like their undisturbed state.

Perhaps the most noticeable effect the Grand Canyon has had on human beings is simply the total impression it has on the senses. It is one of the wonders of the world, not just because of its grand proportions, but because it *looks* grand. There is another canyon many times larger, but it is on Mars, and few people will stand on its rim to decide if it is grander. The spectacle of the Canyon has drawn visitors from all over the world, and those who would provide the services they want. So railroads and highways snaked

their way up to the brink of a gorge they would otherwise have avoided. Miners who came to find gold in the Canyon's ore pockets stayed when they found it instead in the tourists' trousers pockets.

But beyond this, one aspect of the Grand Canyon's natural scene is an intangible element, impossible to define. There have always been individuals who have found the Canyon mysterious, filled with awe-inspiring power, strangely both attractive and repellent, beautiful and charged with meaning. From the earliest Indians who placed figurines in its caves to the latest gasp of a visitor, human reactions to the Canyon have involved the heart, mind, and spirit. Artists have been inspired to paint, musicians to compose, and authors to write. One poet said the Canyon has "power upon the soul of man, to lift him up through wonder into joy."[8] Yet other writers have said that words are inadequate to the subject. Some who visit

the Grand Canyon are unimpressed, but others try to relate it to the nature of the universe. Upon mankind as a whole, the Canyon has exerted an esthetic, scientific, emotional, and even a religious challenge. No historian of the Grand Canyon can fail to remark upon these unique effects of its primitive immensity, form, and color, because the meanings that the Canyon has had for human beings are responsible for much of its unusual history. Among other reactions, many have seen it as a treasure that ought to be held in trust for the present and future people of America and the world. Its designation as a national park was intended to accomplish that preservation, so that others who follow will find the natural scene unmarred as history continues in the house of stone and light.

Postage stamps honoring the Grand Canyon and its history.

1. Joseph Wood Krutch, *Grand Canyon* (New York: Doubleday, 1962), pp. 6-7.

2. There is no good geographical or geological reason for the traditional designation of the junction of the Colorado and Little Colorado Rivers as the head of Grand Canyon. Marble and Grand Canyons are continuous, and the place where Marble Canyon visually "widens out" into Grand Canyon is about ten miles (16 km.) north of the river junction, upstream on the Colorado.

3. U. S. Department of the Interior, National Park Service, *Draft Environmental Statement* DES 76-28; *Proposed Wilderness Classification for Grand Canyon National Park* (Denver Service Center, National Park Service, 1976), pp. II-7-10.

4. P. T. Reilly, letter to Merrill D. Beal, Jr., December 1,1968. Reilly's considerable experience on the river adds authority to his estimate of its speed.

5. See the descriptions of Southwestern ecosystems in Victor E. Shelford, *The Ecology of North America* (Urbana, Illinois: University of Illinois Press, 1963).

6. D. G. Metzger, *Geology in Relation to Availability of Water along the South Rim, Grand Canyon National Park, Arizona*, U. S. Geological Survey Water Supply Paper 1475-C.

7. For a good summary of this whole matter see Robert C. Euler, "The Canyon Dwellers," *American West* 4(May 1967): 22-27, 67-71.

8. Henry Van Dyke, *Chosen Poems* (New York: Charles Scribner's Sons, 1929), p. 62.

2

AMERICAN INDIANS

Made of split willow twigs, this 4,000 year old figure is typical of those found in caves in the Redwall limestone.

Ancestral American Indians were the first people who discovered and explored the Grand Canyon, and lived in the Grand Canyon region.[1] Just when the first human beings came to the Canyon rim is not known, but they must have encountered a view much like one that can still be seen today. Among the earliest signs of human use of the Canyon are split-twig animal figurines, found in remote caves in the Redwall limestone cliffs.[2] According to recent corrections of the radiocarbon dating method, these figurines are 3,200 to 5,000 years old.[3] They were undoubtedly made by hunters, since they seem to represent species that were hunted: mountain sheep, deer, or pronghorn antelope. Moreover, many were pierced by small spears made of sticks or agave thorns.

There are no signs to indicate that anyone actually lived in the caves where figurines were found, but strong suggestions of magic and ritual exist. A shrine-like structure of stone, objects resembling prayer-sticks with feathers attached, and a lock of human hair suspended by twine were found, and the figurines themselves were carefully cached as a rule.[4] One can imagine groups of hunters seeking out caves and other mystical spots in which they could place their offerings, hoping that the symbolic slaying of small figurines would draw the animals themselves to appear so that they could be similarly killed in the hunt. Rituals of this general type are known to have been practiced by many early hunting societies.

Similar figurines have been found elsewhere in northern Arizona, Utah, Nevada, and California's Mojave Desert. Archaeologists have identified the figurine makers with the Desert Culture, widespread in western North America during that period. Desert Culture

projectile points and other chipped-stone tools have been discovered on Red Butte, not far south of the South Rim.[5] Archaeological remains of Desert Culture people show that they hunted large and small animals and collected a wide variety of plant foods in season. They had baskets, woven sandals, fiber nets, and grinding stones for wild seeds. Apparently they knew their environment intimately and made good use of the resources available to them.

About 2,000 years ago, groups of people of Desert Culture background adopted maize and squash farming from their neighbors to the south, and agriculture altered their way of life. Maize, originally domesticated in Mexico, had reached southern New Mexico about 5,000 years ago.

In the Grand Canyon region, the earliest farmers are known as Anasazi, from a Navajo word meaning "Ancient Ones." The archaeological term, "Anasazi," includes both the Basketmakers and Pueblo Indians. Those who lived between about

A.D. 1 and A.D. 700 are called Basketmakers because of the variety of well-made and beautifully decorated baskets that they produced, using twisted and coiled grass and yucca leaves. Often the baskets were woven tightly enough to hold water, or waterproofed with pinyon pine resin. Others were large and conical, with tumplines attached for carrying.

By A.D. 600, they had learned to make pottery, baked for durability. Pieces of this pottery indicate that a few Basketmakers occupied the North Rim. Some also lived on the South Rim, but this was mostly the land of another people, the Cohonina.

The Basketmakers' preference for sheltered locations under overhanging cliffs as homesites preserved many of the objects used in their daily lives. Surface shelters were replaced in the later period by pithouses, consisting of an excavated foundation with a roof above supported by poles and covered with bark and earth. They were a short-statured, long-headed people who wore sandals and were fond of ornaments such as necklaces and ear pendants made of stone, shell traded from the Pacific Ocean, bone, seeds, and feathers. They wore robes made of fur strips or deerskins, and fine woven belts, sashes, and loin cloths. Women wore aprons of juniper bark or yucca fibers.

They tilled the earth with sharpened digging sticks, and ground dried maize kernels between stones: a flat metate and a hand-held mano. They had domestic dogs and turkeys. Agriculture did not completely displace the older practices of hunting and foraging for wild foods. They used throwing sticks and spears aided by spear-throwers, or atlatls, and later adopted bows and arrows.

That the Basketmakers had rich religious rituals is clear from the evidence of petroglyphs and clay figurines, showing human beings, animals and kachina-like figures. They smoked native tobacco in tubular "pipes" on ceremonial occasions, and played music on six-hole flutes like those still used in the Hopi flute dance. Medicine men assembled curative plants, minerals and other sacred objects in special bundles, and made prayer sticks adorned with feathers as offerings. The care with which they buried their dead, including grave offerings, indicates that they believed in life after death.

Around 700 A.D. major changes occurred in the Basketmaker way of life, causing archaeologists to apply a different name, Pueblo, to the Anasazi cultural tradition as it developed from that time on. Modern Pueblo Indians, including the Hopi, continue the same tradition and are, at least in part, their descendants. "Pueblo," a Spanish word meaning "town," refers to the fact that their rectangular houses were built above ground, first of poles and adobe mud, and later of stone masonry. Kivas, or special rooms for religious purposes, were built partly underground in the style of the older pithouses. Hard cradle boards flattened and broadened Pueblo skulls.

Pueblo Indians developed several styles of pottery—banded, decorated, and painted in different colored patterns. Stone and bone tools were made. They grew cotton, spun and wove it in beautiful patterns. Men wore kilts or loin cloths and women wore fringed aprons; all donned robes or blankets in cold weather.

Pueblo villages were independent, like Greek city-states. Rules and customs became highly developed. Reflecting their agricultural way of life, the Pueblos' religion sought rain in a dry land, and fertility for life-sustaining crops. Elaborate ceremonies included masked and costumed dancers. With pictographs and murals they decorated kiva walls, caves, and cliffs. The influences of great civilizations flourishing in Mexico traveled northward with trade. Macaw feathers, and even live birds, were prized, and copper bells tinkled among a people who

had never before used metal. Mosaic inlay with turquoise, jet, shell and other materials was known in Mexico long before it was practiced as an art among the Pueblos. Certain motifs in art seem to have come from the south, as do some elements of Pueblo mythology and ceremonial, perhaps including the snake dance. The ancient Pueblos were not "southwesterners"; they were on the northern edge of the widespread Mesoamerican civilization.

The Grand Canyon formed a western frontier area for the Kayenta, one of

the major subdivisions of Pueblo culture. During their developmental period, between A.D. 700 and 1000, there was limited but growing use of the area. Small houses, terraces and irrigation ditches were built in fertile spots on both rims and in the Canyon. Pueblo occupation of the Grand Canyon accelerated between A.D. 1000 and 1100, until hundreds of sites were inhabited on the plateaus and in nooks and crannies of the Canyon itself, from rims to river, constituting the most extensive human population of the abyss in its entire history. Pueblo Indians

These Pueblo ruins, used as living quarters and for food storage, are perched under overhanging cliffs near Point Sublime.

developed a well-balanced ecology in the Grand Canyon area, finding sources of water, growing crops in every available spot, carefully practicing erosion control and other conservation measures,[6] and supplementing their food supply by hunting and gathering. Water and terrain limited and channeled the use of resources. Although more than 2,000 sites have been found in the immediate area of the Grand Canyon, these never rivaled the size and grandeur of Kayenta centers such as Betatakin, or the Pueblo metropoles at Mesa Verde and Chaco Canyon.

Between A.D. 1150 and 1200, Pueblo Indians abandoned the Grand Canyon almost totally. The small ruin called Tusayan on the South Rim, occupied by about 30 people around A.D. 1185, may represent a stage in their withdrawal from the area.

What caused them to leave? Archaeologists cannot yet agree on the reason, or combination of reasons, that led to the exodus. Did hostile tribes move into the region, seriously threatening the Pueblo Indians or actually attacking them? Two groups, Paiutes to the north and Yuman-speaking Indians to the south, were entering the region at about this time. While some Pueblo structures, particularly those on pinnacles or rocky "islands" in the Canyon near the rim, have a defensive appearance, it is hard to imagine how they might have been used, and no evidence of actual violence has been found in Grand Canyon archaeological sites. Was there a "cold war," or competition for resources with invading groups? Did the Pueblos, in spite of their concern with conservation measures, exhaust their farmlands, firewood, or wild game? Had their population expanded beyond the carrying capacity of an arid land? Did the water supply fail due to changes in the climate? Some students of historic climatic change have identified an over-all drying trend during this period in the Southwest, and the Great Drought of A.D. 1276 to 1299 is famous, although it came a bit late to explain the Grand Canyon abandonment.[7]

While none of these reasons is completely satisfactory, the fact remains that after 1300, Pueblo Indians visited the Grand Canyon periodically, but did not live there. Where did they go? Most, probably, to the Hopi towns to the east.

From perhaps A.D. 600, the Coconino Plateau, Havasu Canyon, and parts of Grand Canyon south of the river were occupied by an agricultural and hunting people called Cohonina.[8] This early culture flourished in the area until its disappearance around 1150, near the time of Pueblo abandonment. Although similar to their Anasazi neighbors, the Cohonina seem to have lived a simpler life. Their buildings were of varying styles, mostly surface structures of wood or stone without indoor fires, but sometimes they constructed pithouses. Their pottery was gray ware, often covered with red hematite. They decorated rocks with petroglyphs, but little is known of their social and religious life. At present, archaeology has not quite made clear what happened to them. One theory holds that they retreated into Havasu Canyon and became the ancestors of the Havasupai. Another possibility is that they withdrew or were forced out of the region entirely, and that the ancestors of the Hualapai and Havasupai were instead a Yuman-speaking group from the west.[9]

The Grand Canyon is in the heart of Indian country today. The reservations of the Hualapai, Havasupai and Navajo tribes include parts of the Canyon, and the Paiute and Hopi reservations are not far away. These tribes have important roles in the history of the region, from early times to the present day.

The Hopis are one of the modern Pueblo peoples. Their villages and farms are about 100 miles (160 km) east of the Grand Canyon, located near permanent springs. Old Oraibi, founded about A.D. 1150, is the oldest town continuously inhabited on the same site in the U.S.

Terraced houses in the Hopi Pueblo of Oraibi, the oldest continuously inhabited settlement in the United States.

Two Hopi girls from Mishongnovi.

Havasu Falls in Havasu Canyon. Photo by David C. Ochsner

The Hopi have maintained their old ways of life and traditional religion. The Grand Canyon figures in Hopi religion as the symbolic place where human beings and animals emerged from the underworld, and the place through which the dead return thence.[10] The Sipapu, or entrance to the underworld, is traditionally located in the canyon of the Little Colorado River about 4½ miles (7 km.) above the junction with the Colorado, and was marked by a bright yellow, circular spring about 10 feet (3 meters) in diameter atop a travertine dome about 90 feet (27 meters) in diameter.[11] It has long been an object of pilgrimages for the Hopis, who also make trips to a ceremonial salt deposit near the Colorado River, below the mouth of the Little Colorado.[12] They climbed down into the canyon of the Little Colorado from the northeast. A trade route to the Havasupai brought the Hopi into another part of the Grand Canyon, as did hunting trips and expeditions to gather the sacred Douglas-fir. They also descended along the line of the Grandview Trail to Horseshoe Mesa, where they collected blue copper ore for use in paints.[14] The Tanner Trail, too, is an old Hopi route. Ruins and sherds of Hopi pottery suggest frequent visits to Grand Canyon, as do clan symbols on the rocks. Several Kachinas, helpful spirits that Hopi masked dancers represent, are associated with Grand Canyon in legend.

The tribe most intimately familiar with the Grand Canyon is the Havasupai, since for centuries the southern tributary canyons and plateau have been their home.[15] They take their name, which means "people of the blue-green water," from the beautiful turquoise-colored pools and limestone-saturated water of Havasu (Cataract) Creek, which flows through the canyon that holds their village. The Havasupai were historically the easternmost band of a tribal grouping, all speaking the same Yuman language, who occupied much of northwestern

Arizona. The other bands are called the Hualapai, or "pine tree people," a name referring to the tall ponderosa pines that occur in the highest parts of their traditional land, which also includes a long stretch of the south side of the western Grand Canyon.[16] Some ethnologists refer to the Hualapai and Havasupai together as the "Northeastern Pai."[17]

The Northeastern Pai were hunters, gatherers and planters. They hunted almost every animal, large and small, that lived in the Grand Canyon region, using bows and arrows, and fiber nets. Among their wild plant foods were pinyon pine nuts, the stalk of the agave (which they roasted in pits), and the oily seeds of *sele*, the blazingstar. In canyon bottoms where water was dependable they planted maize and squash, constructing irrigation ditches. Crops were grown in Havasu Canyon and many other locations such as Meriwitica Creek and Diamond Creek (western tributaries), at Indian Gardens, creek deltas in the inner canyon, and even in Moencopi Wash on the eastern fringe of their territory. Those who farmed generally stayed in the canyons only during the summer growing season, spending the winter on the plateau where they hunted.

Northeastern Pai houses were dome-shaped, built of branches and covered with juniper bark held on with stout cords. In summer, a lighter, cooler brush shelter was often preferred. An earth-covered "sauna" sweat house, big enough for four men or so, usually stood nearby.

Skilled dressers of leather whose well-tanned deerskins were valuable in trade with other tribes, the Hualapai and Havasupai dressed in sewn buckskin garments: a shirt, loin cloth, and moccasins for a man, and a double apron and high moccasins for a woman. They made twined or coiled baskets in many shapes, with contrasting designs, and pottery, brown at first and later red. A red ochre clay used as face and body paint was mined at special locations in the Grand Canyon and served as an important trade item.

Their medicine men treated sickness with rituals and plant medicines. Songs and amulets assisted in hunting and healing. Eaglets were captured, raised for their feathers, and often later released. The Havasupai had a planting ritual in which prayers for a good crop were said toward a sacred location, "sweet corn," high on the canyon wall.[18] Each September the Havasupai invited their neighbors to the annual harvest dance. Northeastern Pai mythology placed the origin of mankind on a mountain near the Colorado River. Leaving their relatives the Mojave behind, they say they proceeded eastward to another sacred location, Meriwitica near Spencer Canyon, a tributary of Grand Canyon. From this place, the various people were dispersed over the earth; the Havasupai were led eastward by a frog to their own Havasu Canyon, where they settled because the frog loved the never-failing stream and green plants there.[19] The Hualapai remained in the country round about Meriwitica. These legends probably preserve a core of historical truth; the Yuman-speaking peoples came into the Grand Canyon from the west around A.D. 1150, and the Havasupai have been living in their Canyon home since at least the Twelfth Century.

Neither Hualapai nor Havasupai were much disturbed by contact with non-Indians before the Nineteenth Century. During the Spanish period they were less influenced by the visits of a wandering priest than by plants and animals that had been introduced into the New World by Spanish settlers and had reached the Northeastern Pai through trade with other Indians, particularly the Hopi. In this way they acquired peaches, figs, wheat, melons, cattle and horses. In the Mexican period they encountered a few predatory slave-traders. But almost all their outside contacts were with other Indians, the friendly Hopi, the enemy Yavapai and Mojave, and the ambivalent Paiute and Navajo.

Several bands of Paiutes occupied the plateau country north of the Grand Canyon. They had moved into that area southeastward from the Great Basin in the period after A.D. 1000, replacing an earlier Pueblo-like people.[20] The Paiute language is Shoshonean, distantly related to the Hopi language. In this speech, "Paiute" possibly means "true people." Among the bands whose range included parts of the Grand Canyon itself were the Kaibabits, Uinkarets, and Shivwits. They sustained themselves by hunting and gathering, and went where they could find food, in an annual cycle. In the fall, they came up onto the higher mountains, including the Kaibab plateau, to hunt deer and collect pine nuts. The name Kaibab means "mountain lying down" in the Paiute language, and the high plateau was regarded by them as common land, not the property of any one band or family group.

The Paiutes lived in scattered family groups. They clothed themselves in loin cloths or skirts made of deerskin or the bark of juniper or cliffrose. Their houses were branch and brush shelters. They made baskets and reddish brown pottery, usually conical in shape and decorated with fingernail incisions in rows. The fire drill, bows and arrows, and throwing stick for rabbits were well known to them, as well as grinding stones for seeds. They ventured into the Grand Canyon in search of rock salt and agave shoots, and sometimes crossed it to contact the Havasupai to the south. Some Paiutes ranged in the country east of Marble Canyon, where trade with the Hopis was usual, and hostilities with the Navajos later became common.

The Navajos reached the Grand Canyon later than any of the other tribes in this chapter.[21] Their ancestral home was in

Blind Havasupai woman grinding corn.
Photo courtesy of Southwest Museum,
Highland Park, California

14

western Canada, near other tribes that also speak Athapascan languages. They call themselves *Dineh*, which means "the People." They recognize many northern Athapascan words as similar to their own, and their older hogans and some of their other artifacts are like those of the Indians of western Canada. About A.D. 1000-1400, the Apaches and Navajos, then the same people, migrated southward across mountains and plains. They came as nomads, hunting and raiding. Finally they settled near the Pueblo Indians, and raided them at times. Navajos adopted many Pueblo customs such as raising maize and weaving, and some religious customs. Their Pueblo neighbors called them *Apaches de Nabahu*, or "enemies with cultivated fields," because the Navajo settled and raised crops, while their Apache relatives remained exclusively hunters and raiders. Navajo mobility and striking power increased when contact with the Spanish settlers gave them horses and sheep.

From their early center in northern New Mexico, the Navajos gradually spread westward into the Grand Canyon area.

1. For a synthesis of Grand Canyon prehistory, see Robert C. Euler, "The Canyon Dwellers," *American West* 4(May 1967): 22-27, 67-71. For a historical sketch of Grand Canyon archaeology, see Douglas W. Schwartz, "A Historical Analysis and Synthesis of Grand Canyon Archaeology," *American Antiquity* 31(April 1966): 469-84. Also useful are Joe Ben Wheat, *Prehistoric People of the Northern Southwest* (Grand Canyon Natural History Association, 1959) and Hannah Marie Wormington, *Prehistoric Indians of the Southwest*, 3rd ed. (Denver: Denver Museum of Natural History, 1956).

2. Douglas W. Schwartz, Arthur L. Lange, and Raymond de Saussure, "Split-Twig Figurines in the Grand Canyon," *American Antiquity* 23(January 1958):264-74. See also P. T. Reilly, "The Sites at Vasey's Paradise," *Masterkey* 40(October-December 1966):126-39.

3. Revised dates based on Trevor Watkins, ed., *Radiocarbon: Calibration and Prehistory* (Edinburgh: Edinburgh University Press, 1975).

4. Malcolm F. Farmer and Raymond de Saussure, "Split-Twig Animal Figurines," *Plateau* 27(April 1955):13-23.

5. Robert C. Euler, "Willow Figurines from Arizona," *Natural History* 75(March 1966):62-67. See also Charles McNutt and Robert C. Euler, "The Red Butte Lithic Sites Near Grand Canyon, Arizona," *American Antiquity* 31(January 1966):410-19

6. Hall, E. T., Jr., *Archaeological Survey of Walhalla Glades* (Flagstaff, Arizona: Museum of Northern Arizona, Bulletin 20, 1942).

7. Douglas W. Schwartz, "Climate Change and Culture History in the Grand Canyon Region," *American Antiquity* 22(April 1957):372-77. See also Richard Benjamin Woodbury, "Climatic Changes and Prehistoric Agriculture in the Southwestern United States," *Annals of the New York Academy of Sciences* 95(1961):705-709.

8. John C. McGregor, *The Cohonina Culture of Northwestern Arizona* (Urbana, Illinois: University of Illinois Press, 1951).

9. Douglas W. Schwartz, "The Havasupai 600 A.D.: A Short Culture History," *Plateau* 28(April 1956):77-85; "Prehistoric Man in the Grand Canyon," *Scientific American* 198(February 1958):97-102; and "Culture area and Time Depth: The Four Worlds of the Havasupai," *American Anthropologist* 61(1959):1060-70. See also Alfred F. Whiting, "Havasupai Characteristics in the Cohonina," *Plateau* 30 (January 1958):55-60.

10. Don Talayesva, *Sun Chief: The Autobiography of a Hopi Indian*, ed. by Leo W. Simmons (New Haven: Yale University Press, 1942), p. 241

11. Daniel E. Davis, *A Resume of the Scientific Values and Interpretive Potential of the Lower Portion of the Canyon of the Little Colorado River and Its Environs*, unpublished MS report (November, 1959), Grand Canyon National Park Library.

12. Fred B. Eiseman, Jr., "The Hopi Salt Trail," *Plateau* 32(October 1959):25-32. See also Mischa Titiev, "A Hopi Salt Expedition," *American Anthropologist* 39(April-June 1937):244-58.

13. Harold S. Colton, "Principal Hopi Trails," *Plateau* 36(Winter 1964):91-94.

14. Ernest Beaglehole, *Notes on Hopi Economic Life* (Yale University Publications in Anthropology, No. 15, New Haven, 1937), pp. 56-57.

15. Leslie Spier, *Havasupai Ethnography* (New York: Anthropological Papers of the American Museum of Natural History 29, No. 3, 1928). See also Albert H. Schroeder, "A Brief History of the Havasupai," *Plateau* 25(January 1953):45-52; and Henry F. Dobyns and Robert C. Euler, *The Havasupai People* (Phoenix: Indian Tribal Series, 1971).

16. Alfred Louis Kroeber, ed., *Walapai Ethnography* (Menasha, Wisconsin: Memoirs of the American Anthropological Association, No. 42, 1935).

17. Henry F. Dobyns and Robert C. Euler, *The Hualapai People* (Phoenix: Indian Tribal Series, 1976), and "A Brief History of the Northeastern Pai," *Plateau* 32(January 1960):49-57.

18. P. T. Reilly, "The Disappearing Havasupai Corn-Planting Ceremony," *Masterkey* 44(1970):30-34.

19. Juan Sinyella, "Havasupai Traditions," ed. by J. Donald Hughes, *Southwest Folklore* 1(Spring 1977):35-52.

20. Isabel T. Kelly, *Southern Paiute Ethnography* (Salt Lake City: University of Utah, Anthropological Papers, No. 69, May, 1964), pp. 5-141. See also Robert C. Euler, *The Paiute People* (Phoenix: Indian Tribal Series, 1972), and *Southern Paiute Ethnohistory* (Salt Lake City: University of Utah, Anthropological Papers, No. 78, April, 1966).

21. Ruth Murray Underhill, *The Navajos* (Norman: University of Oklahoma Press, 1956). See also Henry F. Dobyns and Robert C. Euler, *The Navajo People* (Phoenix: Indian Tribal Series, 1972), and Clyde Kluckhohn and Dorothea Leighton, *The Navajo* (Garden City, New York: Natural History Library, 1962).

3

SPANISH EXPLORATIONS

aying in the far northern borderlands of New Spain, the Grand Canyon was discovered early in the Spanish period, although it was more often avoided than visited. In September, 1540, white men saw the Grand Canyon for the first time. This discovery was an incident in the search for the Seven Cities of Cíbola by Francisco Vásquez de Coronado and happened only twenty years after Cortez's conquest of Mexico. Since the riches of Mexico had surpassed all expectations of the conquistadores, they might well have expected to find other rich cities.

Nuño de Guzmán, a rival of Cortez, heard in 1529 from an Indian that seven rich cities lay in the northern interior of New Spain. This reminded him of the medieval tale of Seven Cities of Antilia, reportedly founded by seven Christian bishops who had fled westward across the sea to escape the conquering Moslems. Guzmán tried in vain to find them.

Seven years later, four ragged survivors of an expedition Pánfilo de Narváez had made to Florida showed up in Mexico City and gave new life to the legend of the Seven Cities. The four were Álvar Núñez Cabeza de Vaca, Dorantes, Castillo, and Dorantes' black slave, Estéban. They had come overland most of the way from Florida and reported that in the lands beyond those through which they had passed there were large cities, with riches of pearls and other gems, copper, gold and silver.[2]

The Viceroy of Mexico, Antonio de Mendoza, decided to investigate and, buying Estéban, sent him as guide for the Franciscan friar, Marcos de Niza, on a reconnaissance toward the north. After traveling for a month, Fray Marcos sent Estéban ahead, with instructions to send back a cross whose size would indicate the grandeur of what he found.[3] Soon Estéban sent Indians carrying a cross as

big as a man, with news of seven cities in the north, called Cíbola, where the houses were two and three stories high, and rich in turquoise. Actually, this report is a fairly good description of the Pueblos of Zuñi. Estéban proceeded to Cíbola (Zuñi), where his arrogant behavior provoked the Pueblo Indians to kill him.[4] A report of Estéban's death came to Fray Marcos, who wrote in his diary that he went forward to a hill from which he could see Cíbola, a city that seemed to him larger than Mexico City itself.

Encouraged by the friar's report, Mendoza in the early part of 1540 sent northward a great expedition by land and sea. An army of about 300 young Spaniards in armor, both cavalry and foot soldiers, and hundreds of Indian allies, led by Coronado, included Marcos de Niza, Pedro de Sotomayor, the official historian of the expedition, and Pedro de Castañeda, who, twenty years after the expedition, wrote the only full account that survives.[5] Hernando de Alarcón was appointed to take three ships up the western coast, maintaining contact with the army.

The Hopi pueblo of Walpi.

After four months of difficult travel, Coronado reached Cíbola and conquered it, but the Spaniards were disappointed at the lack of riches in the Pueblos of stone and mud. While at Cíbola, Coronado was told of a larger group of seven cities off to the west, called Tusayan (Tucano or Totonteac, actually the Hopi pueblos). In

Coronado's search for the Seven Golden Cities of Cibola ended in the conquering of stone and mud pueblos. Map courtesy of Southwestern Parks and Monuments Association

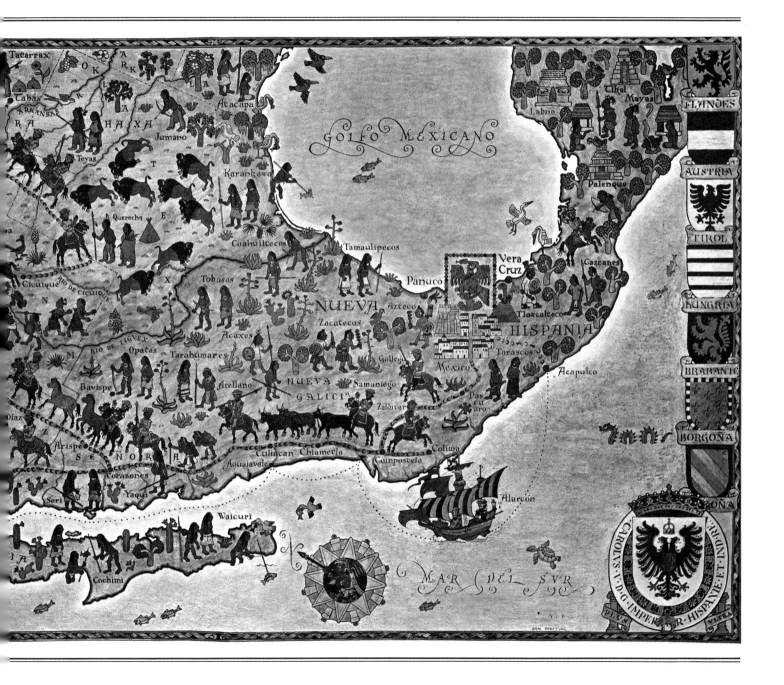

GOLFO MEXICANO

MAR DEL SUR

NUEVA HISPANIA

NUEVA GALICIA

FLANDES

AUSTRIA

TIROL

HUNGRIA

BRABANTE

BORGOÑA

CAROLVS · V · D · G · IMPER · R · HISPANIE · ET · IND · RR
PLVS VLTRA

Tatarrax
Tabas
ARKANSAS
Jumano
Teyas
Querecho
Cicuique
RIO DE CICUIQUE
RIO DE TIGUEX
Opatas
Bavispe
Diaz
Arispe
SEÑORA
Corazones
Seri
Yaqui
Waicuri
Cochimi

OKLAHOMA
HAXA
Atacapa
Karankawa
Coahuiltecos
Tobosos
Acaxes
Tarahumares
Arellano
Samaniego
Zaldivar
Aguaiavale
Culiacan
Chiametla
Compostela
Colima
Alarcon

Tamaulipecos
Azteco
NUEVA
Zacatecos
Gallego
Mexico
Pascuaro
Panuco
Vera Cruz
Tlaxcalteco
Tarascos
Acapulco
Gazcanes

Tikal
Mayas
Labna
Palenque

18

the middle of July, he dispatched Pedro de Tovar with a few soldiers to investigate. Returning after a month, Tovar reported that Tusayan was very much like Cíbola, but that the natives there had told him of a great river not far to the west, and of a land inhabited by people with very large bodies (probably they were referring to the Havasupai, who are generally much taller and heavier than the Hopi).

At the end of August Coronado sent a force under the command of García López de Cárdenas to find the river. Cárdenas, who is recognized as the Spanish discoverer of the Grand Canyon, was a tough, able soldier. He was the young second son of a nobleman, had married a distant cousin of Mendoza in Spain and had come to America in 1535. He led his men to Tusayan, where some Hopis offered to guide him to the river. They traveled for twenty days (according to Cárdenas) through relatively dry country, arriving at the rim of the Grand Canyon late in September.

Castañeda reports the surprise of the men at finding the opposite bank of the river "three to four leagues" (eight to ten miles or 12 to 16 km.) away from them.[6] The river itself appeared to be only six feet (two meters) wide, although the Indians assured the Spaniards that it was much wider than that. Indeed, the depth and vastness of the Grand Canyon were not immediately apparent to Cárdenas and his men. They spent three days searching for a way down to the river and, frustrated, sent three agile young men to clamber down over the rocks. These, the first white men to descend into the Grand Canyon, were infantry Captain Pablo de Melgosa of Burgos, Juan Galeras and a third man whose name is unknown. They discovered unexpected obstacles. "What appeared to be easy from above was not so, but instead very hard and difficult."[7] They managed to get down only one-third of the way, from which point the river seemed as wide as the Indians had said. When

The place where Castañeda first viewed the Grand Canyon was somewhere between Moran Point and Desert View. Photo by David C. Ochsner

they returned in the afternoon, they said that rocks which appeared from above to be about as high as a man proved when they reached them to be taller than the great tower of Seville. That tower, called the Giralda, was then 185 feet (56 meters) high.[8]

The place where Cárdenas and his men first saw the Grand Canyon is not known. Castañeda speaks of the country there as "elevated and full of low twisted pines, very cold, and lying open to the north."[9] The point on the South Rim which best fits this description is the area between Moran Point and Desert View, which is one of the higher sections of the South Rim, is covered with a low piñon-juniper forest, and has a wide view across the Painted Desert to the north and northeast. No other area on the South Rim could be called "open to the north," since the North Rim rises more than a thousand feet higher in that direction. The region around Desert View is closer to the Hopi Pueblos (Tusayan) than any other part of the South Rim, although old Hopi trails touched the Canyon at points from Topocoba Hilltop to the canyon of the Little Colorado.[10] The Hopis would naturally have led Cárdenas along one of their own trails. The most likely of these seems to be one that ran from Oraibi past Coal Canyon to Moenkopi, down Moenkopi Wash and across the Little Colorado, along the base of Gray Mountain, thence parallel to the Grandview Monocline, where there is a line of natural water tanks. This route would have brought them to the Grand Canyon somewhere in the area indicated above.

The accounts of the exploration are vague and general as to distance and direction, so that there is really no way to tell exactly what parts of the canyon rim Cárdenas' men explored. Lack of water handicapped them. Castañeda says it is for this reason that they went no further upstream, and that after four days of

exploring the canyon's rim, they were warned by the Indians that a dry region lay ahead which would take several days to cross.

So they returned, still guided by the Hopis. On the way they discovered a spring where they gathered salt crystals. This seems to indicate that they traveled near the Little Colorado, on which there are several salt deposits known to the Hopis. The ceremonial deposit cannot have been visited by the Spaniards, since it is next to the river, and it is unlikely that the Hopis would have taken the strangers to such a holy place. Indeed, the Hopis could easily have guided the Spaniards down to the river, had they wished to do so, since they knew of other routes into the Canyon besides the Salt Trail. But the Peaceful People did not trust the warlike invaders.

The Spaniards guessed correctly that the river was the Tisón (Firebrand) River, the name they then used for the Colorado. Alarcón had recently tried to sail up this river. The land and sea sections of the expedition to Cíbola never did make contact with one another. Cárdenas was, of course, much too far upstream to contact Alarcón. Another party of Coronado's men, under Melchior Díaz, reached the

Francisco Vasquez de Coronado, leader of the first major expedition of Europeans into the American Southwest (detail from painting by Fredrick Remington page 16). Courtesy Denver Public Library Western History Collection

Tisón only seventy-five miles above its mouth in October, but it was too late. All they found was a letter from Alarcón indicating that he had passed that way. Alarcón had made two trips upstream in August and September, with some help from the Yuman Indians. He estimated that he traveled about 225 miles (360 km.) up the river. The Indians told him that the white men had reached Cíbola, but he could not get any of his own men to attempt the overland trip to contact Coronado.

Coronado traveled on across the buffalo plains with his army, in search of a new legend called Quivira. With the failure of his expedition, the Grand Canyon and its neighboring plateaus were left to the Indians for more than two centuries.

New Spain had little interest in her northern borderlands for the next 40 years, but in 1598 New Mexico was colonized by soldiers, settlers, and Franciscan priests under Juan de Oñate. In 1629, five missions were etablished in the Hopi towns.

The Pueblo Indians came to resent Spanish rule. They were required to render unquestioning obedience and to pay a heavy tribute of handicrafts and other products, but most galling to them was the continuous effort of the Spaniards to stamp out their traditional religion and to compel them to become Christians. "Sorcery," as the Spaniards termed the observance of ancestral Pueblo ceremonials, was punishable by flogging, imprisonment, or even death. In 1680, at the instigation of Popé, a native religious leader, all the Pueblos including the Hopi rose up together in revolt, slaughtering some of the Spaniards and driving away the rest.[11] The reconquest of New Mexico was completed in 1695 by Diego de Vargas, but the Hopi never again submitted to Spain, and when one of their pueblos, Awatovi, admitted Spanish soldiers and a Franciscan priest in 1700, the rest of the Hopi destroyed it.

While the first wave of Spanish

explorers was composed primarily of military men and adventurers, the second wave to enter the Grand Canyon region was led by missionary priests. The Grand Canyon figures in their narratives as an impassable barrier on the routes they sought to follow, huge and inhospitable in aspect. Since conversion of the natives was a major purpose of their exploration, they encountered many of the tribes.

Father Eusebio Francisco Kino, a Jesuit priest from the Tyrol, founded a chain of missions in the Pima and Papago Indian country, which the Spanish called Pimería Alta. These missions included San Xavier del Bac (near present Tucson), founded in 1692. Though he never saw the Grand Canyon, he traveled several times across the lower Colorado River to California. When the Jesuits were expelled from Spanish dominions by the king in 1767, Father Kino's work was continued by Franciscan fathers, one of whom was to rediscover the Grand Canyon.

Francisco Tomás Garcés was a missionary who searched for new Indian tribes, to win their allegiance for his Church and king. He had been appointed priest at San Xavier in 1768, but spent much time exploring the vast country northward.

Garcés' fifth missionary journey began in October, 1775, when he set out with Juan Bautista de Anza on an expedition to found a mission and colony in Alta California. The settlement which became the city of San Francisco was founded by Anza in the eventful year of 1776, but Garcés had left the expedition long before, to explore the Colorado River from its mouth to the upper canyons. He traveled alone, with Indian guides, through the country of the hospitable Hualapais, where he had a view of the deep red gorges of the western Grand Canyon.[12]

On June 20, 1776, he came into the deep canyon of the "Río Jabesua" (Havasu or Cataract Creek) by traveling down a precipitous trail. At one point he had to climb down a ladder of wood.[13] He recognized the creek as a tributary of the Colorado. Its canyon, he noted, was so deep that the sun did not rise until ten o'clock, and its red soil, watered by the

creek, grew trees, grass and rich crops. He marveled at the Havasupais' irrigation system of dams and ditches, and noticed that they had horses and cattle that they had traded from the Hopi, and which he thought had been stolen originally from the Spaniards. The Havasupai prevailed

First to visit the Havasupai Indians, Spanish missionary Francisco Tomás Garcés was later martyred by another tribe.

upon him to stay for five days of generous feasting.

As a giver of names, Garcés has particular importance in the history of the region, for he was the first writer to refer consistently to the "Río Colorado," and the first European to name the Grand Canyon, although the name he selected did not pass into common usage.

He set out for the Hopi pueblos on June 25, 1776, going up another perilous trail onto a plateau covered with grass, pinyons, and junipers. On the following day he viewed the Grand Canyon, which he saw as an endless series of canyons, within which flowed the "Río Colorado" (Red River). He gave the Canyon the name "Puerto de Bucareli" (Bucareli Pass), after Antonio Maria Bucareli y Ursua, then Viceroy of New Spain, although Garces could see that it was a "pass" for the river alone, being far too difficult for human passage. The point at which Garcés reached that spectacular view of the Grand Canyon can only be guessed, but apparently it was from some distance across the plateau:

> From here I saw that in a very large mountain range extending from southeast to northwest and blue with distance a deep passage was cut, steep-sided like a man-made trough, through which the Colorado River enters these lands.[14]

He may also have reached the rim. "I am astonished," he exclaimed, "at the roughness of this country, and at the barrier which nature has fixed therein."[15] Like other early visitors, Garcés was impressed primarily by the Canyon as a barrier, rather than as scenery.

Crossing the Little Colorado, Garcés went on through Moenkopi to the Hopi pueblos. The Hopis would neither lodge nor feed him, or even take his gifts. He returned by the same route, arriving again in Havasu Canyon on July 9, where he was hailed with joy and given a six days' feast. On his second visit, he referred to the

Grand Canyon as "that calaboose [*calabozo,* prison] of cliffs and canyons."[16] Garcés visited the Hualapais again, then returned to San Xavier along the Colorado and Gila Rivers. He was killed five years later during an uprising of lower Colorado River Indians.

The last great Spanish exploration in the Colorado basin took place in 1776, when two Franciscan fathers, Silvestre Vélez de Escalante and Francisco Atanasio Domínguez, with Captain Bernardo Miera y Pacheco, tried to find a practical route between Santa Fe, New Mexico, and Monterey, California. They traveled far to the northwest, reaching "Timpanogotzis" (Utah Valley), and then, their purpose unachieved, returned to the south. They intended to cross the Colorado in that direction and visit the Havasupai, but Paiute Indians told them that the country ahead held little water, and they would not "be able to cross the river in this region because it ran through a tremendous gorge and was very deep, and had on both sides extremely high cliffs and rocks."[17]

Thus they were warned of the barrier which is the Grand Canyon. They turned to the east, seeing upper Marble Canyon as they searched for a ford of the river. This they found on November 7 at "El Vado de los Padres" (The Crossing of the Fathers) in Glen Canyon. They returned to Santa Fe by way of the Hopi pueblos. The Escalante-Domínguez expedition represents the high tide of Spain in the region.

The Louisiana Purchase of 1803 gave New Spain the young United States of America as northeastern neighbor, and although the border was in dispute until 1819, it was far from the Grand Canyon. Meanwhile, Spain's energies were engaged in combating a series of revolutions in Mexico, beginning in 1810, and no explorations were undertaken in the north during the Mexican struggle for independence.

From 1821 to 1848, the Grand

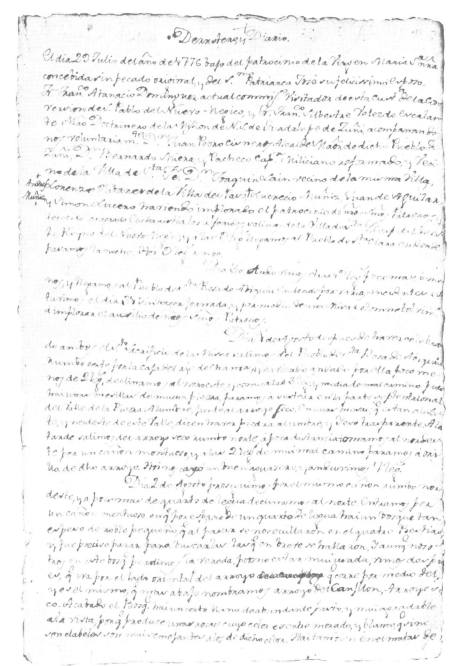

A page from the expedition diary of Father Silvestre Vélez de Escalante. Courtesy of the Ayer Collection, Newberry Library, Chicago, Illinois

Canyon was within the territory of an independent Mexico that was interested in developing trade in the north. A party led by Antonio Armijo traveled from Santa Fe to California to trade woolen goods for horses and mules in 1829-30. Using the Crossing of the Fathers, Armijo's route went north of the Canyon, roughly following the present Arizona-Utah line. A trail further north through central Utah was called the Old Spanish Trail because it was partly based on the route pioneered by Domínguez and Escalante. For the quarter-century of Mexican rule, no record exists of any visits to the Grand Canyon by Mexicans. American trappers are another story, one the next chapter will tell.

Formerly there were considered to be two great branches of the Colorado River. The longer of the two, the Green River, rises in Wyoming. The other was called the Grand River, with its source in Colorado. But many Coloradans wanted their state to have the river it was named after at least partly inside its borders, so at the urging of their representatives, Congress in 1921 changed the name of the Grand River to Colorado River.

1. Herbert E. Bolton, *Coronado on the Turquoise Trail: Knight of Pueblos and Plains* (Albuquerque: University of New Mexico Press, 1949), p. 6.

2. Álvar Núñez Cabeza de Vaca, *Adventures in the Unknown Interior of America,* trans. and ed. by Cyclone Covey (New York: Collier Books, 1961), pp. 108, 110, 119, 124, 132.

3. Fray Marcos de Niza, *Discovery of the Seven Cities of Cíbola* trans. and ed. by Percy M. Baldwin (Albuquerque: Historical Society of New Mexico, Publications in History, Vol. 1, November 1926), pp. 42-43.

4. Letter from Francisco Vásquez Coronado to Antonio de Mendoza, trans. by George Parker Winship, in *Fourteenth Annual Report of the Bureau of Ethnology, 1892-1893* (Washington: Government Printing Office, 1896), p. 563.

5. Pedro de Castañeda, "Relación de la Jornada de Cíbola," trans. and ed. by George Parker Winship, in *Fourteenth Annual Report of the Bureau of Ethnology, 1892-1893* (Washington: Government Printing Office, 1896), pp. 413-546.

6. *Ibid.* Compare the parallel account in the anonymous "Relación del Suceso," trans. by George Parker Winship, in *Fourteenth Annual Report of the Bureau of Ethnology, 1892-1893* (Washington: Government Printing Office, 1896), pp. 574-75.

7. *Ibid.*

8. The upper part of the tower, raising it to 295 feet (90 m.), plus a bronze figure 14 feet (4.3 m.) tall, were added in 1568, and thus were not known at the time to Cárdenas' men. *See* "Seville," *Encyclopedia Britannica,* 11th Edition, Vol. 24 (Cambridge, England: Cambridge University Press, 1911), p. 732a.

9. Castañeda, p. 429.

10. Katharine Bartlett, "How Don Pedro de Tovar Discovered the Hopi and Don García López de Cárdenas Saw the Grand Canyon, with Notes upon their Probable Route," *Plateau* 12(January 1940):35-45.

11. *See* Fray Angelico Chavez, "Pohe-Yemo's Representative and the Revolt of 1680," *New Mexico Historical Review* 42(1967):85-126. The black-faced kachina, often a protector of game, known as Chakwaina among the Hopi, is almost certainly aboriginal in Pueblo religion. Frederick J. Dockstader, in *The Kachina and the White Man* (Bloomfield Hills, Michigan: Cranbrook Institute of Science, 1954), pp. 11-12, 14, suggests that this figure was inspired by the arrival of Estéban, but this seems untenable in light of the unfavorable attitude of the Zuñis toward him. Chavez' theory of Black leadership in the Pueblo Revolt has more to commend it, but is also unlikely. Rather, the black-faced kachina is probably the origin of the rumors he has uncovered.

12. Francisco Tomás Hermenegildo Garcés, *A Record of Travels in Arizona and California, 1775-1776,* trans. and ed. by John Galvin (San Francisco: John Howell, 1967), pp. 63-64.

13. Francisco Tomás Hermenegildo Garcés, *On the Trail of a Spanish Pioneer: The Diary and Itinerary of Francisco Garcés (Missionary Priest),* trans. and ed. by Elliott Coues (New York: Francis P. Harper, 1900), pp. 335-46.

14. Garcés (Galvin), p. 67.

15. Garcés (Coues), p. 351.

16. *Ibid.,* p. 408.

17. Herbert E. Bolton, "Pageant in the Wilderness: The Story of the Escalante Expedition to the Interior Basin, 1776. Including the Diary and Itinerary of Father Escalante Translated and Annotated," *Utah Historical Quarterly* 18(1950):207

4

AMERICAN
EXPLORATIONS

While it was still part of Mexico, the Grand Canyon was first visited by men from the United States. Trappers and fur traders had tried to enter New Mexico in earlier days, but had met opposition from Spanish authorities. The new Mexican Republic was less opposed, and although non-Mexicans were required to have licenses to trap beaver after 1824, practically no Mexican supervision existed in the canyon and plateau country around the Grand Canyon, and the mountain men traveled there, searching for beaver and other furs, pretty much as they pleased.

Trappers steered clear of the Grand Canyon most of the time. The river with its water and beaver was at the bottom of a mile-deep chasm, and no record has survived of any mountain man entering the Canyon, although some probably did.

In 1825, one of the leading fur traders descended the upper Green River through several of its canyons, distinguishing himself and his six men as the first to attempt a boat trip down the Colorado's "mainstream." William Henry Ashley was a frontier businessman who made a fortune through his Rocky Mountain Fur Company. During his eventful trapping expedition of 1825, he constructed two frame canoes covered with buffalo hides, called "bullboats," put aboard a good load of furs, and began the venture down the Green River in what is now Wyoming.[1] He portaged around some of the most difficult rapids, including Ashley Falls, but after losing some of his cargo in rough water, being forced to shift to a wooden dugout canoe, suffering from hunger, and meeting Indians who supplied him with horses, he left the river below the mouth of the Uinta. The journey brought him nowhere near the Grand Canyon, but he set a precedent for later river runners on the Colorado.

James Ohio Pattie did see the Grand Canyon during the next year, if his story can be believed. A young man, he left Iowa with his father, Sylvester Pattie, in 1824 and came to New Mexico, trapped beaver on the Gila and mined some. But the wanderlust held him, and by January, 1826 he had left his father and was traveling with a group of trappers including Ewing Young, Michel Robidoux, "Old Bill" Williams, and Ceran St. Vrain.

The trappers fanned out over the wilderness; Pattie with a group which went from the Gila and Salt to the Red River (the Colorado), where they traveled upstream in search of beaver. At the end of March, they came to a place on the river "where the mountains shut in so close upon its shores" that they "were compelled to climb a mountain, and travel along the acclivity, the river still in sight, and at an immense depth below . . . ."[2] This was the Grand Canyon, which Pattie estimated to be not more than a mile (1.6 km.) wide and about 300 miles (480 km.) long. They followed a course roughly parallel to the Canyon rim for some distance, passing through snow 12 to 18 inches (30 to 45 cm.) deep. It was a depressing journey for Pattie. He had to eat the bark of shrubs, and the scenery did not impress him, as his narrative shows:

> We arrived where the river emerges from these horrid mountains, which so cage it up, as to deprive all human beings of the ability to descend to its banks, and make use of its waters. No mortal has the power of describing the pleasure I felt, when I could once more reach the banks of the river.[3]

Then, his provisions renewed with beaver and elk, Pattie went on from the Grand Canyon to other adventures in Colorado, California, and even in Mexico City.

Pattie's route is hard to trace; from his description one cannot be sure whether he traversed the North Rim or the South Rim. George C. Yount, a member of another group of trappers that had split off from Pattie and his party, left a memoir describing his own passage through several precipitous canyons on his way from the Mojave Indians to Zuni.[4] Probably these were southern tributaries of the western Grand Canyon.

Even harder to trace are the paths of those who did not leave personal narratives. Christopher "Kit" Carson is an example. In 1826, a boy of 16, he ran away from the saddler to whom he had been apprenticed and came to New Mexico, where he traveled widely. He joined one of Ewing Young's trapping expeditions to California in 1829, and may have seen the Grand Canyon on that trip, although he did not record his impressions.[5] Jedediah Smith once traveled down the Virgin River near the lower reaches of the Grand Canyon. Others who knew Arizona well, and traveled widely, may have happened upon the Grand Canyon from time to time. Among these could have been trappers like Antoine Leroux, William Wolfskill, John Hatcher, and Pauline Weaver, who in spite of his name was a grizzled, leathery frontiersman. Almost certainly one of them was William Sherley "Old Bill" Williams, an erratic, trailblazing loner who ranged much of the West.[6] He was apparently among the Hopi in 1827, and a town, a peak and a river in the Grand Canyon country still bear his name. He was typical of the tough, self-reliant breed of frontiersmen that survived and sometimes prospered in the wilderness.

A French-Canadian trapper, Denis Julien, left his name and the date, 1836, on a number of rock walls in the Colorado and Green River canyons.[7] He worked for Antoine Robidoux, the proprietor of a trading post on the Uinta River in Utah. Most of Julien's "autographs" are near the Green River, or the Colorado in Cataract Canyon. One shows the rough outline of a boat and is in a place that would be

In 1857, the steamboat Explorer *was used by Lieutenant Joseph Ives to navigate the lower 350 miles of the Colorado River.*

inaccessible except in a boat, so it is possible that he made the attempt to go down through the canyons by boat, like Ashley. But unlike Ashley, Julien may have been drowned; there are no more of his inscriptions below those in Cataract Canyon.

John Charles Fremont's wide-ranging military surveys of the West passed near, but did not touch, the Grand Canyon. He passed along the Virgin River in May, 1844, but his maps only sketch in the Colorado River without showing or naming the Canyon. Fremont's superior, Colonel John James Abert of the Corps of Topographic Engineers, was honored by having his name given to the tassel-eared squirrel that is found on the South Rim and many other places in the mountain West.[8]

The Grand Canyon became United States territory as a result of the Mexican War, which was ended by the treaty of Guadalûpe Hidalgo, ratified on May 30, 1848. The Territory of New Mexico, including Arizona and the Grand Canyon, was created in 1850. When the United States acquired the Southwest, much of the new territory was unknown. Honest maps showed large blank areas, while other maps were filled with wild speculations. The course of the Colorado River had never been surveyed, and the Grand Canyon did not have an established name.

The American government decided to map the area, find new routes across it, and establish strong points within it. The Latter-day Saints under Brigham Young settled in Utah Valley in 1847 and commenced exploration and colonization of that region, which Congress soon organized as the Territory of Utah. And in 1848, gold was discovered in California, providing the impetus for increased travel along routes to the gold fields, passing both north and south of the Grand Canyon. To map and secure these routes, expeditions of military men were dispatched. For the next few years,

F. W. Egloffstein, illustrator for the Ives Expedition, depicted the landscape of the canyon as ominous and forbidding. From Report Upon the Colorado River of the West by

Lt. Joseph C. Ives, 1861. Reprinted courtesy of the Da Capo Press, New York

27

soldiers were the region's most noted explorers. Fort Yuma on the lower Colorado River was established in 1850. In the next year Captain Lorenzo Sitgreaves explored a route from Zuni to Fort Yuma. Sitgreaves followed the Little Colorado drainage, seeing Grand Falls and the Wupatki ruins, but his guide, Antoine Leroux, warned him that if he continued down the Little Colorado he would end up in the great canyon, so he struck west, passing near the site of Williams and visiting Peach Springs.[9] Leroux's advice suggests that the trapper was familiar with the Grand Canyon. He had come out West with Ashley about 1822.

Fort Defiance was founded in Navajo Country in 1852. In 1853-1854, Lt. Amiel Weeks Whipple traveled across present Arizona, passing near enough to the Grand Canyon to name Red Butte. In 1857-1859, Edward Fitzgerald Beale followed Whipple by building a wagon road from Fort Defiance to California along the general route of the present Santa Fe Railroad. His exploration was the only one in the history of the American desert outfitted with camels.

In the summer of 1857, the War Department authorized Lieutenant Joseph Christmas Ives to explore the Colorado River "to ascertain how far the river was navigable for steamboats."[10] Although George Alonzo Johnson and others had been operating steamboats on the lower Colorado since 1852, Ives decided to have a 50-foot (15.24 m.) stern-wheeler, *The Explorer*, manufactured in Philadelphia, tested upon the Delaware River, and shipped in sections to the mudflats at the mouth of the Colorado, where mechanics assembled it. It was ready to churn upstream in December.

The trip was not easy. *The Explorer* was no match for the swift currents, rapids and shallows of the Colorado. Many times the boat stuck on sand bars, and the men had to tow it upstream from the banks. After two months of hard labor, *The*

Explorer steamed into Black Canyon, 350 miles (560 km.) above the Colorado's mouth, near the present site of Hoover Dam. There, going full speed ahead, while the men were "eagerly gazing into the mysterious depths beyond…, the Explorer, with a stunning crash, brought up abruptly and instantaneously against a sunken rock. For a second the impression was that the cañon had fallen in."[11] Some men were thrown overboard, and the boat was wrecked. Ives concluded that Black Canyon was the head of navigation.

Meanwhile, Johnson, incensed at the fact that he and his steamboat had not been hired, had already steamed up the river in the *General Jesup* with Lt. James L. White and trapper Pauline Weaver aboard, and proceeded nearly to the mouth of the Virgin River.[12] On his return trip, Johnson met Beale and his camels and helped them cross the river.

Ives and his men abandoned the steamer at Black Canyon and explored on to the east. Soon they came to the edge of what Ives called the "Big Cañon," and descended to the bottom along Diamond Creek. The expedition's artists, F.W. von Egloffstein and H.B. Mollhausen, were the first to sketch the Grand Canyon, although their sketches appear dark and forbidding, and fail to convey an impression of its beauty. Egloffstein seems to have sketched the landscape of nightmares. Ives was the first man to record his admiration for Grand Canyon's scenery, writing, "We paused in wondering delight, surveying this stupendous formation through the Colorado and its tributaries break their way." He compared the Canyon, however, to the gate of hell, and noted "the difficulty of getting out."[13]

Egloffstein discovered this difficulty when he attempted to descend an old ladder into Havasu Canyon. The fragile rungs of the ladder broke, and he was precipitated into the canyon. According to

Ives' report, Egloffstein, unhurt, visited the Havasupai village while the rest of the white men waited above, and he was rescued from the gorge when the men tied together their gun slings and pulled him out. He was probably the first white man to visit the Havasupai in more than 80 years.

Dr. John Strong Newberry, a geologist, accompanied the expedition and has the honor of being the first scientist to study Grand Canyon, "the most splendid exposure of stratified rocks that there is in the world."[14]

Ives' descriptions of the Canyon seem to combine Newberry's geological explanations with something of Egloffstein's exaggerated vision:

The extent and magnitude of the system of canyons is astounding. The plateau is cut into shreds by these gigantic chasms, and resembles a vast ruin. Belts of country miles in width have been swept away, leaving only isolated mountains standing in the gap. Fissures so profound that the eye cannot penetrate their depths are separated by walls whose thickness one can almost span, and slender spires that seem to be tottering upon their bases shoot up thousands of feet from the vaults below.[15]

But Ives, like Pattie, did not envision any possible human use for the Grand Canyon:

The region is, of course, altogether valueless. It can be approached only from the south, and after entering it there is nothing to do but leave. Ours has been the first, and will doubtless be the last, party of whites to visit this profitless locality. It seems intended by nature that the Colorado river, along the greater portion of its lonely and majestic way, shall be forever unvisited and undisturbed.[16]

He failed to see that the very majesty which impressed him would draw millions of others to the rim of his "Big Cañon."

Ives continued on across the Little Colorado River, through the Hopi and Navajo country, to Fort Defiance. He produced a monumental report accompanied by Egloffstein's startling illustrations and a map that marked the location of the "Big Cañon of the Colorado River."

The Southwest felt the effects of the Civil War. Forts were closed and most federal soldiers withdrawn in 1861 to serve in the East. Some secessionist citizens in the Tucson area proclaimed Arizona a territory of the Confederacy. Union troops from California entered Arizona in May, 1862, and after a brief skirmish, drove out some Confederate Texas soldiers and raised the stars and stripes again over Tucson.

It is interesting to note that had the South won the war, the Grand Canyon would have remained in New Mexico, since the Confederate line dividing the larger territory was drawn east and west, with an "Arizona" to the south and a "New Mexico" to the north. However, the bill signed by Abraham Lincoln on February 24, 1863, establishing Arizona Territory, used the present north-south line. Arizona's first capital was located at Del Rio. But in the next year, the first governor, John N. Goodwin, arrived and founded a new capital city, named Prescott after the famous American historian, William H. Prescott (1796-1859), author of *The History of the Conquest of Mexico.*[17] Prescott is about 100 miles (160 km.) south of the Grand Canyon, and is the county seat of Yavapai County, which originally included much of the Grand Canyon.

The decades during and after the Civil War were times of conflict between Indians and non-Indians in northern Arizona and southern Utah. The removal of federal troops at the start of the war gave some opportunities to Navajos and Apaches whose way of life then included a pattern of raiding, but the basic problem was the movement of soldiers, travelers and settlers into country that had always been Indian homeland. The non-Indians were often the aggressors during the time of troubles. In June, 1863, after a successful campaign against the Mescalero Apaches, Christopher "Kit" Carson was sent to round up the Navajos and bring them to a reservation at Bosque Redondo (Fort Sumner), New Mexico. He rebuilt Fort Defiance and began to destroy Navajo crops and herds. Faced with starvation, the Navajos fled to isolated hiding places, possibly including the Grand Canyon. Carson rounded up a large group in Canyon de Chelly, and gradually most of the Navajos came in to surrender to Fort Defiance and were led away into captivity. Others remained in the Grand Canyon region, sometimes raiding the southern Utah settlements.[18] After five years at Bosque Redondo, the Navajos signed a peace treaty with the United States, and were allowed to return to their traditional lands. The reservation then established was expanded to include sections of the eastern Grand Canyon in 1884, 1900, and 1930. The Navajo Reservation now includes the entire eastern rim of Grand Canyon and Marble Canyon northward from the Little Colorado River.

Some of the American explorers across northern Arizona contacted the Hualapais, and the contact was not always friendly. Brief hostile incidents occurred with Sitgreaves in 1852, Francis Xavier Aubrey (who gave his name to the Aubrey Cliffs) in the following year, Beale in 1857, and an emigrant train in 1858.[19] A series of killings that climaxed with the murder of Chief Wauba Yuma in 1866 provoked a three-year war led by the Hualapai chief, Sherum, a tactical genius, along with Sukwatama, Leve-leve, and another chief named Hichi-hichi, whose band ranged the plateau just south of the Grand Canyon. The U. S. Army used search-and-destroy missions against the Hualapais, burning their dwellings and food wherever found. The Hualapais made peace in 1869, and many of their warriors served as scouts for General George Crook in his campaign against their traditional enemies, the Yavapais. The Havasupai band escaped the brunt of conflict, but their chief Navajo (for whom Navajo Falls was named) was one of Crook's scouts.[20] Most of the Hualapais were removed to a reservation on the lower Colorado River in 1874, but the Havasupais and the plateau bands near the Grand Canyon remained and offered shelter to a few others. Those who went to the reservation suffered many deaths from illness in the hot lowland climate. Threatened by starvation when conflict between military and civilian agents deprived them of their rations,[21] the Hualapais escaped from that reservation and returned to the area around Kingman and Peach Springs. Lieutenant Colonel William Redwood Price recommended that the area of the present Hualapai Reservation be set aside, and this was confirmed by order of President Chester A. Arthur on January 4, 1883. The reservation embraces almost 1,000,000 acres (more than 400,000 hectares) south of the southern bend of the Colorado River, including a large section of the western Grand Canyon and its southern tributaries such as Spencer Canyon, Peach Springs Canyon, and Diamond Creek.

A Havasupai Reservation was created during the same period. More non-Indians were wandering into Havasu Canyon, and since white men did not always treat Indians kindly in those days, the Havasupai in 1878 appealed to Governor John C. Fremont who gave them a letter stating that they were peaceful people and asking all visitors to respect their rights.[22] They made repeated statements of their friendship for the United States in the years following.

A proclamation by President Rutherford B. Hayes in 1880 established the Havasupai Indian Reservation, an area 5 miles (8 km.) wide and 12 miles (19 km.) long surrounding the village and the cultivated portion of the canyon.[23] The Army Corps of Engineers sent in a surveying party in the following year. They found the canyon topography incredibly rough and impossible to survey accurately, so they ran a new boundary line at the base of the cliffs, including only the village and cultivated fields. Engineer Carl F. Palfrey attributed the desire for a smaller reservation to the Havasupai themselves in these words, "affected,

probably, by a fear of encroachments and finally of removal, [Chief] Navajo appeared to prefer having the boundaries close upon the lands he actually occupied."[24] President Arthur accepted the survey's recommendation and in 1882 reduced the reservation to an area of 518.6 acres (209.9 hectares). With that survey in 1881 was the versatile Dr. Elliott Coues, soldier-naturalist, surgeon, ornithologist, and historian of Western exploration, who made a mildly humorous reference to "the Grand Canyon of the Colorado itself" as the "most wonderful crack of the ground in America."[25]

Another visitor to Havasu Canyon

Chief Navajo photographed by George Wharton James. Courtesy of Southwestern Museum

in the same year was the colorful Frank Hamilton Cushing of John Wesley Powell's Bureau of American Ethnology. Cushing, who went so far as to be adopted into the Zuñi pueblo and its sacred societies, was no ordinary anthropologist. His article, "The Nation of the Willows," was the first description of the Havasupai and the beauty of their isolated home in the popular press.[26]

The last military expedition to Havasu Canyon was General Crook's friendly visit to the home of his former scout, Chief Navajo, in 1884. Captain John Gregory Bourke, Crook's aide-de-camp, recorded the trip along with some romantic impressions of the Grand Canyon scenery. "A tremendous gash in the bosom of Nature," he called it, "a scene of utter desolation. Before us frowned hideous escarpments, and on each hand other walls hemmed us in." It was "a chasm which seemed to fairly yawn for victims," and "the glad sunshine refused to follow us into this gloomy cavernous depth." He felt himself "immured in a dungeon."[27]

North of the Grand Canyon, the Paiutes encountered many of the mountain men and travelers on the "Old Spanish Trail." Settlement began among them in the 1850's. During the 19th century, Paiutes suffered decimation through diseases brought in by the pioneers, shootings and the theft of their children. Their best lands were taken from them. But if relations with their new Mormon neighbors were often amicable, it was largely due to the efforts of one man.

An explorer of the Grand Canyon region and a peacemaker among the Indian tribes, Jacob Hamblin was a quiet-spoken missionary of the Latter-day Saints.[28] Brigham Young, the Mormon leader, sent Hamblin to scout the area around the Colorado River, work among the Indians, and report on movements of expeditions sent out by the government in Washington. In March, 1858, Hamblin saw the Ives expedition.

Hamblin made several trips in an attempt to establish a mission among the Hopi; in the course of these trips he crossed and recrossed the Colorado River, locating the later sites of Pierce's Ferry and Lee's Ferry. In 1862, he made the first recorded circle trip around the Grand Canyon.[29] Going south in the following year, he traveled through Hualapai country and visited the Havasupais. In the period 1865-1870, there were clashes between the Mormons and the Indians in southern Utah, particularly the Navajos but also the Paiutes. Hamblin, a man whose honesty and courage the Indians always respected, helped make peace with them. Doubtless Hamblin knew the North Kaibab Plateau and possibly also the North Rim country. The place on the Kaibab known as Jacob Lake is named after him.

In the same period, much attention focused on the Colorado River. On September 7, 1867, a raft was pulled out of the river at the tiny frontier landing of Callville, Nevada, below the Grand Canyon, with a watersoaked, sunburned, starving, half-dead man on it. When he was revived enough to speak, he gave his name as James White and began to tell the story of a trip down the river through the rapids, lashed to a makeshift raft. His condition and what he managed to say convinced the river boatmen who rescued him that he had come down through what was then called the "Big Canyon."[30] That idea started arguments that have raged from that day to this. Where he left the river is known, but where did he enter it? White himself did not know, because he was completely lost. Some men made impossible claims on his behalf, stating that he began above the junction of the Grand and the Green, while others insisted that he had entered the river at Pierce's Ferry, 60 miles (96 km.) above Callville, and had never been inside the Grand Canyon at all.

James B. White was born in Rome,

30

New York, on November 19, 1837, and grew up in Kenosha, Wisconsin. At the age of 23 he left for the Colorado gold diggings, where he failed to strike it rich. He drifted on to California, where he enlisted in the Union Army. After discharge, he returned to Colorado and Kansas, where he met Captain Charles Baker and George Strole. In the spring of 1867, according to his own story, the three engaged in a bit of horse-stealing and had some trouble with a fourth man named Joseph Goodfellow, who had joined them in Colorado City (Colorado Springs). The trouble ended in the San Luis Valley when White wounded Goodfellow twice in an old-fashioned gunfight, White escaping unhurt.

Baker, Strole and White then set out on a prospecting trip, traveling near the present site of Silverton, Colorado, and then over to the Mancos River, where they saw some of the Mesa Verde cliff dwellings. They traveled from the Mancos down the San Juan River until it entered a deep canyon. They were then south of the San Juan, and crossed it to try to pass north through Ute country to the Colorado River. Going down into a dry tributary canyon, they found no way out on the other side, and when they turned back to retrace their steps, they were attacked by Indians. Baker was shot and killed. Strole and White left their horses, taking weapons, ropes and about 10 pounds of flour, and went down the canyon until they reached the Colorado River, where they made a raft out of five cottonwood logs lashed together with rope, and poled downstream through quiet water all that night and the next three days. The geographical description and the presence of so much quiet water suggest that White and Strole were then, as White himself was later to decide after much reflection, "*below* where the Grand River and the Green River meet." He described the rocks as "light yellowish sandstone."[31] All this sounds like someplace in Glen Canyon.

After three days, they struck the first rapid, which upset the raft. This was only the first of a series of rapids which were constantly upsetting and breaking their raft. The last of their flour was wet, so they scraped it off the inside of the flour sack and ate it. They built a new and larger raft.

A whirlpool washed George Strole overboard and drowned him on the morning of the fifth day, leaving White the lone survivor. He tied himself to the raft and continued down the river, beaten by terrible waves and caught in endlessly revolving eddies. At one place his raft

stuck in some rocks, and he was forced to build a third and smaller one. There was one big rapid on the eleventh day which stood out in White's memory. He described walls rising several hundred feet and then "flaring out." The rocks here, he said, were "darker, a kind of grayish rock with white streaks running through it."[32] He got some mesquite bread and the hind quarters of a dog from Indians; previously he had eaten only a few mesquite beans from an island in the river, and his rawhide knife scabbard. He said that the journey from the time he entered the river until he was pulled from it took 14 days, traveling all day almost every day and stopping at night.

This is the outline of White's own story. The most convincing argument against it is the considered opinion of experienced river runners that it simply would be impossible for a man to go through the Grand Canyon on a makeshift raft. Of course, White did say that his rafts were constantly overturned and at

A controversy still rages today as to whether James White was the first to traverse the Colorado through the Grand Canyon.

least twice smashed. Those who maintain that White entered at some point far downstream such as Diamond Creek or Pierce's Ferry simply discredit his story, or must explain how he managed to get from the San Juan across all of the intervening country to one of those points. Such a trip would be almost as incredible as the river trip itself, especially since White said that he traveled only three days before entering the river.

White eventually settled in Trinidad, Colorado, and died there in 1927 at the age of 89. Was he really "first through the Grand Canyon?" One cannot answer the question with certainty. But if so, it was a voyage which he did not plan or intend. He did not know where he started, where he went, or the significance of his journey. His feat by no means rivals the careful scientific expeditions by boat of Major John Wesley Powell beginning two years later, nor does it deprive the voyage of 1869 of any of its daring or renown.

Powell's is the greatest single name in the history of Grand Canyon and the Colorado River. He played a leading role in the second opening of the West—its opening to science, conservation, and coherent use.[33]

Before Powell began his exploration in 1869, honest maps of this region showed a large white blank. The course of the Colorado River was uncertain, its character guessed at. Stories were told of giant waterfalls and places where the river flowed underground. One of the nation's greatest rivers was yet to be traveled and charted. Powell did both—twice. When he completed his work, the river's path was known, its vast canyons named and measured, their ancient book of geology laid open for scientific study, and the civilization of the Indian inhabitants, ancient and modern, recorded for posterity.

His father, Joseph Powell, was a Welsh-English tailor and a Methodist lay preacher who came to America with his wife and became a frontier circuit rider. He named his second son, born on March 24, 1834, after John Wesley because he hoped that he would be called to the ministry. But Wes grew up to have interests in geology and exploration instead. He was tutored and taken on excursions by George Crookham and William Mather, Illinois naturalists and geologists. He read widely and made himself responsible for his own education.

During the 1850's, Powell taught school in Wisconsin and Illinois and attended classes at several colleges without taking a degree. He became Secretary of the Illinois State Natural History Society and curator of its museum. On long scientific collecting expeditions on the Mississippi, Ohio, Illinois and other rivers, he learned how to handle a boat.

In May, 1861, John Wesley Powell answered President Abraham Lincoln's call for volunteers in the United States Army. By June, he was a Lieutenant. Although he rose to the rank of brevet lieutenant-colonel, he preferred the designation, "Major Powell," for the rest of his life.[34]

In November, he married Emma Dean in Detroit while on leave. Powell's artillery battery fought at the Battle of

Shiloh, where on April 6, 1862, he received a severe wound in his right arm that required amputation. He was back in action at Vicksburg after little more than a year, and later accompanied Sherman on raids into Georgia. He was mustered out of the service in January, 1865.

After the war, Powell became professor of geology at Illinois Wesleyan University and Illinois Normal University, and resumed his positions with the Natural History Society. Under the sponsorship of these institutions, and with some federal support, he carried on explorations in the Rocky Mountains and the headwaters of the Grand and Green rivers in Colorado and Wyoming in 1867 and 1868. He studied the Rocky Mountain parks, describing the Morrison rock formation with its interesting dinosaur fossils, and made the first recorded ascent of Long's Peak. He began his study of Indian languages, customs and religion. There, too, he conceived the dream of exploring the canyons of the Colorado River, because "the Grand Canyon of the Colorado will give the best geological section on the continent."[35]

Powell gathered all the available information on the river from Ives' report with Newberry's geological observations, and from men who had seen the river and boated on it. He tried running the White River, a swift Colorado tributary, himself. He gained support from educational institutions, railroads issued free passes for his men and equipment, the Smithsonian Institution lent scientific instruments, and Congress authorized army posts to issue rations and supplies.

Powell was convinced that his proposed expedition would succeed, and decided to begin in 1869 from the Union Pacific Railroad's bridge over the Green River in Wyoming. He designed boats and had them built in Chicago. Three heavy 21-foot (6.4m.) boats of white oak and a lighter, 16-foot (4.8m.) pilot boat of white pine were constructed with watertight

compartments fore and aft, and equipped with a pair of oars each. They were packed with supplies sufficient for 10 months, with tools for repairs, weapons for hunting, and some trade articles. Powell named the light boat the *Emma Dean* after his wife. Two of the heavy boats were called, respectively, the *Maid-of-the Canyon* and *Kitty Clyde's Sister*, and the last was left with *No-Name*.

The men who set out with Powell in the four boats were his younger brother Walter, a captain in the Union army who had suffered extremely in Confederate prisons; a Colorado editor, Oramel Howland and his brother Seneca, a Union veteran of Gettysburg; Jack Sumner, Union veteran, Indian trader and guide; Bill Dunn, a real Western mountaineer and trapper of the old school; Billy Hawkins, another mountaineer and Union veteran who became cook of the expedition; Andy Hall, a bright and brave Scottish lad of 18; Sergeant George Bradley, a Union veteran of Fredericksburg for whom Powell had obtained a discharge so that he could participate; and Frank Goodman, a talkative English adventurer who showed up unexpectedly at Green River. The members of the expedition were to share in taking measurements of longitude, latitude, river distance and direction, elevations and canyon altitudes. Powell took the major responsibility for these, and served as pilot in the lead boat, the *Emma Dean.*

Powell's expedition left Green River on May 24, 1869. They went swiftly downstream through the rapids, naming canyons and making observations along the way. On June 9, in a place later called Disaster Falls, the *No-Name* was smashed in a rapid and lost with 2,000 pounds of provisions. Her crew, the Howland brothers and Goodman, were saved narrowly from drowning. The barometers and a jug of whiskey were salvaged from the wreck.

In late June, Powell stopped and went overland to the Uinta Indian Agency

to obtain provisions. Goodman, discouraged after his near-drowning, left the expedition there. Powell sent a letter to his wife that temporarily quieted the spreading rumors that he and all his men had drowned. At least two impostors had claimed to be the "only survivor."

The nine remaining men continued on, passing the confluence of the Grand and the Green on July 17. Food and water were problems for them by this time. The bacon and flour were bad and most of the other provisions were short, though the men eked them out by shooting mountain sheep and deer, and catching fish. The muddy Colorado, "too thin to plow and too thick to drink," did not make the best thirst-quencher, so they tested the tributary streams for potability. On July 28 they reached a creek "as filthy as the washing from the sewers of some large, dirty city, but stinks more than Cologne ever did."[36] Disappointed, Powell adopted Dunn's name for it, the Dirty Devil.

The expedition located the mouth of the Paria River on August 4. More rapids followed in Marble Canyon, requiring exhausting work in the white water and in portages. On August 10, the men were at the mouth of the Little Colorado River in the Grand Canyon. Powell wrote,

We are three-quarters of a mile in the depths of the earth, and the great river shrinks into insignificance, as it dashes its angry waves against the walls and cliffs, that rise to the world above; they are but puny ripples, and we but pigmies, running up and down the sands, or lost among the boulders. We have an unknown distance yet to run, an unknown river yet to explore. What falls there are, we know not; what rocks beset the channel, we know not; what walls rise over the river, we know not.[37]

Soon the great walls of the Inner Gorge of the Grand Canyon closed in around them. Their provisions were

During his first expedition in 1869, Powell referred to the Canyon as "our granite prision." Photo by David C. Ochsner

reduced to flour, coffee and dried apples, and they could no longer hunt for mountain sheep or deer.

The walls, now, are more than a mile in height. A thousand feet of this is up through granite crags, then steep slopes and perpendicular cliffs rise, one above another, to the summit. The gorge is black and narrow below, red and gray and flaring above, with crags and angular projections on the walls, which, cut in many places by side cañons, seem to be a vast wilderness of rocks. Down in these grand, gloomy depths we glide, ever listening, for the mad waters keep up their roar; ever watching, ever peering ahead, for the narrow cañon is winding, and the river is closed in so that we can see but a few hundred yards, and what there may be ahead we know not; but we listen for falls, and watch for rocks, or stop now and then, in the bay of a recess, to admire the gigantic scenery.[38]

The "Grand Cañon," as Major Powell called it, had the worst rapids he had seen. Oars were splintered and boats badly damaged. Some notes and maps were lost.

The expedition stopped on August 15 at the mouth of a clear, cold stream. This the Major was to call the Bright Angel in compensation for the Dirty Devil, and thus give a most distinctive name to one of the Grand Canyon's features, a name which came originally from Milton's *Paradise Lost*. Here the men repaired the boats, made an oar, and caught fish. Powell found Indian ruins, and made other observations:

While the men are at work making portages, I climb up the granite to its summit, and go away back over rust colored sandstones and greenish yellow shales, to the foot of the marble wall. I climb so high that the men and boats are lost in the black depths below, and the dashing river is a

rippling brook; and still there is more cañon above than below. All about me are interesting geological records. The book is open, and I can read as I run.[39]

The trip from this point was one rapid after another. "The boat glides rapidly, where the water is smooth, or, striking a wave, she leaps and bounds like a thing of life, and we have a wild, exhilarating ride....The excitement is so great that we forget the danger until we hear the roar of a great fall below..." "...the rushing waters break into great waves on the rocks, and lash themselves into mad, white foam." "...we have to make another portage."[40] Cold rain drenched them and produced cataracts of muddy water; then the sun came out and the extreme August heat of the Inner Gorge baked them. They found an Indian garden, which they raided, adding a little green squash to their diet.

Powell referred to the Canyon as "our granite prison."[41] On August 27, the men were discouraged by the sight of a particularly bad rapid ahead. At this point, Oramel Howland asked Powell that the expedition abandon the river and hike out north to the Mormon settlements. Powell refused after a difficult night of decision, and most of the men backed him, but the Howland brothers and Bill Dunn were determined to leave, as to go further downstream seemed suicide to them. The last of the flour was baked into biscuits and divided equally, and the deserters were given weapons, ammunition and copies of Powell's diary and notes.

The three men left the rest at Separation Rapid and climbed northward to the plateau, where some Paiute Indians mistook them for prospectors who had mistreated and killed one of their women, and killed them in revenge. 1869 was a year of conflict between Whites and Indians in the Grand Canyon region.

Meanwhile, Powell and his five

faithful companions abandoned the damaged *Emma Dean* and in the remaining two boats made their way through the difficult rapids and out into quiet water in one day's time. They had gone all the way through the Grand Canyon. Soon they reached a Mormon settlement at the mouth of the Virgin River.

The Major and his brother left the river there, returning east through Salt Lake City. The other four went on down the already well-known lower river to Fort Yuma, where Sumner and Bradley left. Andy Hall and Billy Hawkins went all the way to the Gulf of California, and thus deserve the title of "first down the Colorado River from Wyoming to Mexico." For the scientist, the purpose of the expedition had been fulfilled when he reached known country again, but for Andy and Billy, it was the adventure of once in a lifetime.

Powell returned to "civilization" with much new geological and geographical knowledge, but he had lost many of his notes, and additional exploration was needed. He planned a second river voyage, this one to be broken into sections with supply points located along the river, and it received government support. After the success of the first expedition, Congress had established the Geographical and Geological Survey of the Rocky Mountain Region with Powell in charge.

During 1870, Powell explored the plateaus north of the Grand Canyon to locate routes of supply for his second river expedition, investigate the deaths of the three men who had deserted his first trip, and study and photograph the Indians. Jacob Hamblin, whose knowledge of the country and tribes was valuable to Powell, served as guide and interpreter. Hamblin induced the Kaibab Paiute chief, Chuarrumpeak, to find out how Powell's men had died, and to locate springs and trails for Powell. Hamblin also guided Powell across the future site of Lee's Ferry to

the Hopi towns.

The second Colorado River
expedition left Green River, Wyoming, on
May 22, 1871. This time Powell's
companions were amateur scientists and
other educated men, rather than the
soldiers and frontiersmen of the 1869
voyage. The members were Powell's
brother-in-law, Almon H. Thompson, the
geographer; Walter Clement (Clem)
Powell, the Major's young cousin; Frank
Richardson, who left the party on June 8;
Fred Dellenbaugh, a young artist and
writer; S. V. Jones, mathematician and
surveyor; John F. Steward, amateur
geologist; Francis M. Bishop, surveyor
and teacher; Andy Hattan, the cook; and
E. O. Beaman, a professional photographer.
When Beaman left, photographs were

taken by Clem Powell, then James
Fennemore, and finally by John K. (Jack)
Hillers, whose work became deservedly
well-known.[42] The boats, named the
Emma Dean, Nellie Powell and *Cañonita*, were
of improved design. The Major sat in an
armchair atop the *Emma Dean*, from
which he could signal the following boats.
On October 23, after many rapids and
delays, they reached Lee's Ferry and

Powell's boat, Emma Dean, *in Marble
Gorge during the second expedition. He lashed a
captain's chair to the deck so that he could
signal to the boats following.*

went into winter camp at Kanab. Bishop
resigned at that point.

After explorations in the area north
of the Grand Canyon, the expedition
started down the river again, leaving Lee's
Ferry on August 17, 1872, in the *Emma
Dean* and the *Cañonita*, abandoning the
Nellie. Soon they were in the Grand
Canyon, where the wild rapids of a high
river constantly threw the men into the
water. Since maps and notes survived
from 1869 for the lower Grand Canyon,
and because of the dangers ahead, the
second expedition left the river at Kanab
Creek on September 8.

During the summer of 1872, Powell
explored the Kaibab Plateau and the North
Rim of the Grand Canyon with Professor
Harvey C. DeMotte, after whom

DeMotte Park was named.

After 1872, Powell continued his studies of American Indian customs, languages and myths, particularly those of the Paiutes north of the Grand Canyon. He was founder and first director of the Bureau of American Ethnology, which preserved and published Indian lore. He also continued his geological and geographical survey work in the Colorado River basin. This work was placed under the United States Geological Survey, which Powell had worked hard to bring into being. He was the second director of the Geological Survey, serving from 1881 to 1894. His unusually acute ideas on the importance of water, irrigation and a federal policy for land use in the West were a half century ahead of their time, and did not find immediate acceptance. Indeed, they caused pressures that resulted in his resignation from the Geological Survey directorship. He died on September 23, 1902, after receiving many honors and awards.

While he was not the first to use the name "Grand Canyon," Powell was the one who more than anyone else caused it to be accepted.

The nearby Indian tribes had names for the Grand Canyon. The Havasupai refer to it as Wikatata, or Rough Rim, and to the Hopi it is the place of emergence from and descent into the underworld. The Paiutes knew of water "deep down in the earth."

Cardenas evidently did not name the Canyon he discovered; Castañeda refers to it only as a "Barranca" or large canyon. Garces in 1776 was the first white man to name it, calling it Puerto de Bucareli.

Pattie in 1826 made reference only to "these horrid mountains," but in the early period of American exploration, it was variously called Big Canyon, Great Canyon, or Grand Canyon. Ives referred to it as Big Cañon, *cañon* being the Spanish spelling of canyon, a word adopted from Spanish.

"At the Mouth of the Little Colorado," by Thomas Moran.

The first map containing Grand Canyon as a place name accompanied General William J. Palmer's railroad survey report in 1868.[43] By Palmer's time, the name was widely used.

The honor of the first consistent and authoritative use of the name "Grand Canyon" belongs to Major John Wesley Powell, whose definitive and widely read reports caused the name to be adopted permanently after 1869.

While Powell was making his second trip downstream in 1871, Lieutenant George M. Wheeler was working other boats laboriously upstream. His U.S. Geographical Surveys West of the 100th Meridian went up the Colorado from Camp Mojave, beyond Ives' "head of navigation" into Grand Canyon's lower entrance and 53 miles (85 km.) further, reaching the mouth of Diamond Creek. With Wheeler were Dr. W. J. Hoffman, naturalist, P. W. Hamel, topographer, and Timothy H. O'Sullivan, a photographer who had been the famous Matthew Brady's apprentice. O'Sullivan is the first photographer known to have taken pictures of the Grand Canyon.[44] Grove Karl Gilbert, the geologist of the expedition, was an associate of J. S. Newberry (who had been with Ives in 1857-58) and later worked with Powell and the U.S. Geological Survey. Wheeler remarked that the Grand Canyon's walls were "magnificent beyond description," and went on to speculate:

> These stupendous specimens of extended rock-carving that make up the system of the cañons have been partially described and made known. They stand without a rival upon the face of the globe, must always remain one of the wonders, and will, as circumstances of transportation permit, attract the denizens of all quarters of the world who in their travels delight to gaze upon the intricacies of nature.[45]

Through the work of Powell and those who went with him and followed him, the nation became aware that the Grand Canyon possessed not only size, but also beauty and scientific interest. Soon artists' canvases and a scientist's glowing prose told Americans that the Grand Canyon would be worth seeing, for those hardy enough to make the trip to that country still beyond the frontier.

With Powell in the North Rim country in the early 1870's were Professor Almon Harris Thompson, who was making a topographic survey, and a young artist named Thomas Moran.[46]

Moran, Thompson thought, kept getting in the way of serious work. But the sketches of the Grand Canyon which the artist was making, and the paintings which were to follow, did more to make the Grand Canyon's beauty known to America than perhaps any other means. Born in England in 1837 into a family of painters who soon moved to America, Thomas and his brothers Edward and Peter Moran were deeply influenced by the Turner school of landscape painting. Joining the Hayden expedition to the Yellowstone in 1871, Thomas Moran produced a painting, "The Grand Canyon of the Yellowstone," and later made another splendid landscape as a

Thomas Moran, at left, and J. E. Colburn on the Powell Expedition to the North Rim country in 1873.

companion piece, "The Grand Chasm of the Colorado." These were purchased by Congress for $10,000 each, and hung for a time in the National Capitol building. Powell called on Moran to prepare illustrations for his great report, "The Exploration of the Colorado River of the West," published in 1875. Moran became an artist of international renown, and he often returned to Grand Canyon, where Moran Point is named for him.

His second visit was in 1880, when he was again invited to accompany a scientist on a trip to the Grand Canyon. This was a protege of Powell, Clarence Edward Dutton of the new United States Geological Survey. He had been trained for the Christian ministry and, like Powell, was a Union veteran of the Civil War. He had accompanied the Powell Survey in 1875, and now was returning to the Canyon country as the leader of a full-fledged geological expedition. His survey of 1880-1881 gave him the information for his excellent report, "The Tertiary History of the Grand Cañon District, with Atlas." This is the first important geological book on the Grand Canyon. Dutton was a fine geologist, but also a fine writer. He saw the Grand Canyon not only as a geological exhibit, but also as a place of mystery and beauty, and his descriptions of the scenery, never excelled by any other writer, are classic. He recognized the ever-changing aspect of the Canyon:

> It is never the same, even from day to day, or even from hour to hour. In the early morning its mood and subjective influences are usually calmer and more full of repose than at other times, but as the sun rises higher the whole scene is so changed that we cannot recall our first impressions. Every passing cloud, every change in the position of the sun, recasts the whole. At sunset the pageant closes amid splendors that seem more than earthly. The

direction of the full sunlight, the massing of the shadows, the manner in which the side lights are thrown from the clouds determine these modulations, and the sensitiveness of the picture to the slightest variations in these conditions is very wonderful.[47]

Dutton often chose architectural terms in describing Canyon forms, and his interest in oriental religions led him to see a resemblance between great buttes in the Canyon and the temples of India and China. He began naming the Canyon's features after the eastern gods: Brahma Temple, Vishnu Temple, Shiva Temple, The Tower of Babel, the Hindu Amphitheater, and many more on the same pattern.

Dutton's book has a few illustrations by Thomas Moran, but many more by William Henry Holmes, another artist who traveled with the 1880 survey. While Moran painted landscapes as an artist, Holmes sketched the earth's structure with scientific precision so that a geologist could recognize every rock layer.

Clarence Edward Dutton

Moran's cliffs are lost in the clouds, but Holmes' have the clarity of the desert atmosphere.

Another geologist, Charles Doolittle Walcott, traveled with Powell into the Grand Canyon in 1882-1883.[48] In order to take in its horses and equipment, this expedition contructed the Nankoweap Trail, leading down into the eastern end of the Canyon along the route of an old Indian trail.[49] It was winter, and they had to face blinding snow and wind. Walcott studied the Grand Canyon Series of rock layers, and decided that they were much older than had been thought. He published his findings in a series of scientific papers. In 1894, he became Powell's successor as director of the United States Geological Survey. In 1891, Powell and G. K. Gilbert brought a large group of the International Congress of Geologists to the Grand Canyon, for by that time it had achieved recognition as one of the world's most outstanding geological exhibits.

1. William Henry Ashley, *The West of William H. Ashley,* ed. by Dale L. Morgan (Denver: Fred A. Rosenstock Old West Publishing Co., 1964), quoted in T. H. Watkins, ed., *The Grand Colorado: The Story of a River and its Canyons* (New York: American West Publishing Co., 1969), pp. 62-66. The oft-repeated story of Ashley's disaster in Ashley Falls apparently exaggerates what really happened.

2. James Ohio Pattie, *The Personal Narrative of James O. Pattie of Kentucky,* ed. by Timothy Flint and Reuben Gold Thwaites (Cleveland: Arthur H. Clark, 1905), p. 97.

3. *Ibid.*

4. Charles L. Camp, ed., *George C. Yount and His Chronicles of the West, Comprising Extracts from His "Memoirs" and from the Orange Clark "Narrative"* (Denver: Fred A. Rosenstock Old West Publishing Co., 1966), p. 36.

5. Christopher "Kit" Carson, *Kit Carson's Own Story of His Life: As Dictated to Col. and Mrs. D. C. Peters about 1856-57, and Never Before Published,* ed. by Blanche M. Grant (Taos: Santa Fe New Mexican Publishing Corp., 1926), p. 14, says only, "on the fourth day we arrived on the Colorado of the West,

"The Panorama From Point Sublime Looking East," by W. H. Holmes appeared in the Atlas *accompanying* Tertiary History of the Grand Canyon District.

below the great Cañon." Dewitt C. Peters, *Kit Carson's Life and Adventures, etc.* (Hartford: Dustin, Gilman and Co., 1874), p. 40, apparently on the strength of this statement, says Carson "came in sight of the great Cañon of the Colorado."

6. Alpheus H. Favour, *Old Bill Williams: Mountain Man* (Norman: University of Oklahoma Press, 1962), pp. 125-26.

7. J. Cecil Alter, *James Bridger: Trapper, Frontiersman, Scout and Guide: A Historical Narrative* (Columbus, Ohio: Long's College Book Co., 1951), p. 551, in a note on the date, March 14, 1824, mentions Denis Julien "on his way to the Indians." *See also* Charles Kelly, "The Mysterious 'D. Julien,'" *Utah Historical Quarterly* 6(July 1933): 82-88. This article contains an incorrect version of the Fruita, Colorado, inscription, of which there is a photograph in Donald V. Hague, *Canyon Graphics and Graffiti* (Salt Lake City: Utah Museum of Natural History, 1975), p. 13. The last word in this inscription is not White, but WINTE, a fairly common trappers' spelling for Uinta(h). The date, comparing the other two instances of the figure "1," must be 1837.

8. William H. Goetzmann, *Army Exploration in the American West, 1803-1863* (New Haven: Yale University Press, 1959), pp. 66, 71; map D.

9. Lorenzo Sitgreaves, *Report of an Expedition Down the Zuni and Colorado Rivers* (32d Congress, 2d Session, Sen. Exec. Doc. No. 59, Serial No. 668. Washington: Robert Armstrong, Public Printer, 1853), pp. 8-9.

10. Joseph Christmas Ives, *Report upon the Colorado River of the West; Explored in 1857 and 1858* (Washington: Government Printing Office, 1861), p. 21.

11. *Ibid.*, p. 81.

12. Arthur Woodward, *Feud on the Colorado* (Los Angeles: Westernlore Press, 1955), pp. 56, 88-104.

13. Ives, pp. 99-100.

14. *Ibid.*, p. 101.

15. *Ibid.*, p. 109.

16. *Ibid.*, p. 110.

17. William Hickling Prescott, *History of the Conquest of Mexico, with a Preliminary View of the Ancient Mexican Civilization and the Life of the Conqueror, Hernando Cortés* (New York: A. L. Burt, 1843).

18. C. Gregory Crampton and David E. Miller, eds., "Journal of Two Campaigns by Utah Territorial Militia Against the Navajo Indians, 1869," *Utah Historical Quarterly* 29(April 1961):148-76.

19. *Walapai Papers: Historical Reports, Documents, and Extracts from Publications Relating to the Walapai Indians of Arizona* (74th Congress, 2d Session, Sen. Doc. No. 273, Serial No. 10012. Washington: Government Printing Office, 1936), pp. 11 ff. *See also* Henry F. Dobyns and Robert C. Euler, *The Hualapai People* (Phoenix: Indian Tribal Series, 1976), pp. 31-38.

20. Dobyns and Euler, p. 47.

21. *Walapai Papers*, p. 98.

22. John C. Fremont, open letter of November 23, 1878, in History File, "Havasupai," Grand Canyon National Park Library.

23. Executive Orders of June 8 and November 23, 1880.

24. Carl F. Palfrey, report of July 20, 1881, quoted in Stephen Hirst, *Life in a Narrow Place* (New York: David McKay Co., 1976), p. 58.

25. Elliott Coues, *Birds of the Colorado Valley: A Repository of Scientific and Popular Information Concerning North American Ornithology* (U.S. Department of the Interior Geological Survey of the Territories, F. V. Hayden, Miscellaneous Publications No. 11. Washington: Government Printing Office, 1878), p. 165.

26. Frank Hamilton Cushing, "The Nation of the Willows," *Atlantic Monthly* 50(September-October 1882):362-74, 541-59. Reprint, with foreword by Robert C. Euler (Flagstaff: Northland Press, 1965).

27. Frank E. Casanova, ed., "General Crook Visits the Supais, as Reported by John G. Bourke," *Arizona and the West* 10(Autumn 1968):263, 268. Navajo, said by Bourke to be 40 years old in 1884, lived until 1900.

28. Paul Bailey, *Jacob Hamblin: Buckskin Apostle* (Los Angeles: Westernlore Press, 1948), pp. 181, 261.

29. Jacob Hamblin, *Jacob Hamblin: A Narrative of His Personal Experience, as a Frontiersman, Missionary to the Indians and Explorer*, ed. by James A. Little (Salt Lake City: Deseret News, 1909), pp. 88-90.

30. R. E. Lingenfelter, *First through the Grand Canyon* (Los Angeles: Glen Dawson, 1958).

31. Robert Brewster Stanton, *Colorado River Controversies*, ed. by James M. Chalfant (New York: Dodd, Mead & Co., 1932), p. 52.

32. *Ibid.*, p. 53.

33. William Culp Darrah, *Powell of the Colorado* (Princeton: Princeton University Press, 1951). *See also* Wallace Stegner, *Beyond the Hundredth Meridian: John Wesley Powell and the Second Opening of the West* (Boston: Houghton Mifflin Co., 1953).

34. Powell probably avoided using "Colonel" because it was so often an empty honorific at this time.

35. Darrah, p. 92.

36. *Ibid.*, p. 135.

37. John Wesley Powell, *Exploration of the Colorado River of the West and its Tributaries* (Washington: Government Printing Office, 1875), p. 80.

38. *Ibid.*, p. 83.

39. *Ibid.*, p. 89.

40. *Ibid.*, pp. 82, 91.

41. *Ibid.*, p. 89.

42. John K. Hillers, *"Photographed All the Best Scenery:" Jack Hillers' Diary of the Powell Expeditions, 1871-1875* (Salt Lake City: University of Utah Press, 1972).

43. Francis P. Farquhar, *The Books of the Colorado River and the Grand Canyon: A Selective Bibliography* (Los Angeles: Glen Dawson, 1953), p. 20. This use of the name was noted by Robert Brewster Stanton.

44. Robert A. Weinstein and Roger Olmsted, "Image Makers of the Colorado Canyons," *The American West* 4(May 1967):28-39.

45. George M. Wheeler, *Report upon United States Geographical Surveys West of the One Hundredth Meridian*, Vol. 1: *Geographical Report* (Washington: Government Printing Office, 1889), p. 168.

46. Thurman Wilkins, *Thomas Moran: Artist of the Mountains* (Norman: University of Oklahoma Press, 1966).

47. Clarence Edward Dutton, *Tertiary History of the Grand Canyon District, with Atlas* (Washington: Government Printing Office, 1882), p. 152.

48. Charles Doolittle Walcott, "Study of a Line of Displacement in the Grand Cañon of the Colorado, in Northern Arizona," *Bulletin of the Geological Society of America* 1(No. 7, 1889):49.

49. Edwin D. McKee, "The Canyon Trails," in Roderick Peattie, ed., *The Inverted Mountains: Canyons of the West* (New York: Vanguard Press, 1948), p. 299.

5

THE AMERICAN FRONTIER REACHES THE GRAND CANYON

The American frontier came late to the Grand Canyon region. Dry climate and rough topography discouraged settlers, so the frontier swept on around northern Arizona before filling it in. Settlement speeded after the early 1880's, when railroads pushed into the area.

Many of those who came early were looking for ways to make themselves rich. Prospectors roamed everywhere, seeking the mineral wealth they thought must be there. Hunters and trappers found wildlife plentiful, especially on the Buckskin Mountains (Kaibab Plateau) and Greenland (Walhalla) Plateau. Cattle and sheep were grazed on both rims, and timber was cut.

Ranchers, settlers, and colonists arrived. Arizona Territory quadrupled its non-Indian population between 1870 and 1880, from under 10,000 to over 40,000, and more than doubled it again to 88,000 by 1890, when the U.S. Bureau of the Census declared the frontier at an end. The settlement of Southern Utah proceeded earlier than that of northern Arizona, as the Latter-day Saints moved down from the north under the guidance of their powerful Church.

Mormon colonization was remarkable in organization and extent. Cedar City had been founded in 1851. Kanab, an outpost since 1864, was founded as a town in 1870, and soon afterward a fort was constructed at Pipe Spring. The Mormons made several attempts to colonize the basin of the Little Colorado River, beginning in 1873, and met with eventual success. James S. Brown and others settled in 1875 at Moenkopi, and the Mormons founded nearby Tuba City in 1878, a site later bought by the U.S. government in 1903.

Timber for construction in the Southern Utah towns was often obtained from the Kaibab Forest, where Levi Stewart operated a portable steam sawmill beginning in 1871 near Big Springs.[2] Lumber from Mt. Trumbull, further west, was used in the Mormon Temple at St. George, completed in 1877.[3]

Cattle and sheep grazing on the ranges north of the Grand Canyon made a profitable business before overgrazing depleted the grass.[4] The Canaan Cooperative Stock Company and then the Winsor Castle Stock Growing Company successively grazed cattle north of Grand Canyon. The Kaibab range was controlled for about a decade after 1877 by the United Order of Orderville, Utah, who wintered their herds in House Rock Valley at the eastern base of the plateau, and moved them in summer up to the extensive meadows of DeMotte Park, often called V. T. Park, in the Kaibab Forest.[5]

The Kaibab Land and Cattle Company was formed in 1887 by John W. Young, a son of Brigham Young.[6] While on a mission in England, he got "Buffalo Bill" Cody to agree to take a group of Englishmen along with him in 1892 on a trip to the North Rim country, where they could see the possibilities of establishing hunting lodges and keeping horses and hounds on the Kaibab. They got off the train in Flagstaff, where the local people were much impressed.[7] Some Kanab businessmen including Dan Seegmiller met them with wagons and took them up to the South Rim, then via Lee's Ferry and Houserock Valley to the Kaibab. After such a rugged trip it is no wonder the honored guests decided that the Grand Canyon country was too far

"Buffalo Bill" Cody on the North Rim in 1892 with a group of Englishmen interested in establishing hunting lodges on the Kaibab.

from England.

Money had been borrowed on the security of the Kaibab Land and Cattle Company's range rights, so when English backing failed, a finance company took over the mortgage and put the astute A. W. Ivins in charge. Later, B. F. Saunders and then E. J. Marshall's Grand Canyon Cattle Company controlled the northern grazing lands in the Kaibab area. Further to the west, Preston Nutter, a cattleman who had served in the Colorado legislature, purchased range and water rights north of the Grand Canyon following 1893.[8]

An essential link for Mormon development in northern Arizona was the Colorado River crossing at Lee's Ferry. There are only a few places in the Grand Canyon region where the Colorado can be approached and crossed with relative ease. One of these is Pierce's Ferry, below the Grand Wash Cliffs at the mouth of Grand Canyon, a site found by Jacob Hamblin and operated as a ferry by Harrison Pierce beginning in 1876.[9] More famous is the crossing near the mouth of the Paria River, located by Hamblin with the help of Naraguts, a Paiute Indian, in 1858.

John Doyle Lee, a controversial Mormon, moved there in 1871, and established a ferry.[10] Although his name for the place, suggested by one of his wives, Emma, was Lonely Dell, it has been called Lee's Ferry ever since. Lee went to Lonely Dell partly because of trouble stirred up over his role in the massacre of a group of pioneers by Mormons and Paiutes in Mountain Meadows several years before. He was arrested on this charge in 1874, convicted and executed in 1877, although no one else involved in the massacre was ever brought to trial.

The first boat used by Lee as a ferry was a rough scow called the *Cañon Maid*, constructed by Powell in 1870 to cross the river on his way from Kanab to the Hopi towns, repaired by Lee to carry a band of Navajos across the river on January 18,

1872, and then taken by prospectors and wrecked in a Marble Canyon rapid. Powell had also cached two boats, the *Emma Dean* and *Nellie Powell*, at the mouth of the Paria when he had completed the first leg of his second river expedition in 1871. These were "borrowed" and used by travelers, and by Lee himself. When he resumed his second expedition, Powell abandoned the *Nell* at the Paria, where Lee continued to operate her as an auxiliary boat at the ferry. In 1873, with a new boat called the *Colorado*, Lee instituted regular ferry business with a charge of $3 per wagon and 75¢ per animal.

Lee sometimes had to flee from the ferry when he received word that lawmen were approaching; in 1873 he was staying at Moenave, and in a letter written from there he reported that he had gone for a brief visit to the Havasupai. Contrary to legend, however, he did not hide there for any considerable length of time, nor did he introduce peaches to the Havasupai, who had obtained them long before from the Hopi.[11]

After Lee's arrest, Emma continued to run the ferry. It was purchased from her in 1879 by the Latter-day Saints Church for $3,000, most of it in cattle. Warren Marshall Johnson and his sons, who had been operating the ferry for Emma Lee since 1875, continued in charge for 20 years, followed by James S. Emett from 1896 to 1909.[12] A cable and other improvements were added, but the crossing was often dangerous, sometimes fatal, throughout the ferry's history. The Grand Canyon Cattle Company controlled the ferry for a brief period before selling it to Coconino County. Warren Johnson's sons, Jerry, Frank and Price, operated it until a tragic accident in June, 1928, drowned three men. Since Navajo Bridge, which was to replace the ferry, was under construction, the ferry never reopened.

As a result of the Colorado River Compact in 1922, Lee's Ferry is the point from which distances are measured along

the Colorado River by government surveys. Mile 61, for example, refers to a point in Grand Canyon 61 miles (98 km.) below Lee's Ferry. Boat trips through the Grand Canyon often start at Lee's Ferry, as it is virtually the only practical approach to the river above Grand Canyon.

In the years after the Civil War, railroad-building enthusiasm swept the country. One line pushed across northern Arizona. This was the Atlantic and Pacific Railroad, which followed a route surveyed by General William J. Palmer in 1867-1868, passing near the San Francisco Peaks and Bill Williams Mountain. Railroad camps such as Flagstaff, Williams, and Peach Springs were established. There were post offices and sawmills by the time the railroad tracks were laid, in 1882. Flagstaff took its name from an event which probably occurred on July 4, 1876, when a group of settlers from Boston stopped near the later site of the town and, stripping a large pine of its branches, raised the Stars and Stripes to celebrate a century of independence.[13] The coming of the railroad to northern Arizona made the Grand Canyon much more accessible to ranchers, tourists, prospectors, and miners.

At this time, most people who had heard of the Grand Canyon had a hazy and fantastic idea of its actual appearance. But as artists depicted the Canyon, scientists studied, mapped and described it in more detail, and professional travelers wrote guide books, it became more widely and better known and more people wished to see it. Early visitors had to be hardy travelers, willing to spend days on horseback or in lurching wagons and stagecoaches. The stop at Peach Springs on the Hualapai Reservation was the railroad's closest approach to the Grand Canyon, and tourists began to make the 20-mile (32 km.) journey fairly often in 1883. They went down Peach Springs Wash to its junction with Diamond Creek, and then two miles (3 km.) along that creek to

Until the opening of Navajo Bridge in 1929, Lee's Ferry was the only place to cross the Colorado for hundreds of miles. It remains prominent as the starting point for river trips through the Grand Canyon.

the Colorado River at the bottom of the Canyon. Ben Wittick, the early Southwestern photographer, made the trip with his son in that year.[14] Soon a road was built and the first tourist stagecoaches ran from the railroad to the river. J. H. Farlee built a frame hotel at the junction in 1884, called the Farlee Hotel or Diamond Creek Hotel. An early visitor described it as a board shanty of a single room below, with kitchen attached, and two bedrooms under the roof above. It was the first hotel in the Grand Canyon. Mr. Farlee was "stage proprietor, road-owner, driver, guide, landlord, and cook."[15] Charles F. Lummis, the writer and naturalist, walked down Peach Springs Wash during a cross-country tramp in early 1885.[16] But few hotel guests stayed very long, and as access to the rim further east was developed by Flagstaff and Williams entrepreneurs, the Diamond Creek Hotel was eclipsed. It closed in 1889.

The arrival of the railroad brought change in the lives of the Indians. Contacts with non-Indians became more frequent, and there were conflicts over the land. Whites killed much of the wildlife, and gained control of sources of water and grazing land in Hualapai and Havasupai country.[17] Overgrazing became a chronic problem. In the 1880's, many Hualapais were living in railroad towns such as Kingman, Hackberry, and Peach Springs. The railroad was to claim that its land grant entitled it to every alternate section of land in the reservation, and in 1888, Mohave County asked in vain for the abolishment of the Hualapai Reservation. Along with these encroachments and threats came epidemics, accidents, and acts of violence. By this time, Indians generally wore clothing of "White" style, and many were working for non-Indians.

The Ghost Dance was an Indian religious protest against the destruction of their land and culture by the whites. It began to spread rapidly among many tribes in 1889, due to the work of the Nevada Paiute prophet, Wovoka. He taught that if Indians would dance, sing special songs, and return to the old ways, the earth would be renewed. All the dead Indians, deer, antelope, and other living things that existed in past ages would reappear, the non-Indian strangers would depart, and Indians would again have full possession of the land.

The Southern Paiutes were the first Indians near Grand Canyon to adopt the Ghost Dance.[18] The Hualapais learned it from the Paiutes near St. George, and Chief Sherum, who visited the Paiutes to find out more about the Ghost Dance, was an enthusiastic leader of the movement among the Hualapais during the years 1889-91. They danced around a spirally painted pole with eagle feathers at the top for many days at a time.

The Havasupais were a little later in adopting the Ghost Dance, but with the encouragement of Chief Navajo, the ceremony survived longer among them than other tribes. When it was clear that the dead had failed to return and the environment was not renewed, the Ghost Dance rituals faded away, leaving only a few songs as survivals.

At about the same time government supervision of Grand Canyon Indians was increased. The Bureau of Indian Affairs placed the Hualapais and Havasupais under the jurisdiction of Fort Mohave Indian School in 1890.[19] A government farmer was sent into Havasu Canyon two years later. Schools were established at Hackberry and Kingman for the Hualapais, and at the Havasupai village, where in sandstone buildings near the junction of Havasu and Hualapai Canyons, there were soon about 70 pupils studying under two teachers.[20] The Havasupai day school included only the lower grades; older children were sent out to boarding schools.

By 1896, a B.I.A. agent named Henry P. Ewing was appointed to the Walapai Indian Agency, which supervised both tribes. He began to collect fees for grazing and timber cutting on the reservation. The agent recommended that the Havasupai Reservation be enlarged to include some plateau lands; the issue was to simmer for 90 years.[21] John Muir met some of the Havasupais at Grand Canyon, and described them from his own viewpoint:

> The cañon Indians I have met here seem to be living much as did their ancestors...They are able, erect men, with commanding eyes, which nothing that they wish to see can escape. They are never in a hurry, have a strikingly measured, deliberate, bearish manner of moving the limbs and turning the head, are capable of enduring weather, thirst, hunger, and over-abundance, and are blessed with stomachs which triumph over everything the wilderness may offer. Evidently their lives are not bitter.[22]

The prospectors of the late Nineteenth Century were incurable optimists. Pay dirt, it seemed to them, was always over the next rise. Rich mines were found in the West by a lucky few, and this encouraged the unlucky majority to search on and on. Lonely men with burros, or on foot, prospected the Grand Canyon region in the '70's, '80's and '90's. Doubtless they saw every alcove and side canyon of the great gorge itself. It seemed as if the Grand Canyon ought to contain vast mineral wealth, and rumors of John D. Lee's lost gold mine lent luster to that idea.

Of course, it would be impossible to record the movements of all these men. The hills were full of them, and they wandered everywhere. George Riley, a prospector who accompanied Powell's 1871 reconnaissance, was rumored to have found gold in Kanab Creek, which precipitated a minor gold rush.[23] Other tributaries, and the River itself, were searched at the same time with few results.

Prospective miners became a plague to the Havasupai Indians. Charles Spencer, a long-time resident among the Hualapais, found a silver lode in Havasu Canyon in 1873. W. C. Beckman and H. J. Young in 1879 located a lead-silver claim near the base of Bridal Veil (Havasu) Falls. In the next year they returned with others including Daniel W. Mooney, a sailor turned miner, and attempted to descend the cliff near the highest falls downstream.[24] They lowered a rope over the side, and Mooney slid down it, but the rope was too short; he fell to the rocks below and was killed. The falls have since been called Mooney Falls. The other miners later placed a ladder there and buried Mooney's body.

In the 1870's, copper mining districts were opened near the Grand Canyon in the Grand Wash Cliffs and Mt. Trumbull areas.[25] The Grand Gulch Mine, about 15 miles (24 km.) north of the Canyon's lower end, was equipped with a smelter. There was activity to the east at the same time; in 1874 two prospectors, William Ridenour and S. Crozier, claimed that Indians had chased them out of the Grand Canyon.[26] The plateau south of the western Grand Canyon was busy in the 1880's, with mines at Pine Springs, Music Mountain, and the "Grand Cañon" mine located on the rim near Prospect Valley.

During his river survey in January, 1890, Robert Stanton met Felix Lantier, a Flagstaff prospector, at the bottom of the Tanner Trail.[27] About a month later, Ben Beamer took up residence in an abandoned Pueblo ruin near the confluence of the Little Colorado and Colorado, and tried to support himself by plowing the streamside alluvium when he wasn't prospecting.[28] Apparently a "copper rush" began in 1890, when William Ashurst, Senator Henry F. Ashurst's father, found rich ore near the "Number Seven" which

is visible from Hopi Point.[29] He had been prospecting the Canyon since 1880, and continued to do so until he lost his life there in a rockslide in 1901. James S. Best led a prospecting party in 1891 that came in by boats on the Colorado River from Green River, Utah, to Lee's Ferry, by horseback across the Kaibab Plateau to Jacob Lake, and then into Grand Canyon down Bright Angel Creek on foot. Mormons developed copper mines near Jacob Lake, and opened a smelter about 1900 at Ryan on the Kanab Plateau west of Kanab Creek. Kanab men prospected the North Rim, too, and in 1902 copper was rumored near Point Sublime.[30]

Few Grand Canyon prospectors were successful. Some returned to "civilization" with glowing tales. Some never returned at all.

In order to provide themselves with a supply of pack animals, prospectors released burros in the Canyon where they thrived on the sparse vegetation and multiplied. Other burros were lost, and the population reached an estimated two thousand burros in modern times. Much destruction of plant cover and fouling of springs resulted. Burros are not native to America.

Hundreds of claims were located in the Grand Canyon. To patent his claim a prospector had to do work to "prove" it. Those who mined in the Grand Canyon were faced with prohibitive difficulties. Trails had to be built and the ore packed out on animals. Water was scarce. Railroads were distant. Finally, the Canyon's ore deposits proved to be of limited extent; none of them brought great financial return with the exception of the Orphan Mine, and that one had to wait until the advent of the atomic age before it panned out.

Some miners who stayed on at the Canyon discovered that their trails and their land had value as tourist facilities which equalled or exceeded its mineral value. These men went into the guide business

and then into the tourist camp and hotel business.

One of these was "Captain" John Hance, a memorable storyteller, tourist guide, trailbuilder and miner, who arrived at the Grand Canyon about 1883 and soon became the first White resident.[31] He built a log cabin east of Grandview Point at the head of the Old Hance Trail, which he improved. Across the river he located an asbestos mine. But his major activity was entertaining tourists. He would give them bed and board at his cabin, guide them down his trail on foot, horse or mule, and tell them stories, of which more than a hundred have been remembered and written down. Apparently he never spun the same tale twice in exactly the same way.

Some of them had dozens of alternate endings or "punch lines." Others he invented on the spot and never told again. His gift seems to have been to start out with something barely believeable, proceed to the merely plausible, and end up with the completely absurd without losing his listeners along the way. At the end, they laughed with him, and laughed partly at themselves for being led as far as they had been.

Among his stories that people still love to repeat is the one about the time the Canyon filled up solid with clouds from rim to rim, and he walked across on snowshoes, barely escaping death when a clearing trend occurred and he was marooned on a pinnacle. Or the one in which, riding his faithful horse Darby, he was being pursued by Indians when he came upon the Canyon rim and was forced to jump his horse across toward the North Rim. Failing to make it, he fell down toward the river, only saving himself by dismounting handily just above the ground—or by grabbing the limbs of a pine tree—or by shouting "whoa!" to his obedient horse—or perhaps he was killed, depending on which version of the story he happened to be telling.[32]

The first tourists known to have visited John Hance at the Grand Canyon were Edward Everett Ayer and his family and friends. Ayer was a businessman with wide interests in mining and lumbering, who had built the first sawmill in Flagstaff in 1882. He went on to become a patron of learning, as a founder of Chicago's Field Museum and donor of a unique collection of books on the American Indian to the Newberry Library.

This claim to the Coyote Mine was found in a tobacco can along the West Rim in 1974.

Pat Lynch, Civil War veteran, prospector, and hermit. Hundreds like him wandered the immensity of the Canyon in an effort to strike it rich.

On his 1884 Grand Canyon visit, he hired Philip and William Hull, who had a sheep ranch south of the Canyon, as guides.[33] They made a trip to the bottom of the Canyon, giving Mrs. Ayer the distinction of being the first white woman to make the descent on foot. They used the Old Hance Trail, and John Hance, then working at Hull Ranch, was their guide for the inner canyon hike. Many others followed the Ayers, and by 1886, John Hance was advertising in the Flagstaff newspaper:

> Being thoroughly conversant with all the trails leading to the Grand Canyon of the Colorado, I am prepared to conduct parties thereto at any time. I have a fine spring of water near my house on the rim of the Canyon, and can furnish accommodations for tourists and their animals.[34]

Hance built the Red Canyon, or New Hance Trail, in 1894 when rockslides had made the old trail unusable.[35] He continued to work his mines, raised vegetables, constructed a reservoir or "tank" near his cabin, hunted, and sometimes lived in a second rock cabin down in the Canyon during the winter to avoid the worst of the cold and snow. He kept a guest book in which the tourists could record their impressions:

> God made the cañon, John Hance the trails. Without the other, neither would be complete.
> —Wm. O. O'Neill[36]

Hance impressed his visitors as a kind, generous host with a hard-bitten exterior, but a heart of gold. A lifelong bachelor, he was clean and orderly to the extreme, considering the conditions of his life, and served excellent meals. Although those who knew him before he came to the canyon said he was "a terror when drinking," he was seldom seen in that condition in later years. Perhaps he "drank in" the Grand Canyon scenery, and

Storyteller, tourist guide, trailbuilder, and miner, Captain John Hance. Like others, he soon discovered that tourists were more profitable than mining and built the first hotel on the Canyon's rim near Grandview Point.

found that all he needed. His voice was high-pitched but clear, and carried well. His profanity, as spectacular as fireworks, was used sparingly to illuminate his stories and never wearied his listeners. After all, he had been a muleskinner.

He liked children and could keep them entertained for hours. And he lived at peace with nature. His friends remarked that he never killed an animal except for meat, and never carved on a tree, or cut one down unless it was needed. He loved the wilderness, and the Grand Canyon beside which he lived.

Hance sold his ranch and trail to J. Wilbur Thurber, who operated the stage line from Flagstaff, in 1895.[37] But he stayed on, becoming the first postmaster on the rim of the Grand Canyon when the post office of Tourist, Arizona, was established in 1897 at Hance Ranch.[38] He sold the asbestos mines, but continued to manage them for an eastern firm until 1904. In 1906, Martin Buggeln, former manager of the Bright Angel Hotel, bought Hance Ranch and built a white, seventeen-room frame hotel beside the old log dining room which had been the nucleus of a tourist tent-camp "hotel." Buggeln evidently entertained only a few friends and relatives there.

Hance moved over to Grand Canyon Village, where the Fred Harvey Company provided him with room and board in Bright Angel Lodge, and encouraged him to talk to tourists as a "character," to provide local color, and in general to be his own yarn-spinning self.

John Hance kept his earlier life a secret by telling so many wild tales about it that even the truth is discredited as another "whopper." He was born in 1838 in eastern Tennessee at Cowan's Ferry into a family of abolitionist Republicans and Union sympathizers. He may have fought on either or both sides in the Civil War, and may have been taken prisoner, but the title "Captain" which he bore in later life seems to have been a strictly

honorary one. At the end of the war he was in Kansas near Fort Leavenworth working as a civilian on a mule wagon train which supplied U. S. Army forts. His boss was Lorenzo Butler Hickok, often called "Tame Bill" Hickok because his brother was James Butler "Wild Bill" Hickock.[39]

With his brother George, John came to Arizona in the late fall of 1868 and settled at Camp Verde near Prescott. He worked on his brother's ranch operating ox-drawn wagons. One of the jobs George and John took on was to move the Indians from the Verde Valley to the San Carlos Reservation. Most of the Indians walked, but the Hances hauled the baggage and those who were old, sick, wounded, or with infants. Afterwards John Hance operated a bull team of his own. On a prospecting trip in 1883, he first saw the Grand Canyon, which he came to know and love, and where his body was buried, as he wished, in 1919.

Bass Camp, Bass Trail and the Bass limestone are all named for a man who came to Arizona for his health at the age of 34, and became a Grand Canyon settler, trailbuilder, guide, miner and promoter who lived into his eighties.[40] William Wallace Bass was born in Indiana in 1849, and was a dispatcher on the railroads in New York before coming West.

In 1883 Bass came to Williams, a frontier town of tents, false-front stores, sawmills and saloons. At first he lived in a cave, and later worked and lived on the Scott Ranch along Cataract (Havasu) Creek. He heard many tales of the Grand Canyon and John D. Lee's hidden gold, and went up to take a look. He was so impressed with the Canyon that he forgot all about the gold and felt everyone should see the Grand Canyon.

He set up a camp on the South Rim near Havasupai Point, and built a road to Ashfork about 1890. He located several copper and asbestos claims, made friends with the Havasupai Indians, and soon was guiding parties of tourists from

Williams and Ashfork to the Grand Canyon and Havasu Canyon. Later, when the railroad came, many of his parties came by train to Bass Station, four miles from Bright Angel Lodge. Bass provided buggy and coach service from there.

Bass constructed a trail down into the Canyon from his camp on the rim to Mystic Springs, a source of water which was shown to him by one of his Havasupai friends named Captain Burro. He packed water from the springs to Bass Camp. Later the trail was continued down to the Colorado River; he crossed the river by means of a boat he built on the rocky shore near the mouth of Shinumo Creek.[41] About two miles beyond the river crossing, along the bank of Shinumo Creek, he had a tent camp and a garden where he raised melons, corn, and other vegetables; also an orchard of peach and apricot trees and grapevines. Another old Indian trail, the White Trail, continued up Shinumo Creek and White Creek to Powell (Muav) Saddle and the North Rim. This made a cross-canyon trip possible for tourists on the Bass Trail.

One of the tourists Bass took on a horseback trip to Havasu Canyon in 1892 was Ada Diefendorf, a music teacher from Worcester, New York, and a graduate of the Boston Conservatory of Music. Perhaps a common interest in music attracted them to one another, for Bass played the violin. They were married two years later, and Mrs. Bass moved up to Bass Camp to become the first white woman to raise a family on the rim of the Grand Canyon. The trip to town required an overnight stop enroute and Ada Bass often said she prepared a meal or slept under every tree on the 73 miles (117 km.) of road to Ashfork. Since there was no permanent water at Bass Camp, she sometimes made a three-day trip down to the Colorado River in the Canyon to do laundry. She had four children: Edith, William, Hazel, and Mabel.

Bass operated a regular stage line to

his camp, using an old four-horse stagecoach which had belonged to General Nelson A. Miles. An overnight stop was made at "The Cave." No more than 18 guests could be accommodated at Bass Camp, which in addition to a large main building had several tent cabins, a bunkhouse for guides, barns, corrals and warehouse. There was also a darkroom in a small cave a few feet below the canyon rim. Bass was a self-taught photographer who used the old glass plate cameras.

Bass imported horses, including a thoroughbred stallion. He installed a cableway across the river in 1908 at Bass Crossing with a cage big enough to carry a burro, soon enlarged to permit a mule or horse to be sent across. Mules and horses, being cautious animals, were not always eager to make the trip, and some incidents of humor and danger resulted. Asbestos from Bass' mine was shipped as far as France to be used in fireproof theater curtains. Later he built another cableway three river miles below, near the mouth of Hakatai Canyon. The cables remained in place until 1968, when they were removed as a hazard to aircraft.

Loading a burro with books and provisions, Bass often went into the Canyon for weeks at a time, studying and prospecting. He had his own theory about its formation which was quite different from the usual story one reads. He wrote several poems about the Grand Canyon which he would recite to his passengers on stage trips, and he could hold his audiences spellbound for long periods of time while he lectured on the rim. He also made tours through the East showing lantern slides of his own making. He had a deep and reverent feeling

Pictured here with Big Jim, Bass was an active friend of the Havasupais. He took tourists and mail into their Canyon home and even helped to establish their first school.

Bass's unique theories about the formation of the Canyon are expounded in one of his poems.

for the Grand Canyon and the lessons it teaches.

Bass knew the Havasupai Indians well, and often took tourists to see their canyon home. He blasted cisterns in dry places, and built dams along Havasu Creek to store water for travelers and their animals. He was active in behalf of aid for the Havasupai Indians, helping to get a school started there, obtaining medicine for them during an epidemic of measles, and even going as far as Washington to request congressional action. He carried mail between Havasu and Grand Canyon for a time, and often employed Havasupai Indians at his camp. He also helped to get the first schoolhouse and teacher for Grand Canyon Village in 1911. Eight children were required to hold a school and Bass had four; often there were just enough to keep it going. He also operated horsedrawn tours on the rim drives and later had two automobiles. He and his family continued to operate Bass Camp until 1923, when they moved to Wickenburg. Bass' properties at Grand Canyon were purchased by the Santa Fe Railroad in 1926 and then transferred to the national park.

W. W. Bass died in 1933, and according to his wishes, his ashes were scattered over Holy Grail Temple, also known as Bass Tomb, from an airplane. Ada Bass, his wife, survived him until 1951, when her body was buried near that of her oldest daughter Edith in Pioneer Cemetery at Grand Canyon.

One of the Mormon settlers at Tuba City was Seth B. Tanner, who prospected and traded over a large region. He built a house near a ford of the Little Colorado River above the present town of Cameron. This Tanner's Crossing had a rock bottom, avoiding the quicksands found elsewhere. In 1880, he organized the Little Colorado Mining District, covering a large area southward and eastward from Grand Canyon. Tanner often visited the eastern part of Grand Canyon, and

followed an old Indian trail since called the Tanner Trail to mining claims near the river, where he found a little copper.

The Tanner Trail gained a romantic and also a rather unsavory reputation over the years. It leads down into country where legend says John D. Lee buried several pots of gold. Many attempts have been made to find this treasure, all of them failures and some of them disasters. For

example, a man named Brown, guided by W. W. Bass, is reported to have lost five heavily laden burros over the edge near the top.[42]

There is also a tradition of skulduggery there by thieves, poachers and renegades. From the Tanner Trail, one can cross the river to the Nankoweap Trail and thus go from rim to rim via what was called the Horsethief Trail. According to many old-timers, this trail was used by a

gang who stole mounts in Utah, changed the brands and spirited them across to Arizona, where they sold them and then stole more to bring back and sell to their original victims, whom they again robbed, etc.

In more recent times the Tanner Trail served as an outlet for illicit booze. Park Naturalist Glen Sturdevant discovered a distillery at an abandoned campsite in

1928, with assorted bottles, kegs and other equipment. It has been reported that a bootlegger sold the stuff in Grand Canyon Village during prohibition.[43]

Louis D. Boucher was called "the Hermit" because he was a quiet man who lived in an out-of-the-way beautiful place, Dripping Springs, in an amphitheater of Hermit Basin, the head of Hermit Canyon, a tributary of the Grand Canyon.[44] He had a white beard, rode a white mule with a

Louis Boucher, the "hermit" of Hermit Camp.

53

bell around its neck, and carried the tools of a prospector: a geology pick and a pan, and tools for trailmaking. He hailed from Sherbrooke, Quebec, in French-speaking Canada, and came to the Canyon about 1891. Apparently he was a trail guide at Hance Ranch for a time.

His home camp at dependable Dripping Springs consisted of two tents and a corral for horses, mules and burros. He also kept sheep. He even kept goldfish in a trough. His Silver Bell Trail descended from the rim to Dripping Springs and then out around Columbus Point into Long (Boucher) Canyon, where he planted a splendid orchard and garden and grew oranges, figs, peaches, pomegranates and other fruits, vegetables of every kind including tomatoes throughout the year, chili, cucumbers, melons and grapes. He had 75 trees. This orchard was at the site of Boucher's copper mine, where tourists could stay in cabins. Louie located other mineral claims, including a deposit of graphite, but apparently none of his prospects were pay dirt, because by 1912 he had moved on to Mohrland, Utah, where he worked in a coal mine. He was not a complete hermit, as other men worked with him from time to time, and in 1903 he assisted in the search for P. H. McGonigle and Charles McLean, who had drowned in the river.[45]

Peter D. Berry's life is a page out of the Old West. He was born in 1856 in Ohio but his family soon moved to Missouri.[46] As a young man, he went out to Colorado to work in the mines. One of his brothers, John Berry, had gone to Flagstaff, Arizona Territory, where he ran a saloon and was well-liked. There were trouble-makers in every Western frontier town, and Flagstaff, no exception, had the two Hawkes brothers. One night they got into a rough argument at the Berry Saloon, and when John tried to pour oil on the troubled waters, they filled him full of lead. The sheriff's deputy put them in jail, but as the good townspeople were

not willing to let the law take its slow course, they shot one of the Hawkes boys in the jail and took the other one out and lynched him. Someone let Pete know what had happened. He came to Flagstaff and tried to do what was best by his own rights. His brother's widow and her son seemed to need support, so he married her and settled down in Flagstaff. He built a house there in 1888.

Interest in prospecting and mines at the Grand Canyon was high in those days, and Peter had mining experience. He made friends with two smart, energetic men named Ralph and Niles Cameron, who were at the time running a store in Flagstaff and a sheep ranch nearby, and the three of them went up to the Canyon often during the 1890's as partners to locate claims and work some of them, and incidentally to explore the Canyon and build trails down into it. There were other partners involved with Berry and the Camerons from time to time.[47] But Berry spent months hiking in the Canyon alone, recording his movements in his meticulously kept, atrociously spelled diary.[48]

The first trail constructed by Berry, the two Camerons, and others was the Bright Angel Trail, an old Havasupai Indian track which they widened in 1890 and 1891 as far as Indian Gardens. This was recorded as a toll road, and through mining claims located at strategic spots such as Indian Gardens, its use was controlled. The trail was extended on down to the river about 1898.

Meanwhile, the Camerons and Berry became interested in another part of the Canyon. In 1890, Pete located the "Last Chance" claim on a rich vein of copper ore on Horseshoe Mesa below Grandview Point.[49] He claimed a mill site on the rim and in 1892 built the Grandview Trail from there down to the mine. Ore was packed up the trail on 8 or 10 mules, each carrying 200 pounds (90 kg.). They could make a round trip and a half on the 4-mile (6

km.) trail each day. In the mine, work was done with pick and shovel, explosives and a wheelbarrow, with a mule-operated hoist to the surface and a narrow-gauge track out to the dump. There were several cabins and a mess hall located on Horseshoe Mesa, provided with Arizona Air-Tight Stoves for winter heat. The ore was excellent. At the Columbian Exposition in Chicago it was awarded a prize as over 70% pure copper.

One day in 1894 the Camerons, Berry and James McClure were traveling along the Tonto Platform between the Grandview Trail and the Bright Angel Trail. Ralph Cameron was ahead of the others. In a stream bed he found an old Meerschaum pipe lying on the ground. He picked it up, scratched a date about one hundred years previous on it, and put it where they could not miss it. His companions fell for the joke, speculating on who might have been there so long before. The story was too good not to tell. The stream has been called Pipe Creek ever since.[50]

The miners were constantly receiving visitors, and it was not long before they saw them as a valuable source of income. The rude cabin up on the rim was joined by the Grandview Hotel, a long, two-story log structure that opened for business in spring, 1897, and was for several years the leading tourist mecca at the Grand Canyon. It was managed by Peter Berry. The Grandview Trail was extended down to the river for trailriding visitors, and some natural limestone caverns that the miner's cook had discovered became a popular attraction. Soon stalactites and stalagmites decorated the hotel's front porch, their places in the caves taken by scrawled names and dates.[51]

Mrs. Berry had borne Pete a son, named Ralph after Ralph Cameron. According to some of the old-timers, Mrs. Berry did not like life at the Canyon, and before long she had gone away to Tucson.[52] Pete married Martha Thompson, the

housekeeper at the Grandview Hotel.

The Last Chance Mine seemed to consume more money than it produced. Still, it was a good mine and the ore was rich. In 1901, Berry and his partners sold it to the Canyon Copper Company, an eastern corporation.[53] In 1907, the bottom dropped out of the copper market. New methods had been developed for processing low-grade ore, and the high-grade ore of the Last Chance Mine was no longer worth hauling out of the canyon.

The hotel, too, fell on evil days. The railroad reached the canyon eleven miles (18 km.) to the west in 1901, and few tourists desired to make the arduous three-day stage trip from Flagstaff to Grandview and return. Some did take Fred Harvey trips out along the rim to Grandview and beyond, so Pete and Martha Berry stayed in business serving meals until 1908.

The Berry Copper Company holdings were eventually sold to the William Randolph Hearst interests, who in turn sold them to the National Park Service.[54] Pete guided his last string of tourists down into the Canyon in 1916, and soon afterwards moved down to the ranch below Hull Park which his son Ralph had homesteaded in 1915. Ralph died in the influenza epidemic of 1919. Pete and Martha continued to live at the ranch. Martha died in 1931, and Pete in 1932. The ranch was inherited by a nephew, Ray W. Berry, who sold it to William Belknap. The Belknaps used it at times, but abandoned the ranch house after thieves broke in and stole most of the movables. Today it lies in ruins. The Grandview Hotel is only a dim outline in the ground; but a deteriorating cabin, a pile of vandalized debris, and the excavations remain at the Last Chance Mine.

Daniel L. Hogan, a native of New York and resident of Flagstaff, arrived at the Grand Canyon about 1890, and began to prospect.[55] The best-looking copper ore he could find was down over the rim of the canyon, a thousand feet below Maricopa Point. He located a claim there, including part of the rim, in 1893. Since he was an orphan, he named it the "Orphan Lode" or "Orphan Mine." He also did some prospecting in Hermit Basin, and in 1896 he and some others built the trail down into that area from Horsethief Tank, which he had also constructed. Once he ran across an old counterfeiters' camp in Hermit Basin.

During the Spanish-American War, Hogan and Buckey O'Neill served in Cuba with "T. R." Roosevelt's Rough Riders. The certificate of patent for the Orphan Lode Mining Claim, dated March 23, 1906, bears the signature of President Theodore Roosevelt.[56] After his return, Dan was appointed deputy sheriff and was wounded in 1899 during a fight with some Navajos he was trying to arrest.

Like all the other copper mines in the Grand Canyon, the Orphan was not particularly profitable, and was inactive for many years.

Sanford H. Rowe operated a livery stable in Williams, and provided transportation up to the Grand Canyon.[57] While being guided by a Havasupai Indian named Big Jim in 1890, Rowe noticed damp ground indicating a seep of water. Later he dug a well at this point, and claimed the land by right of discovery. Since he had already homesteaded a farm near Williams, he had to locate Rowe's Well as a mining claim and mill site. The "Lucky Strike," the "Little Mamie" and the "Highland Mary" claims never produced any mineral to boast of, but enough to patent. Rowe and others built a crude smelter there of rock and adobe, which operated on pinyon pine charcoal for fuel, to do the patent work. With Ed Hamilton as partner, Rowe developed the land into an automobile camping

An early tourist accommodation in Grand Canyon Village was the Bright Angel Hotel, started in 1896.

ground. Cabins, a coffee shop, a bar, and a dance hall later ornamented the forest there, using the water from the well, which proved to be insufficient. The claims were acquired by the National Park Service in 1956.

Most tourists who wanted to see the Grand Canyon before 1901 came by horseback, wagon or stage from some point on the Atlantic and Pacific Railroad. As access through Peach Springs declined in popularity, visitors were taking stages from other points further east by making arrangements with W. W. Bass, who operated chiefly out of Ashfork after 1892, or with Sanford Rowe, who drove the route from Williams. But the majority of tourists took the regular stage from Flagstaff, run by E. S. Willcox. Three stages a week traveled from Flagstaff, stopping at stations where travelers refreshed themselves while a change of horses was made. These stations were Little Springs, Cedar Ranch and Moqui Tanks. The trip to Hance's Ranch could be made in one day, and the fare was $15. For this price, one could jounce along in a four- or six-horse stage coach to which, if there were too many passengers, a second coach or "trailer" was attached, making a train measuring 48 feet from the first horses' noses to the tailboard. According to a traveler, "deep wheel-ruts in the yellow soil cause the coach to act like an over-laden schooner in a heavy sea."[58]

In 1895, J. Wilbur Thurber took over the operation of the stage line, and purchased Hance's trail and hotel. The line was extended over to the present site of the Bright Angel Lodge, where Thurber erected a cabin and tourist tent camp. Thurber always referred to himself as the "gentlemanly" driver of the Grand Canyon stage.

As the railroad approached the Canyon in 1900, stages were driven from the railhead at Anita to Thurber's "Bright Angel Hotel" at the head of the Bright Angel Trail. But with the arrival of the rails in 1901, the stagecoaches were limited to the trips along the rim, which they continued to take until the 1920's.

One cannot leave the subject of transportation to the Grand Canyon without mentioning the intrepid members of the Coconino Cycling Club of Flagstaff, who made their First Annual Run to the Grand Canyon in 1894.[59] The trip was not an easy one, and so few attended that only four Annual Runs were held. For example, in 1896 there were 60 reservations for the trip, only 13 starters, and only 6 who completed the trip, one with a broken chain. The usual August thundershowers dampened the cyclists' enthusiasm.

A few well-known visitors to the Grand Canyon in the late Nineteenth Century should be mentioned. General John J. Pershing, then a 29-year-old second lieutenant, visited the Canyon with three companions in 1889.[60] Lost and nearly perishing of thirst, he was guided to Hance's place by Captain Burro, the Havasupai Indian. In later years, Pershing was said to have remarked that if it were possible to move it, the Grand Canyon would make a wonderful border between France and Germany.

John Muir, the great conservationist, visited the Canyon many times and urged its establishment as a national park. He described it as a scene without parallel on earth:

No matter how far you have wandered hitherto, or how many famous gorges and valleys you have seen, this one, the Grand Cañon of the Colorado, will seem as novel to you, as unearthly in the color and grandeur and quantity of its architecture, as if you had found it after death, on some other star; so incomparably lovely and grand and supreme is it above all the other cañons in our fire-moulded, earthquake-shaken, rain-washed, wave-washed, river and glacier sculptured world.[61]

Muir made an 1896 visit with Gifford Pinchot, the founder of the U. S. Forest Service, and the two men scorned a comfortable hotel room to spend a night out sheltered from the freezing wind by a grove of trees on the canyon rim.[62] Several years later, Muir returned with the naturalist, John Burroughs, who called the

Canyon "The Divine Abyss," a place where one might look *"into* the earth as through a mighty window or open door."[63] Burroughs' description of his muleback trip down the Bright Angel Trail will sound familiar to anyone who has taken it:

My mule was named "Johnny," and there was soon a good understanding between us. I quickly learned to turn the whole problem of that perilous descent over to him. He knew how to take the sharp turns and narrow shelves of that steep zigzag much better than I did. I do not fancy that the thought of my safety was "Johnny's" guiding star; his solicitude struck nearer home than that. There was much ice and snow on the upper part of the trail, and only those slender little legs of "Johnny's" stood between me and a tumble of two or three thousand feet. How cautiously he felt his way with his round little feet, as, with lowered head, he seemed to be scanning the trail critically! Only when he swung around the sharp elbows of the trail did his forefeet come near the edge of the brink. Only once or twice at such times, as we hung for a breath above the terrible incline, did I feel a slight shudder.[64]

J. W. Thurber and passengers on the rim of the Canyon.

Among the early visitors were two who wrote travelogues, George Wharton James and Burton Holmes. James' guidebooks were standards on the Grand Canyon for many years. The photographers Henry G. Peabody and William Henry Jackson captured canyon images around the turn of the century.

Scientists continued to find the Grand Canyon region a subject for study. John Gill Lemmon, the California botanist, published his observations from an 1888 trip.[65] But in the following year, C. Hart Merriam made one of the most influential biological surveys on record.[66] Although most of his work was done in the San Francisco Peaks, he did study the animals and plants of the Grand Canyon as well. The result of this study was the concept of "life zones," that is, that different communities of animals and plants are found at certain elevations throughout the region, forming bands that are more or less horizontal. He was the first to give a scientific statement of the fact that in traveling upward in elevation from the bottom of the Grand Canyon to the top of the San Francisco Peaks, a gain of 10,000 feet (3200 m.), one encounters changes in climate, animals and plants similar to those one would encounter in traveling northward at low elevation from the Mexican desert to the Canadian arctic. Merriam wrote a type description of the white-tailed Kaibab squirrel that lives only in Grand Canyon's North Rim country. "The Grand Canyon of the Colorado is a world in itself," he wrote, "and a great fund of knowledge is in store for the philosophic biologist whose privilege it is to study exhaustively the problems there presented."[67] These words describe his own contributions to ecological understanding.

Railroads were still pushing forward in the last two decades of the Nineteenth Century, when the iron horse was the major means of long-distance travel. The construction of a railroad to the Grand

Canyon was an idea proposed by many. But the idea of building a railroad *through* the Grand Canyon along the Colorado River also had its day, occurring first to a prospector named S. S. Harper.[68] He had watched the westward progress of the Atlantic and Pacific Railroad and thought that a water-level route might have advantages. A look at the Colorado River near Lee's Ferry convinced him that it was possible, and he had soon sold the idea to Frank Mason Brown, a former California State Senator who had turned to the mining and real estate businesses in Denver.

To Brown, the idea of a railroad from Denver to San Diego through the Grand Canyon was irresistible. After talking to Powell, he and others formed the ambitious Denver, Colorado Canyon and Pacific Railroad Company on March 25, 1889. Soon afterwards, they appointed Robert Brewster Stanton, the designer of Colorado's famous Georgetown Loop, as chief engineer of a survey of the route.

Robert Brewster Stanton's first trip down the river ended in disaster. Three months later he returned, still intent on proving the feasibility of putting a railroad through the Grand Canyon of the Colorado.

A better man could hardly have been chosen, for once Stanton began a project, he always saw it through to completion or grand failure. He was a graduate of Miami University in Ohio, where his father was president. He had studied civil engineering, and had experience in railroad surveys and mining in the West. Now he undertook to repeat Powell's feat of taking a survey party by boat down the Colorado River.

The expedition left Green River, Utah, on May 25. Stanton took Powell's book along as a guide. President Brown, who came too, had provided them with five light boats of thin red cedar and had vetoed life preservers as unnecessary. In Cataract Canyon two boats were lost along with almost all the food, but miraculously all the men survived and Stanton managed to carry the survey through.

Provisions were renewed at Lee's Ferry, but in Marble Canyon on July 10 a boat overturned, tossing Brown into the river, where he drowned. Another disaster took the lives of Peter M. Hansbrough and Henry C. Richards a few days later. The surviving men then retreated from what was, to them, "death's canyon."[69]

Stanton was not defeated. He had larger boats constructed of sturdy oak with airtight compartments all around, and provided them with life preservers and waterproof rubber bags for the food. By December 10 he was leading a new survey party down the Colorado. After a fine Christmas dinner with the Johnsons of Lee's Ferry, they plunged into Marble Canyon, where disaster again overtook them. The photographer, Franklin A. Nims, fell down a cliff, breaking a leg and hitting his head. He remained unconscious for several days, and had to be taken overland by stretcher to Lee's Ferry.[70] Stanton took all the photographs from that point on. Miraculously, not one of the 2200 negatives was lost.

Testing their experience against the violence of the rapids, the men lost a boat and several fell overboard, but the life preservers did their work and no one was drowned. One man walked out, and three left by the railroad at Peach Springs. But Stanton and six others went all the way to the Gulf of California with the two remaining boats and completed the first run of the Grand Canyon in almost twenty years.

Stanton firmly believed that a railroad could have been built down the Colorado River, from an engineering standpoint, and perhaps he was right.[71] But he always tended to be overly optimistic about the business such a line would carry, located at the Canyon's bottom.

Stanton devoted much time in his later years to compiling a monumental history of the Colorado River that was too long to find a publisher. The courageous but frustrated life of this hardheaded dreamer ended in 1922.

In the years between Stanton's survey and the turn of the century, two trappers, Flavell and Galloway, took boats down the river through Grand Canyon.[72] George F. Flavell left Green River, Wyoming, on August 27, 1896 in a flat-bottomed boat named the *Panthon* with a companion, Ramon Montez. By October 20, they had reached the mouth of the Little Colorado. Flavell's log records the journey with flashes of a trapper's humor:

> If we had lowered over all the bad places, it would have taken a month. By risk it was run in a day. Still I feel confident we will get through. We must expect some accidents and expect to hit some rocks. There is only one stone we must not hit. That we must miss at all hazzard: our Tomb Stone![73]

After running all the rapids in Grand Canyon, without knowing their names, Flavell reached quiet water at the Grand Wash Cliffs on October 31, and then took his time, trapping beaver and visiting friends, downriver to Yuma.

Nathaniel T. Galloway, a Utah trapper, and William C. Richmond ran the river through the Grand Canyon in the winter of 1896-1897.[74] "Than," as his friends called Galloway, was a tall, slim, athletic man of 45, bald but possessing a large black moustache. He initiated a new method of running rapids. Instead of taking them head on, as Powell and the others had done, he turned the boat around and ran the rapids stern first so that he could watch where he was going, guide himself and check his speed with the oars. This method was adopted by almost all his successors, so that today if a violent rapid twists a boat around and forces the oarsman to run bow first, he is said to be "Major Powelling."

Galloway's boats were relatively flat-bottomed rowboats, 16 feet (4.9 m.) long, made of one-inch fir, with canvas covers and compartments added. Less enthusiastic about the scenery than Flavell, Galloway said that his trip was of "no profit."[75] He did manage to trap six beaver in the Grand Canyon. And the river had some hold on him, it seems, because he repeated his trip 12 years later.

While Stanton's project for a railroad down the length of the Canyon seems a trifle visionary even today, the suggestion of a spur line from the Atlantic and Pacific Railroad had much to recommend it, including potential business from tourists who wanted to see the scenic wonder. However, it was almost 20 years from the time the railroad reached Flagstaff and Williams to the completion of a line to the Grand Canyon.[76]

Businessmen in Flagstaff began the agitation for a line in 1886 by organizing the Flagstaff and Grand Canyon Railroad Company and running a survey,[77] but financial backing could not be secured. The Arizona legislature passed a bill in 1887 exempting from taxation for a period of six years from its completion the first railroad to be built from the Atlantic and Pacific line to the Grand Canyon.

Several further attempts were made by Flagstaff people to interest backers in the project, and a town meeting in 1891 promised help in securing right of way for any company that might build the railroad. In the same year, Flagstaff became the county seat of a new county, Coconino, carved out of Prescott's Yavapai County.[78] This gave Flagstaff new importance and encouraged its citizens in the project of a rail line to the Grand Canyon, now within Flagstaff's own county. Another company was formed, and in 1896 was granted right of way across the Grand Canyon Forest Reserve by Congress, but after a total of 15 years of sporadic effort, there was still no railroad from Flagstaff to the Grand Canyon.

By that time, Williams had its turn at promoting the railroad. In 1894, citizens contributed $1,000 to finance a survey.[79] The moving spirit behind this action was the young sheriff of Yavapai County, William Owen O'Neill, known to everyone as "Buckey," a name which stems from a gambling term, "Bucking the Tiger," meaning "to bet all on one throw."[80]

Buckey O'Neill was born in Missouri, received a legal education in Washington, D. C., came to Arizona in 1879, and in a brief but brilliant career became an author, reporter, editor, judge, and superintendent of schools, and was involved in several business ventures in the vast territory between Tombstone and the Grand Canyon. As sheriff, he was famed for the capture of the men who robbed the A. and P. train at Canyon Diablo in 1889, after trailing them to the Utah border country. Later he was the candidate of the People's Party for territorial delegate, and twice defeated. O'Neill had prospected a bit and located what he thought was a rich copper mine near Anita, 14 miles (23 km.) south of the Grand Canyon.[81] Like other miners in the area, he was faced with the prohibitive cost of

shipping out his ore. What was needed was a railroad. He succeeded in interesting the Chicago firm of Lombard, Goode and Company in the mines, the railroad and the Canyon, and sold out to them in 1898 shortly after his election as mayor of Prescott and just before he went to Cuba with Theodore Roosevelt's Rough Riders, where he lost his life in the charge up San Juan Hill. He is memorialized by O'Neill Butte, towering above the Kaibab Trail.

In July, 1897, the Santa Fe and Grand Canyon Railway Company was organized by Lombard, Goode and Company, to build a railroad and telegraph line from Williams to Grand Canyon by way of the mines at Anita. In order to do this, a new act of Congress was required, granting right of way across the Grand Canyon Forest Reserve. The act was passed in May, 1898 and construction had already begun. By 1900 the tracks reached Anita, but the copper deposits were limited, production had ceased at the mine, and the railroad company went bankrupt. The Santa Fe Railroad, which by this time had absorbed the Atlantic and Pacific, bought the property on July 18, 1901 for $150,000.

The Grand Canyon Railway Company, a subsidiary of the Santa Fe Railroad, completed the line from Anita to the Grand Canyon, and the first scheduled train to travel from Williams to the Grand Canyon made its historic trip on September 17, 1901.[82] This date marks the end of one era and the beginning of another at Grand Canyon. A relatively smooth rail journey of less than three hours, costing $3.95, replaced the jouncing all-day stage ride that cost $20. The number of tourists increased, and most of them came to Grand Canyon Village rather than to Grandview, Hance Ranch or Bass Camp. Frontier days were over.

1. Leland Hargrave Creer, *Mormon Towns in the Region of the Colorado* (Salt Lake City: University of Utah, Anthropological Papers 32, 1958). See also C. Gregory Crampton, *Land of Living Rock: The Grand Canyon and the High Plateaus: Arizona, Utah, Nevada* (New York: Alfred A. Knopf, 1972), pp. 86, 146.

2. Robert W. Olsen, Jr., "Winsor Castle: Mormon Frontier Fort at Pipe Spring," *Utah Historical Quarterly* 34(Summer 1966):222. See also Angus M. Woodbury, "A History of Southern Utah and its National Parks," *Utah Historical Quarterly* 12(July-October 1944):190.

3. P. T. Reilly, letter to J. Donald Hughes, December 31, 1976.

4. Crampton, pp. 138-39. See also Don D. Walker, "The Cattle Industry of Utah, 1850-1900, an Historical Profile," *Utah Historical Quarterly* 32(Summer 1964):182-97.

5. Woodbury, pp. 160-61, 183-84. See also Mark A. Pendleton, "The Orderville United Order of Zion," *Utah Historical Quarterly* 7(October 1939):154, and P. T. Reilly, "Kanab United Order: The President's Nephew and the Bishop," *Utah Historical Quarterly* 42(Spring 1974):144-64.

6. Woodbury, pp. 190-91.

7. *Coconino Sun*, Flagstaff, Arizona, November 10, 1892.

8. Virginia N. Price and John T. Darby, "Preston Nutter: Utah Cattleman, 1886-1936," *Utah Historical Quarterly* 32(Summer 1964):232-51.

9. Crampton, pp. 108, 136.

10. W. L. Rusho and C. Gregory Crampton, *Desert River Crossing: Historic Lee's Ferry on the Colorado River* (Salt Lake City: Peregrine Smith, 1975).

11. Alfred F. Whiting, "John D. Lee and the Havasupai," *Plateau* 21(July 1948):12-16. See also Charles Kelly, ed., *Journals of John D. Lee* (Salt Lake City: Western Printing Co., 1938), p. 230.

12. P. T. Reilly, "Warren Marshall Johnson, Forgotten Saint," *Utah Historical Quarterly* 39(Winter 1971):3-22.

13. Harold S. Colton, "How Flagstaff Was Named," *Plateau* 15(October 1942):17-21.

14. Thomas Wittick, "1883 Expedition to the Grand Canyon: Pioneer Photographer Ben Wittick Views the Marvels of the Colorado," *American West* 10(March 1973):38-47.

15. "A. G.," "How to Reach the Grand Cañon," *Science* 5, O.S.(June 26, 1885):516-17.

16. Charles Fletcher Lummis, *A Tramp Across the Continent* (New York: Charles Scribner's Sons, 1892), p. 242.

17. Henry F. Dobyns and Robert C. Euler, *The Hualapai People* (Phoenix: Indian Tribal Series, 1976), and *The Havasupai People* (Phoenix: Indian Tribal Series, 1971). See also U. S. Senate, 74th Congress, 2d Session, Sen. Doc. 273, Ser. 10012, *Walapai Papers, Historical Reports, Documents, and Extracts from Publications Relating to the Walapai Indians of Arizona* (Washington, D. C.: Government Printing Office, 1936).

18. Henry F. Dobyns and Robert C. Euler, *The Ghost Dance of 1889 Among the Pai Indians of Northwestern Arizona* (Prescott, Arizona: Prescott College Press, 1967). See also James Mooney, "The Ghost-dance Religion and the Sioux Outbreak of 1890," *Fourteenth Annual Report of the Bureau of Ethnology* (Washington, D. C.: Government Printing Office, 1896), pp. 641-1110.

19. Earl Y. Henderson, *The Havasupai Indian Agency, Arizona* (Lawrence, Kansas: Haskell Printing Department, 1928), p. 8.

20. Joseph Wampler, *Havasu Canyon: Gem of the Grand Canyon* (Berkeley, Calif.: Howell-North Press, 1959), pp. 60, 77, 81-82.

21. Stephen Hirst, *Life in a Narrow Place* (New York: David McKay, 1976), pp. 62, 65.

22. John Muir, "The Grand Cañon of the Colorado," *The Century Magazine* 65(November 1902):115.

23. Crampton, pp. 149, 151.

24. Helen Humphreys Seargeant, "Mooney Falls," *Arizona Highways* 35(August 1959):23-24. George Wharton James, *In and Around the Grand Canyon* (Boston: Little, Brown, 1900), p. 300, says his first name was James, but mining records prove this wrong.

25. Crampton, pp. 151, 153.

26. Margaret M. Verkamp, "History of Grand Canyon National Park," M. A. thesis, University of Arizona, 1940, p. 24.

27. Robert Brewster Stanton, *Down the Colorado*, ed. by Dwight L. Smith (Norman: University of Oklahoma Press, 1965), p. 146.

28. See chap. 2, n. 11.

29. Daniel L. Hogan, interview transcribed by William E. Austin, February 3, 1939, in *Grand Canyon Items*, Vol. 2, MS, Grand Canyon National Park Library. See also *Coconino Sun*, March 2, 1901.

30. *Coconino Sun*, November 22, 1902.

31. Hamlin Garland, "John Hance: A Study," in C. A. Higgins, et. al., *The Grand Canyon of Arizona, Being a Book of Words from Many Pens* (Chicago: Passenger Department, Santa Fe Railroad, 1902). See also Lemuel A. Garrison, "John Hance: Guide, Trail Builder, Miner and Windjammer of the Grand Canyon," *Arizona Highways* 25(June 1949):4-11; and Frank C. Lockwood, *More Arizona Characters* (Tucson: University of Arizona Bulletin, Vol. 13, No. 3, 1942); and *Prescott Journal-Miner*, Prescott, Arizona, January 11, 1919.

A new era began on September 17, 1901 when the first scheduled passenger train arrived at the Canyon from Williams, Arizona.

32. Burton Holmes, *Travelogues*, Vol. 6 (New York: McClure, 1901), p. 170. See also *Prescott Morning Courier*, Prescott, Arizona, June 4, 1902.

33. Bert Cameron, interview transcribed by William E. Austin, June 21, 1939, in *Grand Canyon Items*, Vol. 2, MS, Grand Canyon National Park Library. See also Verkamp, p. 19.

34. *Arizona Champion*, Flagstaff, Arizona, 1886.

35. J. Harvey Butchart, "The Grandview Trail," *Plateau* 31(October 1958):38.

36. G. K. Woods, ed., *Personal Impressions of the Grand Canyon of the Colorado River Near Flagstaff, Arizona, as Seen Through Nearly Two Thousand Eyes, and Written in the Private Visitors' Book of the World-Famous Guide Capt. John Hance, Guide, Story-Teller, and Path-Finder* (San Francisco: Whitaker and Ray, 1899), p. 64. (January 25, 1893).

37. *Coconino Sun*, November 7, 1895; October 26 and November 16, 1901.

38. Byrd H. Granger, ed., *Will C. Barnes' Arizona Place Names* (Tucson: University of Arizona Press, 1960), p. 145.

39. Frances Hance Rose, letter to Lemuel A. Garrison, July 31, 1948, History File, Grand Canyon National Park Library.

40. W. W. Bass papers, La Siesta Motel, Wickenburg, Arizona; copy in History File, Grand Canyon National Park Library. See also Nell Murbarger, "Trail-Blazer of Grand Canyon," *The Desert Magazine* 21(October 1958):5-9.

41. Edwin D. McKee, "On Canyon Trails, Part II," *Grand Canyon Nature Notes* 8(September 1933):193, gives 1895 as date. See also Duncan Jones, letter to Harold Child Bryant, February 5, 1947, History File, Grand Canyon National Park.

42. James, pp. 246-47.

43. Daniel L. Hogan, interview, January 17, 1944; and William Dowling, interview, January 11, 1945, both transcribed by Harold Child Bryant, MS, in History File, Grand Canyon National Park. See also Glen E. Sturdevant, "A Reconnaissance of the Northeastern Part of Grand Canyon National Park," *Grand Canyon Nature Notes* 3(December 1928):4.

44. McKee, Part II, p. 191. See also George Wharton James, *The Grand Canyon of Arizona: How to See It* (Boston: Little, Brown, 1910), pp. 45-48. See also Woods, pp. 34, 43.

45. *Coconino Sun*, August 8 and 15, 1903, and July 10, 1908.

46. Peter D. Berry, interview transcribed by Hugh H. Waesche, July 19, 1932, and Ray W. Berry, interview transcribed by Lon Garrison, October 4, 1951, in History File, Grand Canyon National Park Library. See also the Dowling interview. The Berry papers are accession no. 1031 in Grand Canyon National Park Museum.

47. Among these were T. F. McMillan, Robert Ferguson, Ed I. Gale, and C. H. McClure.

48. The Peter D. Berry daybooks are accession no. 1206 in Grand Canyon National Park Museum.

49. Hugh H. Waesche, "The Grand View Copper Project," *Grand Canyon Nature Notes* 8(March 1934):257-58.

50. Hugh H. Waesche, "How Pipe Creek Received Its Name," *Grand Canyon Nature Notes* 8(June 1933):155-56. Waesche received his information in an interview with Emery Kolb.

51. *Coconino Sun*, June 11, 1896, and February 19, 1898. The vandalism of the cave can be inferred by comparing the present condition of the Grandview Cave with pictures on file at the Museum of Northern Arizona, Flagstaff, that show the porch of the Grandview Hotel covered with broken formations.

52. Ray W. Berry said she ran away with a traveling salesman; Dowling said with a gambler. Perhaps he was both, and a tourist as well.

53. *Coconino Sun*, January 25, 1902, gives date of sale as August 21, 1901.

54. The Berry holdings were sold in 1913, and all property involved was transferred to the National Park Service in 1940. File L-1425, Grand Canyon National Park.

55. Hogan interviews (see notes 29 and 43 above).

56. General Land Office no. 43506, Cert. No. 660, Book 32 of Deeds, pp. 278-80, Coconino County, Arizona. Rec. GLO, Vol. 430, pp. 205-8. File L-1425, Grand Canyon National Park.

57. Hogan, 1939. Some additional material on Rowe, including a newspaper clipping dated April 24, 1936, was found in File L-1425, Grand Canyon National Park.

58. Holmes, p. 129.

59. *Coconino Sun*, May 28, August 20 and 27, 1896.

60. Donald Smythe, "'Never Have I Witnessed a Sight So Marvelous:' 'Black Jack' Pershing's Brilliant Career Almost Ended in an Attempt to View Arizona's Awesome Grand Canyon in 1889," *Montana* 13(Spring 1963):11-23.

61. John Muir, "The Wild Parks and Forest Reservations of the West," *Atlantic Monthly* 81(January 1898):28.

62. Michael Frome, *Whose Woods These Are: The Story of the National Forests* (Garden City, New York: Doubleday, 1962), pp. 50-51.

63. John Burroughs, "The Divine Abyss," in *The Writings of John Burroughs*, Vol. 14, *Time and Change* (Boston: Houghton Mifflin, 1912), p. 49.

64. *Ibid.*, pp. 66-67.

65. John Gill Lemmon, "Grand Cañon of the Colorado," *Overland Monthly* 12, N. S. (September 1888):244-56.

66. Clinton Hart Merriam and Leonhard Stejneger, "Results of a Biological Survey of the San Francisco Mountain Region and the Desert of the Little Colorado, Arizona," *North American Fauna*, No. 3 (Washington, D. C.: Government Printing Office, 1890), pp. 1-113.

67. Joseph Wood Krutch, *Grand Canyon* (Garden City, New York: Doubleday, 1962), p. 12.

68. Stanton, pp. 20-37.

69. *Ibid.*, pp. 76, 88.

70. Dwight L. Smith, ed., *The Photographer and the River, 1889-1890: The Colorado Cañon Diary of Franklin A. Nims with the Brown-Stanton Railroad Survey Expedition* (Santa Fe: Stagecoach Press, 1967).

71. Robert Brewster Stanton, "Availability of the Cañons of the Colorado River of the West for Railway Purposes," American Society of Civil Engineers, *Transactions* 26, No. 523(April 1892):323-32.

72. Otis Marston, "River Runners: Fast Water Navigation," *Utah Historical Quarterly* 28(July 1960):292.

73. George F. Flavell, "Journal of the *Panthon* of Green River, Wyoming, 1896," in Otis Marston, ed., "Some Colorado River Journals and Diaries," MS, Grand Canyon National Park Library, entry of October 22, 1896, p. 34.

74. William C. Richmond, "Journal," in Marston, "Colorado River Journals."

75. Nathaniel T. Galloway, letter to Mr. and Mrs. James Coupe, January 15, 1897, in Marston, "Colorado River Journals."

76. Verkamp, p. 24.

77. *Arizona Champion*, December 31, 1886. See also George H. Tinker, *Northern Arizona and Flagstaff in 1887: The People and Resources*, ed. by Ben H. Tinker (Glendale, California: Arthur H. Clark, 1969), pp. 7-10.

78. Harold S. Colton, "How Coconino County Received Its Name," *Plateau* 31(October 1958): 47-48.

79. James R. Fuchs, *A History of Williams, Arizona, 1876-1951* (Tucson: University of Arizona Bulletin 24, No. 5, 1953), p. 78.

80. Ralph Keithley, *Buckey O'Neill, He Stayed With 'Em While He Lasted* (Caldwell, Idaho: Caxton Printers, 1949), p. 20.

81. Hugh H. Waesche, "The Anita Copper Mine," *Grand Canyon Nature Notes* 7(February 1933):111.

82. *Williams News*, Williams, Arizona, September 21, 1901.

6

FOREST
RESERVE AND
NATIONAL
MONUMENT

N ational Parks are an American idea. Government reserves had long been made for various purposes, but a national park in the sense of a large area of scenic wilderness set aside for the benefit and enjoyment of all the people was first advocated in the mid-Nineteenth Century United States. As early as 1832, George Catlin suggested that an area in the West be preserved as "a *nation's park*, containing man and beast, in all the wild and freshness of their natures' beauty." "What a beautiful and thrilling specimen for America to preserve and hold up to the view of her refined citizens and the world, in future ages!"[1]

Yellowstone became the first national park, and the Grand Canyon was naturally suggested for similar designation, since to many people it was America's greatest scenic wonder. But a generation was to pass before Grand Canyon National Park came into being.

By 1896, Yosemite, Sequoia and General Grant had joined Yellowstone as national parks, but Grand Canyon had to wait until these and eleven others had been created. Proclaimed a forest reserve by President Benjamin Harrison in 1893, Grand Canyon was placed under the General Land Office of the Department of the Interior in 1897.

Local feeling was divided on the question of Grand Canyon National Park. While the people of northern Arizona favored the publicity and the increased tourist business that might be expected, miners, stockmen and settlers in the area were quick to voice their opposition to anything that might threaten their interests. The Flagstaff paper gave its support to the park idea in two editorials in 1898, while stating that local mineral and grazing rights should be protected.[2] Grand Canyon National Park remained an idea.

Theodore Roosevelt, a vigorous

Theodore Roosevelt and John Hance (on second mule) at the head of the Bright Angel Trail. Courtesy of Kolb Studio

outdoorsman, became president in 1901, and succeeded in doing more than any other individual to establish conservation as a national policy. In 1903 he took a trip through the West, visiting the Grand Canyon for the first time on May 6. The local people were excited, and a special train was advertised. With the governor and members of his old regiment, the president rode on horseback to Grandview, where he dined on simple frontier fare.

Roosevelt was deeply moved by the beauty of the Grand Canyon, and remarked that it was "to me the most impressive piece of scenery I have ever looked at."[3] In a speech at the Canyon, he expressed the conviction that all Americans should be able to see and feel what he had seen and felt on the wild and lonely rim:

> In the Grand Canyon, Arizona has a natural wonder which, so far as I know, is in kind absolutely unparalleled throughout the rest of the world. I want to ask you to do one thing in connection with it in your own interest and in the interest of the country—to keep this great wonder of nature as it is now...I hope you will not have a building of any kind, not a summer cottage, a hotel or anything else, to mar the wonderful grandeur, the sublimity, the great loveliness and beauty of the Canyon. Leave it as it is. You cannot improve on it. The ages have been at work on it, and man can only mar it. What you can do is to keep it for your children, your children's children, and for all who come after you, as the one great sight which every American...should see"[4]

Theodore Roosevelt did much to protect the Grand Canyon. When Senator Reed Smoot of Utah, another friend of conservation who had visited the North Rim, succeeded in getting through Congress a bill for the protection of wild animals in the Grand Canyon Forest Reserve, Roosevelt signed the bill and then on November 28, 1906,[5] proclaimed the Grand Canyon Game Reserve. This action protected the deer and other "game animals," but was not considered to apply to predators.

Meanwhile, a new forest policy had been enacted. Gifford Pinchot became head of the Division of Forestry in the Department of Agriculture in 1898. He worked with Roosevelt's help to gain supervision over the forest reserves. He succeeded in 1905, and his agency was renamed the Forest Service. Two years later, the forest reserves were redesignated national forests, and thus Grand Canyon National Forest came into being. Unlike national parks, which were to be preserved in a natural state for recreational, scientific, and aesthetic purposes, the national forests were administered for many kinds of continuing land use and development, including hunting, grazing, mining, and timber cutting, while assuring the protection and regeneration of the forests. Many people, including Roosevelt, believed that national park status would be most appropriate for Grand Canyon, but Congressional action was delayed. In 1906, however, Congress had passed the Act for the Preservation of American Antiquities, giving the president the power to set aside areas which contained "objects of historic or scientific interest" as national monuments. Roosevelt established Grand Canyon National Monument under this law on January 11, 1908. Roosevelt's proclamation was challenged, but upheld by the Supreme Court.[6] The monument was placed under the Forest Service, since it had been created out of a national forest. The rest of Grand Canyon National Forest was divided into two parts, one becoming Kaibab National Forest and the other becoming part of Coconino National Forest.

Arizona became a state in 1912, and this strengthened the movement to create a national park. Representative Carl Hayden and Senator Henry Fountain Ashurst of Arizona set out to give Arizona a great national park which would not include vast tracts of grazing land or forests. In early 1917, they introduced bills in the House and Senate designating a national park including only the eastern part of the Grand Canyon, with very narrow strips along the rims. Provisions were made in Ashurst's bill to protect the rights of owners of valid land claims already established in the area, and a special clause prohibited the building of any structure between Hearst's lands and the rim. Concessions were to be let to the "best and most responsible bidder." Several amendments were added, protecting the rights of the Havasupai Indians, allowing the Secretary of the Interior to grant rights of way for railroads, and limiting mining and power and reclamation projects to those "consistent with the primary purposes of the park."[7] As to the primary purpose, it had been defined in the Act of August 25, 1916, creating the National Park Service, "To conserve the scenery and the natural and historic objects and the wildlife therein and to provide for the enjoyment of the same in such manner and by such means as will leave them unimpaired for the enjoyment of future generations."[8] Ashurst's bill provided that the "administration, protection and promotion of said Grand Canyon National Park shall be exercised under the direction of the Secretary of the Interior, by the National Park Service."[9] That young agency gave the measure strong support; its acting Director said, "The Grand Canyon should be a National Park,"[10] and pointed out that his mail showed that many Americans thought it already was. The bill passed both houses and was signed by President Woodrow Wilson on February 26, 1919. On that date Grand Canyon National Park came into being.

From 1903 to 1924, travelers down the Bright Angel Trail were required to pay a toll at this gate operated by Ralph Cameron. Courtesy of Kolb Studio.

The period between the arrival of the railroad at Grand Canyon in 1901 and the establishment of Grand Canyon National Park in 1919 was an eventful one, as tourism gained greater importance than any other economic activity. On the South Rim, it was the age of the passenger railroad. Grand Canyon Village grew around the railroad terminal, and the Fred Harvey company, a subsidiary of the Santa Fe Railroad, opened new hotels and other facilities.[11] Development of the North Rim lagged behind due to its isolation, but it was a popular hunting ground, and there will be more to say about it later in this chapter.

The Bright Angel Hotel had been started in 1896 by J. Wilbur Thurber near its present site.[12] There was a cabin that was used as an office, and several tents that were rented to tourists. When the arrival of the railroad put Thurber's stage line out of business, his Bright Angel development was acquired by Martin Buggeln, who managed the hotel in association with the Santa Fe Railroad until 1905, when he moved out to the old Hance Ranch.

When El Tovar was built, the Bright Angel Hotel was temporarily closed and then reopened as Bright Angel Camp in 1905. Fred Harvey ran both establishments, charging 75 cents a day at Bright Angel Camp, European plan. As the years went by, Bright Angel Camp collected a series of cabins and tents from various sources.

In those years Ralph Cameron had control of the Bright Angel Trail, which he managed as a toll trail, charging $1.00 for every tourist who rode down into the Canyon.[13] His right to do this was questioned by the Santa Fe Railroad, whose station grounds were not far from the head of the trail, and who planned to build a new hotel there. Beginning in 1902, Cameron located mining claims on the Santa Fe station grounds, on the site where the hotel was to be built, on Indian Gardens halfway down the trail, and on scenic points on the rim. Eventually these claims, consisting of some 13,000 acres (5300 ha.), virtually surrounded the railroad's lands and were in a position to control the tourist trade. Since there was no mineral of value located on the claims, they could not be patented, but were the subject of long legal battles by the railroad, the Forest Service, and the National Park Service. At least one case went all the way to the Supreme Court, and Cameron's claims were invalidated in 1920, but meanwhile he held onto them, blocking plans for developing access to the Canyon.

Cameron built a hotel on one of his claims, next to the railroad terminal and the Bright Angel Hotel. His hotel was a log cabin that had been a stage station at Red Horse.[14] It was moved up to the Canyon rim log by log, reassembled, and a second story added. After 1910 it became the post office, and is now one of the cabins at Bright Angel Lodge. To keep passengers from seeing Cameron's Hotel first, the railroad moved its terminal several hundred feet east, so people would have to pass the Bright Angel Hotel if they were going to Cameron's. Cameron sold some of his troublesome claims to the railroad in 1916, but continued to collect tolls on Bright Angel Trail. Ownership of the trail reverted to Coconino County in 1906, and Cameron was given a franchise to collect tolls for the county. He maintained his claims at Indian Gardens, the location of the only spring on the trail. Cameron's caretaker would not allow trail riders to drink from the spring, and sanitary conditions there were bad. This was the situation facing the new administration at Grand Canyon in 1919.

A first-class hotel was desired as soon as the railroad reached Grand Canyon, and the Santa Fe asked Charles F. Whittlesey to design a 100-room structure, to be called Bright Angel Tavern, which would combine the architecture of the "Swiss chateaux" with that of the

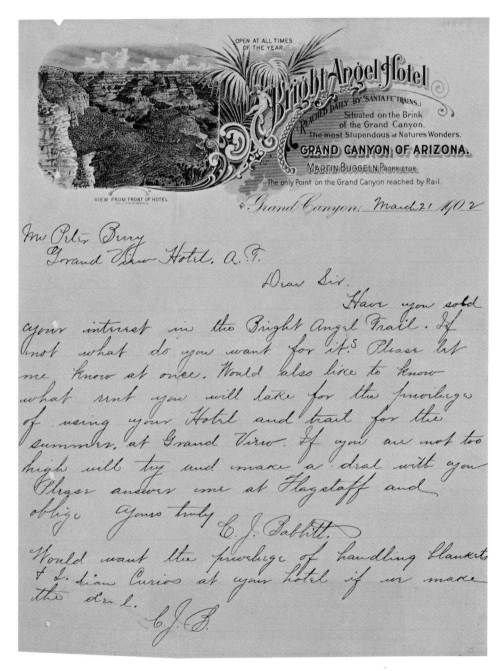

For years, a bitter controversy raged over the rights to the Bright Angel, a Havasupai trail which was later rebuilt by Pete Berry and Niles and Ralph Cameron. This 1902 letter from

C. J. Babbitt offers to buy Berry's interest in the trail.

El Tovar

"castles of the Rhine" in native boulders, Douglas fir logs and boards.[15] The building cost $250,000 to construct, and by the time it opened on January 14, 1905, it had been renamed El Tovar in honor of the Spanish explorer who had visited the Hopi towns, but not Grand Canyon, in 1540. The Fred Harvey company, which ran all the hotels and restaurants along the Santa Fe lines, already had a Cardenas Hotel in Trinidad, Colorado. Their new El Tovar boasted the most fashionable accommodations, including a dining room overlooking the Canyon, large fireplaces, a lobby decorated with animal heads and Indian pottery, a Music Room, Art Room, Ladies' Lounging Room, Barbershop, Amusement Room, Club Room, Solarium, Grotto, and roof gardens. It was equipped with electric lights powered by a steam generator. Fresh fruits and vegetables were grown in greenhouses, and fresh eggs and milk came from the hotel's own chicken house and herds. All water for the hotel, and for all operations at Grand Canyon Village, was brought in by railroad tank car from Del Rio, 120 miles (200 km.) away.

A replica of an Indian pueblo, called the Hopi House, was constructed nearby. Hopi Indians were encouraged to live there, demonstrate crafts, wear native costumes, and put on dances. Navajo hogans in replica were also built. The Hopi House was the first full-fledged curio shop at Grand Canyon, although hotels had long sold Indian crafts.

One of the tents of the Bright Angel Hotel served as a curio stand run by John G. Verkamp for the Babbitt Brothers' Trading Company.[16] After a few weeks Verkamp sold his stock, returning in 1905 to build a curio store east of the Hopi House.

One way for the Santa Fe people to avoid tolls and trouble on the Bright Angel Trail was to build a trail of their own. Permission was granted by the Forest Service, and in 1910-1912, the Hermit Rim Road was built out along the rim west of

Completed in 1905, El Tovar Hotel boasted its own dairy, greenhouse for flowers and fresh vegetables, and the most fashionable of accommodations.

Bright Angel Camp. This was a road for open-top touring stages; no automobiles were allowed on it, so as not to frighten the horses, until 1919.

Hermit's Rest, a stone-and-log building where weary travelers could find refreshment, was built at the end of the road where the trail begins, in 1914. The architect was Mary Jane Colter, who also designed The Lookout, built on the rim by Bright Angel Camp at about the same time. Hermit's Rest included a huge fireplace within which tourists could sit. Miss Colter also brought a bell from New Mexico and had it hung in a stone gateway.

The new trail was constructed down

the east side of Hermit Basin and through Hermit Canyon to the river. The Hermit Trail was better made than any other in Grand Canyon, paved with sandstone in some sections, with rock walls along the outer side. A rest house was constructed at Santa Maria Spring, two miles down the trail, in 1913. Hermit Camp was located on a flat area of the Tonto Plateau near a source of water.[17] Mule trips operated to the camp, where tourists could stay overnight in comfort. To supply the camp, an aerial tramway was erected, with the upper terminus on the west side of Pima Point. The car could be lowered the distance of

The sale of curios at the Canyon originated in this tent operated by John George Verkamp.

more than 3000 feet (920 m.) in half an hour. A telephone line reached Hermit Camp by 1916.

Hermit Camp continued in operation until 1930, when the opening of the Bright Angel Trail to free travel and the construction of the new South Kaibab Trail and Phantom Ranch had made it redundant. The trail was abandoned and later the buildings and tramway were removed.

The eclipse of the railroad as the major means of reaching Grand Canyon was heralded by the arrival of automobiles at both rims. On January 4, 1902, a remarkable steam-driven automobile, a new Toledo Eight-horse, chugged out of Flagstaff toward the Grand Canyon. The driver was Oliver Lippincott, the guide was Al Doyle, and the passengers were Thomas M. Chapman and a Los Angeles journalist who wrote a story describing the historic journey, the intrepid Mr. Winfield C. Hogaboom.[18]

The machine managed to get out of sight of the people of Flagstaff before it broke down the first time. Delayed, the men had to seek shelter for the night in a cowboy's cabin, and since it was very cold, the motor froze. Expecting to make the trip in one day, they had not brought food or extra water. They broke a water

Hermit Camp, which operated from 1912-1930.

gauge and a sprocket chain, and finally ran out of gas 18 miles (29 km.) from the Canyon. Hogaboom had to walk to Grandview for help. Pete Berry rescued the other three men, and hauled gas from the railroad terminal to the machine, which was finally nursed up to the rim five days after it had left Flagstaff. Lippincott and Berry made the return trip in seven hours.

The first automobiles to go to the North Rim, a Locomobile and a Thomas Flyer, left Kanab in June, 1909, and made the trip in three days.[19] Gasoline had been cached in advance by team, 10 gallons (38 liters) for every 30 miles (48 km.), but the passengers had to do road repair work on the way. The two machines wore out nine tires, which were exhibited by the U. S. Rubber Company to illustrate their durability. The trip was sponsored by the North Rim promoter, E. D. Woolley and his nephew, E. G. Woolley, Jr., of Salt Lake City.

By this time, automobiles were a common means of travel, and in spite of poor roads, automobile travel to the Grand Canyon increased at a much faster rate than the increase in railroad passengers. By 1926 automobiles overtook the railroad as the most popular way to get there.

With increasing tourist travel just before World War I, it became necessary to charge 25¢ a day for water at automobile campgrounds and place water distribution in charge of the railway agent.[20] All water was being brought in by railroad tank car, although alternative plans were explored. Perhaps the most ambitious was one advanced in 1917 to collect water from the San Francisco Peaks, pipe it to the craters of extinct volcanoes nearby, which would serve as natural reservoirs, and then deliver it by pipeline to Grand Canyon Village. This helpful suggestion came to nothing, and wells drilled south of the Canyon proved to be dry.

To protect the forests, a fire tower was erected at Hopi Point in 1909, and firefighters were sent out whenever the smoke of a forest fire was spotted. Game management consisted of protecting deer and killing predators, and for this purpose game wardens were hired.

Cattlemen received grazing permits, and with no fences, range cattle and horses were seen constantly around the railroad terminal, hotels, and scenic points. Some visiting ladies were frightened by horned beasts so near the Canyon rim, and Forest Service saw the need for fences.

The increased number of people living near the railroad terminal, including railroad and hotel people as well as earlier settlers, posed a problem for the Forest Service. Buildings, shanties and tents dotted the area without plan, and rubbish heaps marred the landscape. In 1910, Forest Supervisor W. R. Mattoon proposed the first townsite plan for Grand Canyon Village, including construction of roads and fences, relocation of the railroad workers' camp, construction of a new headquarters and the location of a public campground. Due to lack of funds, this plan was not followed in detail, but some

Due to breakdowns, the first automobile trip to the Canyon in this Toledo Eight took five days. Shown here on the rim near the Grandview Hotel, it arrived on January 12, 1902.

progress was made in beautification of the area and establishment of a community south of the railroad tracks. The Forest Service was the first agency to view the Grand Canyon community as a whole, and to make plans for its orderly development.

During the early years of the twentieth century, a few men ran the Colorado River by boat. Apparently Arthur R. Sanger, John A. King and their boatman, E. B. "Hum" Woolley, were miners. They left Lee's Ferry on August 17, 1903, in an eighteen-foot (5.5 m.) oaken boat, and by the end of October had reached Yuma. Sanger's meager diary describes the "great underground river" whose walls are "miles high," and the "terrible rapids," but makes no mention of minerals.[21]

Between September, 1907, and February, 1908, the miners Edwin R. Monett and Charles S. Russell ran the river from Green River, Utah, to Needles, California.[22] Albert Loper was with them as far as Cataract Canyon, where his boat was damaged. He made repairs, but when he reached Lee's Ferry the others had already gone on. A second boat was lost in Hance Rapid. They took the third as far as the Bright Angel Trail, and spent three days resting at El Tovar. Going downstream, they were lining the last boat through Hermit Creek Rapid when it was torn out of their hands and lost. Monett and Russell hiked up to Louis Boucher's cabin, and "the Hermit" helped them find and repair their boat.

Beginning in 1909, the reason given by many parties for attempting a Colorado River trip was simply the journey itself. The first sportsman's river trip was made by Julius F. Stone, an Ohio manufacturer.[23] Stone's companions were Seymour S. Deubendorff and the experienced Nathaniel Galloway, who designed a boat decked over except for a cockpit in which a single oarsman sat. The trip from Green River, Wyoming, to Needles was made in only ten weeks, and neither Stone nor

Galloway had a single upset. Stone's brother-in-law, Raymond A. Cogswell, took a fine series of photographs.

Ellsworth L. Kolb and Emery C. Kolb came to the Grand Canyon in 1902.[24] Ellsworth took a job as bellhop at the Bright Angel Hotel, and Emery had intended to work in the Hance mines, but they were not operating. Soon the brothers bought a little photographic studio in Williams, brought it up to the Canyon, and went into business taking pictures of parties starting down the Bright Angel Trail. They explored the Grand Canyon itself, making the first trip to Cheyava Falls in Clear Creek Canyon in 1908, but the Kolb brothers are nationally known for their boat trip down the Colorado River in 1911-1912, the first to be recorded on motion picture film.[25] They left Green River, Wyoming, with two flat-bottomed, 16-foot (4.9 m.) boats on September 8, 1911. In November they arrived at the Bright Angel Trail and hiked up to their Canyon home. A month later, they started again with Hubert R. Lauzon and completed the trip at Needles on January 18, 1912.

By May, 1913 Emery was in the East, giving lectures illustrated with his motion pictures and slides to packed houses in many cities. In 1915 he erected a showroom at the head of the Bright Angel Trail, where he began to give lectures on the river trips and the Canyon. These were a regular feature at Grand Canyon for sixty years, although in a recorded form after 1948, when an illness weakened his voice. He lived in the home on the rim as Grand Canyon's best-known resident, until his death on December 11, 1976, at the age of 95. His body lies beside those of his wife and brother in Pioneer Cemetery at Grand Canyon.

Not everyone who embarked on the voyage through the Grand Canyon succeeded. In fact, some never reached even the upper end of Grand Canyon. Others gave up part way through. J. H.

Hummel and David Miller started out at Green River, Wyoming in 1914. Miller quit at the confluence of the Grand and Green and a discouraged Hummel stopped at Bright Angel Creek and gave his boat to Emery Kolb.[26]

Charles S. Russell attempted another voyage with Goddard Quist in 1914, but climbed out of the Canyon on the Bass Trail. Russell tried again the next year with A. J. Tadje and a motion picture photographer named Clemens, but that trip ended with a lost boat at Crystal Rapid.

A monument on the Canyon rim to John Wesley Powell and the men of his two Colorado River expeditions was proposed soon after the great explorer's death.[27] Congress made a small appropriation in 1909 that was supplemented by private donations, and the memorial, a truncated stone pyramid with a bronze plaque, was constructed on Sentinel Point, now called Powell Memorial Point, in 1916. Two years later the Secretary of the Interior dedicated the monument with, among other things, a libation of Colorado River water.

Scientific exploration continued, as geologists studied the magnificent series of rocks in the Grand Canyon, making many discoveries of fossils, archaeologists traced early inhabitants, and topographers produced new maps. The first topographic map of Grand Canyon was one of the finest ever made; it is the masterpiece of its maker, Francois Emile Matthes.[28] He began his map for the U. S. Geological Survey in 1902 on the South Rim, establishing bench marks and using triangulation, leveling and plane-table methods to establish the position and elevation of points which could be seen from the rim. Observations were also taken within the Canyon under difficult conditions; during scorching days on the Hance Trail, the rocks became so hot that the men had to shift continually from one foot to the other to avoid burning

The Grand Canyon of Arizona

The Kolb brothers, Ellsworth and Emery, are intimately linked with the human history of the Canyon. The Kolbs did more to record that history on film than anyone else. Operating their first darkroom in an abandoned mine shaft covered with canvas, they later built their studio on the rim and began photographing mule trips at the head of the Bright Angel Trail. The tradition was to continue for some 70 years. The Kolbs were also the first to make a motion picture of running the Colorado river through the Grand Canyon during their famous 1911-12 trip from Green River, Wyoming to the Gulf of Mexico.

Kolb Studio, 1904.

A typical Kolb photo of mule riders at the head of the Bright Angel Trail.

Emery and Ellsworth during their 1911-12 trip.

Making the first motion picture of running the Colorado.

themselves on the hobnails in their boots, and the air bubbles in the levels grew smaller, disappearing around noon each day. Water had to be packed in, and every man drank a gallon a day.

When the survey had to cross to the North Rim, there was no established route. Matthes was assured that Bright Angel Canyon was impassable, the incomplete Bass Trail was practical only for burros, not horses, and Lee's Ferry was too far away. He decided to use the Bass Trail and after the survey had worked its way down to the river, they discovered that Bass' boat was on the north side. Matthes and another man had to swim the river and bring the boat back. Then the horses and mules had to be tricked into entering the water—they were literally pushed in—and guided across to the other side with the boat, which was leaky and required constant bailing. The entire crossing from one rim to the other required six days.

Once on the North Rim, the men had to get their supplies from Kanab, 75 miles (120 km.) distant by trail. As winter approached, Matthes had to cross the Canyon again. By this time he had reached the head of Bright Angel Canyon, and decided to examine it. He was startled to see "two haggard men and a weary burro" emerge from the depths. Matthes' men immediately began improving the trail for their animals, down to the mouth of Bright Angel Creek. "So steep was it," said Matthes, "that the animals fairly slid down on their haunches."[29] In going to the River, they had to ford Bright Angel Creek 94 times. A prospector lent them his boat to cross the river. From this time on, the survey used Bright Angel Canyon.

Triangulation during the survey required signalling by sun mirror from Cape Royal to Kendrick Peak in the San Francisco Peaks, fifty miles (80 km.) away. The Vishnu, Bright Angel and Shinumo quadrangles were finished in 1905, and the remaining areas in 1920-1923 by Richard T. Evans. Special care

A section of Matthes' Bright Angel Quadrangle.

Plane table station for the first topographical mapping of the Grand Canyon. The mapping was directed by Francois Matthes who continued Dutton's practice of giving heroic names to the temples and buttes in the Canyon.

was taken to make the maps accurate, clear and beautiful. To preserve the detail, they were done on a larger scale than usual in Geological Survey maps. The usual method of drawing contours was modified so as to reveal better the sculpturing of cliffs. Matthes was faced with the fact that many formations in the Grand Canyon were larger than most mountains east of the Mississippi, yet had no names. It was his decision to continue the "heroic nomenclature" begun by Dutton, although Matthes incorrectly thought that this class of names had been given by Powell.[30] So Dutton's Vishnu Temple was joined by Matthes' Krishna Shrine, Solomon Temple, Wotan's Throne and Walhalla Plateau. He has been criticized for doing this, but perhaps it is good for the wonder of the world to bear the names of gods and heroes of every nation.

Francois Matthes was a naturalized American, born in Holland in 1874, who had lived in Switzerland and studied at Frankfurt, Germany, and the Massachusetts Institute of Technology. He served in the Department of the Interior for fifty-one years, and after his work at the Grand Canyon he mapped Yosemite Valley, the San Andreas Fault and Mount Rainier, and wrote the monumental *Geologic History of the Yosemite Valley*. He died in California in 1948.

After Matthes' topographic map was completed, Levi F. Noble prepared a geologic map of the Shinumo Quadrangle for the U. S. Geological Survey,[31] showing the different kinds of rocks in that part of the Canyon, and tracing the faults.

Fossil footprints of four-footed animals were found in the Coconino sandstone and Hermit Shale by Charles Schuchert of Yale University in September, 1915. Fossil plant impressions were also found. This aroused great interest in the world of science. More of the tracks were collected by Noble and others, and Schuchert and Richard S. Lull

published papers concerning them in 1918.[32] Since no bones were found, there was some discussion as to whether the creatures which made the footprints were reptiles, amphibians or some other ancestral animals.

Archaeologists had long been aware that the Grand Canyon held much to interest them. The Bureau of American Ethnology hailed the proclamation of Grand Canyon National Monument as a means of protecting "innumerable antiquities, including cliff-dwellings, pueblos, dwelling sites, and burial places."[33] They sent the first professional archaeologist to investigate the Grand Canyon, Neil M. Judd, whose surveys between 1915 and 1920 included areas north of the River.[34] George A. West of the Milwaukee Public Museum also reported Grand Canyon sites.

The Grand Canyon isolates the northwestern corner of Arizona, and before the late 1920's, made it all but inaccessible from the south. The North Rim and the rest of the territory to the north of the Canyon is called the "Arizona Strip." It was settled by people from Utah who shared the dominant Latter-day Saints religion of Utah, and it seems understandable that Utah should have desired the area. In February, 1865, the Utah Legislative Assembly asked Congress to detach land in Arizona north of the Colorado River and add it to Utah Territory.[35] One reason given was the isolation from the rest of Arizona caused by the Grand Canyon.

Soon after Utah received statehood in 1896, while Arizona was still only a territory, a similar resolution was passed by the Utah State Legislature, and bills introduced in both houses of Congress.[36] Among reasons now given for the change was that the area provided a haven for evaders of the law. Arizona, having access to the area only by way of a ford across the Little Colorado River and Lee's Ferry, made few attempts to enforce justice in the

Strip. It was a place of settlement for Mormon polygamists who refused to surrender their practice. In another annexation attempt in 1902, a bill was introduced in Congress and Utah legislators were delegated to confer with the Arizona territorial legislature. The Arizonans voted not even to listen to the delegates, but Utah did not give up. Still another bill was introduced in the Senate in 1904, drawing protests from Mohave County. Local sentiment in the Arizona Strip opposed the efforts of Salt Lake City, and the project was dropped when Arizona became a state in 1912.

The North Rim remained isolated territory, covered by deep snows each winter. E. D. Woolley, one of the most prominent men in Kanab, conceived the idea of building a trail across the Grand Canyon, with a cable crossing at the river, to bring tourists across from the Santa Fe terminal.[37] In 1903, with several men including David D. Rust, his son-in-law, "Uncle Dee" Woolley formed the Grand Canyon Transportation Company to develop the route used by Francois Matthes the year before. The trail was improved and the cable was brought down rolled up from both ends and loaded on two mules at once. In spite of the clumsiness of this arrangement, only one mule was killed. The cable was installed near the mouth of Bright Angel Creek in 1907. A cage big enough for a mule was suspended from it on pulleys, and pulled back and forth by a lighter cable wound on drums. A trail continued up the other side to the Tonto Platform, then east along the shelf to Indian Gardens by way of Burro Spring. This was the old "Kaibab Trail" or "Cable Trail," which continued in use until the 1930's, when the River Trail made it obsolete.

A camp was established during the trail construction near the mouth of Bright Angel Creek, which became a stopping place for tourist parties guided by Dave Rust, and was called Rust's Camp. He

Cable car constructed by David Rust in 1907.

constructed irrigation ditches and planted cottonwoods for shade and various fruit trees. In 1913, Theodore Roosevelt stopped there briefly, so it became Roosevelt's Camp until 1922, when it was named Phantom Ranch.

Grand Canyon Game Reserve was set aside in 1906, and soon afterwards James T. "Uncle Jim" Owens was appointed warden by the Forest Service. He was a Texan who had worked at the Goodnight Ranch and served as game warden in Yellowstone.[38] He had a cabin near the rim and another one in a cave near a spring. In those days the idea of game management was to protect harmless forms of life and to kill off predatory animals such as coyotes, bobcats, owls, hawks, eagles, and especially mountain lions. In some 12 years of hunting on the North Rim, Uncle Jim claimed to have shot 532 mountain lions, and has been credited with more. He collected a bounty on every one he shot, making as much as $500 in a single day. The logs of his cabin were studded with mountain lion claws, and nearby was a sign, "Lions Caught to Order, Reasonable Rates."

Hunting lions with dogs became a sport on the northern edge of the Grand Canyon, and Uncle Jim served as guide to many parties. In 1908, Zane Grey, writer of Western novels, hired Uncle Jim and with "Buffalo" Jones, Jim Emett, and a Navajo Indian, went out to the Powell Plateau.[39] Their dogs would follow a lion's trail and tree the creature. Buffalo Jones would climb the tree, lasso the lion and pull it out. Uncle Jim and Emett would tie the lion's feet, muzzle it and clip its claws, and then chain it to a tree. Grey took pictures. They packed the lions on horses, two on each horse, and fed and watered the lions as they traveled. One lion was brought across the Canyon on horseback, taken across the river in the cage on the cable at Bright Angel Creek, and put on display at El Tovar.

Uncle Jim joined Buffalo Jones, E. D. Woolley, and others in a plan to save the buffalo from extinction and breed a cross between buffalo and cattle, the "cattalo," a new animal that would be adapted to the western range and produce good beef.[40] In 1906, the Secretary of Agriculture gave Jones permission to keep the animals in the Grand Canyon Forest Reserve, and Forest Ranger T. C. Hoyt was sent to help bring the buffalo from the railroad at Lund, Utah, across the desert to the Kaibab Plateau, where they were pastured near Bright Angel Point. One bull escaped, scaring a team of horses and upsetting a hay wagon. The buffalo did not thrive in the forest, preferring the open land of House Rock Valley, where the herd survives. The cross-breeding scheme failed, but Uncle Jim kept the herd until he sold it to the Arizona State Game and Fish Commission in 1926.

Many stories are told about Uncle Jim. He is said to have raised a mountain lion kitten that played with a pup, and followed its owner around like a dog. A less credible tale said that he fell from a cliff onto the back of a mountain lion and rode it for several feet. In his later days at Grand Canyon he was a lean, bent figure with long white hair and a drooping white moustache. He retired around the time of the creation of the national park, and died in 1936.

The Havasupai Indian community in its alcove of Grand Canyon was less isolated than before.[41] "Supai" peaches sold well in Williams and Flagstaff, and some Havasupais found jobs at Grand Canyon Village. The English language and "Western" clothes were adopted to a greater extent. Among the leaders in this period were Big Jim, who sometimes lived at Indian Gardens, and Manakaja. Supai Post Office, opened in 1903, required the mail carrier to travel over a long, rough trail. The Bureau of Indian Affairs sent a Superintendent into Havasu Canyon in 1904. In the years following, the Indian agency made several requests to expand the land in Grand Canyon under its own

trust authority, but this was not done. Instead, the Indians were given special grazing permits in the national forest and monument lands.

The flood of 1910 was the most disastrous in Havasupai memory.[42] It swept away most of the homes, as well as the school. Fortunately most of the people were absent from the Canyon on their annual trip to the rim, and there was only one death. The government began relief work. After the flood, a resident physician who doubled as Superintendent was sent in. His wife was a registered nurse. The school was reopened in a tent. Soon there was a new wooden school building with the bell rescued from the original school, and the old school tent, with frame construction added, became the general store. The government also constructed two-room frame houses for the homeless people, who did not want them. The Havasupai instead rebuilt their old brush shelters or "hawas" and used the wooden houses for storage of food and tools. When asked why they would not live in the houses, they replied that they were too hot in the summer and too cold in the winter. In later years some families moved into these houses.

Even though their reservation was tiny and difficult to reach, the Havasupais were not free from attempts at exploitation. In 1902 the United Gold and Platinum Company began a wagon road from Grand Canyon Village that was planned to descend Topocoba Canyon to Supai. At the same time a bill was introduced in Congress to grant a railroad right-of-way through the Reservation. In recommending the bill, the House Committee on Indian Affairs said, "This small reservation should not interfere with the mineral interests of northwestern Arizona and . . . we believe that the rights of the Indians will be fully protected and that the bill should pass."[43] The bill did pass the House, but died in the Senate Committee on Indian Affairs. Neither the railway nor the road was completed. Meanwhile, the miners had built a camp below Havasu Falls and had constructed a series of tunnels, steps and pegs down through the travertine beside Mooney Falls. On the west wall they erected an iron scaffolding to support wooden ladders ascending 258 feet (78.6 m.) up the vertical cliff to a tunnel entrance.[44] Ore was packed out laboriously. They planned hydroelectric power generation as well, and filed mining claims, mill sites, and even homesteads in an attempt to gain control of the water. But the 1910 flood destroyed the company's buildings and much of the equipment, ending the operation.

The Hualapais were encouraged by their agents to develop the extensive grazing lands in their reservation on the Grand Canyon's southern margin by building fences, charging grazing fees, and starting a herd of their own.[45] They were troubled by the Santa Fe Railroad's claim to half those lands. A tribal council was elected in 1919. Several Hualapai men gave distinguished service in World War I; the American Legion post in Kingman was named for one of these, Sam Swaskagame.

North of the Canyon, slightly more than a hundred Kaibab Paiutes were living at Moccasin Spring. A reservation was created for them in that area in 1907, and enlarged in 1913 and 1917.

The early twentieth century was a "golden age" for paintings of the Grand Canyon by artists. American painters were turning to subjects they found authentically American, particularly Indians and the landscapes of the West. Artists came from Europe to capture the same themes. Taos, New Mexico, became a thriving art colony, and the challenge of the colors and forms of the newly accessible Grand Canyon attracted many. The Santa Fe Railroad served as a patron of artists who painted Southwestern subjects, and made a fine collection of canvases.[46] William Robinson Leigh, for example, was given a free railroad ticket to Arizona in 1906 in return for a promise to paint canvases of Grand Canyon; the company later commissioned six of them. Louis Akin arrived in Flagstaff about the same time, and in the next few years made 35 paintings of the Grand Canyon. His largest canvas, entitled "Evening—Grand Canyon," painted in 1911, hangs on display in John G. Verkamp's studio.[47] Akin, who lived and painted for a time in the Hopi town of Oraibi, was also the muralist of the Southwest Indian Room in the American

Pictographs like these found along the
Bright Angel Trail were probably the earliest
forms of art connected with the Canyon.

Carrying the Mail to Supai *by John W. Hampton*

Phantom Ranch, Grand Canyon
by Gunnar M. Widforss

Grand Canyon *by William Robinson Leigh*

The River, Grand Canyon *by Louis Akin*

Grand Canyon from El Tovar *by Walter Ufer*

Grand Canyon *by Thomas Moran*

The Grand Canyon has proved to be a test of faith not only to the early pioneers and explorers who first visited the area, but also to those who have attempted to represent it in various artistic mediums. The scale and constantly changing composure of the Canyon have made it a difficult test. The earliest forms of art were left on the Canyon's walls in the form of petroglyphs and pictographs. It wasn't until the last half of the 19th century that European and American artists arrived to try to capture the Canyon in oils and watercolors. Artists will undoubtedly continue to express their vision of the Canyon and in the process be shaped by it.

Museum of Natural History.

For the National Park Conference in January, 1917, Stephen Mather had a "First Exhibition of National Parks Paintings"assembled in the National Gallery of Art.[48] Of the 45 paintings exhibited, 16 were of Grand Canyon subjects, including works by Leigh, Howard Russell Butler, Elliott Daingerfield, Sheldon Parsons, Frank C. Peyraud, Edward Henry Potthast, William Ritschel, Birger Sandzen, Walter Ufer, and F. Ballard Williams. DeWitt Parshall was represented by three canvases of Grand Canyon scenes. Thomas Moran had two Grand Canyon paintings along with one each of Yellowstone and Rocky Mountain National Parks. The heavy representation of Grand Canyon at the exhibition was no accident; at this time Mather was advocating that it be made a national park, and his efforts were helped toward success by the display of Grand Canyon paintings in the nation's capital.

1. George Catlin, *Letters and Notes on the Manners, Customs, and Condition of the North American Indians*, 2 vols. (Reprint. Minneapolis: Ross and Haines, 1965), I, pp. 261-62. The Hot Springs Reservation, begun in 1832, was not designated as a national park until 1921.

2. *Coconino Sun*, Flagstaff, Arizona, September 24 and October 29, 1898.

3. Theodore Roosevelt, letter to John Hay, August 9, 1903, quoted in *Life* 31(December 10, 1951):156.

4. New York *Sun*, May 7, 1903.

5. S 2732, 59th Congress (S 11-8-06, 40, 787).

6. In its 1920 decision, the Supreme Court held that as one of the greatest examples of erosion in the world, the Canyon was clearly an object of unusual scientific interest and thus could be set aside by proclamation under the Antiquities Act of 1906. See Douglas Hillman Strong, "The Man Who 'Owned' Grand Canyon," *American West* 6(September 1969):36.

7. P. L. No. 277, 65th Congress, Section 7.

8. Robert Shankland, *Steve Mather of the National Parks* (New York: Alfred A. Knopf, 1970), p. 101.

9. P. L. No. 277, 65th Congress, Section 2.

10. Horace M. Albright, *Report of the Director of the National Park Service to the Secretary of the Interior for the Fiscal Year Ended June 30, 1917* (Washington, D.C.: Government Printing Office, 1917), p. 93. Albright wrote this report as acting Director because Stephen T. Mather was ill.

11. James David Henderson, *Meals by Fred Harvey: A Phenomenon of the American West* (Fort Worth: Texas Christian University Press, 1969). See also Charles W. Herbert, "The Fred Harvey Story," *Arizona Highways* 44(June 1968):10-11, 30-35.

12. J. Wilbur Thurber, in correspondence book of the Bright Angel Hotel, Grand Canyon National Park Museum.

13. See Shankland, pp. 225-42, and Strong (note 10 above).

14. Bert Cameron, interview transcribed by William E. Austin, June 21, 1939, in "Grand Canyon Items, Vol. 2," Grand Canyon National Park Library.

15. Fred Harvey, *El Tovar: A New Hotel at Grand Canyon of Arizona* (Chicago: Santa Fe Railroad, 1904). See also *Coconino Sun*, May 17, 1902, March 21 and June 6, 1903, and April 2, 1904.

16. Margaret M. Verkamp, "History of Grand Canyon National Park," M. A. Thesis, University of Arizona, 1940, p. 47.

17. Ian Campbell, "Hermit Camp Today," *Grand Canyon Nature Notes* 9(May 1934):277-80. See also *Coconino Sun*, May 28, 1909 and January 9, 1912.

18. *Coconino Sun*, January 4 and 18, and February 8, 1902.

19. Angus M. Woodbury, "A History of Southern Utah and Its National Parks," *Utah Historical Quarterly* 12(July-October 1944):193.

20. Louise M. Hinchliffe, "Water Use at Grand Canyon: A History;" Report, May 1976, Grand Canyon National Park Library, pp. 1-3.

21. Arthur Randall Sanger, "Dairy" (*sic*) MS journal in Otis Marston, ed., "Some Colorado River Journals and Diaries," Grand Canyon National Park Library.

22. Edward Regan Monett, letter, October 2, 1908, in Marston.

23. Julius Frederick Stone, *Canyon Country: The Romance of a Drop of Water and a Grain of Sand* (New York: G. P. Putnam's Sons, 1932).

24. Kolb, interview. See also Lon Garrison, "A Camera and a Dream," *Arizona Highways* 29(January 1953):30-35.

25. Ellsworth L. Kolb, *Through the Grand Canyon from Wyoming to Mexico* (New York: The Macmillan Co., 1914). See also Emery C. Kolb, "Cheyava Falls," in *History and Exploration of the Grand Canyon Region* (Natural History Bulletin No. 2, Grand Canyon Natural History Association, November 1935), pp. 10-17. See also Ellsworth L. Kolb and Emery C. Kolb, "Experiences in the Grand Canyon," *National Geographic Magazine* 26(August 1914):99-184.

26. *Coconino Sun*, October 2, 1914.

27. Frederick S. Dellenbaugh, "Memorial to John Wesley Powell," *American Anthropologist* n.s. 20(October-December 1918):432-36.

28. Francois Emile Matthes and Richard T. Evans, "Map of Grand Canyon National Park," *The Military Engineer* 28(May-June 1926):188-201. See also Fritiof Melvin Fryxell, *Francois Matthes and the Marks of Time* (San Francisco: Sierra Club, 1962), and "Memorial to Francois Emile Matthes, 1874-1948," *Proceedings*, Geological Society of America, Annual Report, 1955.

29. Francois Emile Matthes, "Breaking a Trail through Bright Angel Canyon," *Grand Canyon Nature Notes* 2(November 1927):1-4.

30. Francois Emile Matthes, correspondence and notes, "Place Names in Grand Canyon" file, accession No. 828, Grand Canyon National Park Museum.

31. Levi F. Noble, *The Shinumo Quadrangle: Grand Canyon District, Arizona*. U. S. Geological Survey Bulletin 549 (Washington, D.C.: Government Printing Office, 1914).

32. Charles Schuchert, "On the Carboniferous of the Grand Canyon of Arizona," and Richard Swann Lull, "Fossil Footprints from the Grand Canyon of the Colorado," *American Journal of Science*, 4th Series, 45(May 1918):347-61, 337-46.

33. William Henry Holmes, "Report of the Chief," *Twenty-ninth Annual Report of the Bureau of American Ethnology*, 1907-1908 (Washington, D.C.: Government Printing Office, 1916), p. 20.

34. Neil Merton Judd, *Archeological Observations North of the Rio Colorado*. Bureau of American Ethnology Bulletin 82 (Washington, D.C.: Government Printing Office, 1926), pp. 76-142. See also Douglas W. Schwartz, "A Historical Analysis and Synthesis of Grand Canyon Archaeology," *American Antiquity* 31(April 1966):473.

35. Donald Bufkin, "The Lost County of Pah-Ute," *Journal of Arizona History* 5(Summer 1964):7.

36. *Coconino Sun*, February 20 and March 5, 1896, March 22, 1902, February 14 and 21, 1903, December 17, 1904, March 11, 1905, and September 16, 1910.

Thomas Moran sketched at the Canyon and then returned to his New York studio to produce his oils. He is pictured here with his two daughters.

37. Woodbury, pp. 191-92. See also *Coconino Sun*, July 11, 1903, and Hugh H. Waesche, "Yesterdays on the Kaibab Trail and Phantom Ranch," *Grand Canyon Nature Notes* 8(November 1933):206-8, and also David D. Rust, "From Salt Lake to the Grand Canyon," *Improvement Era* 13(March 1910):408-12.

38. Robert Easton and Mackenzie Brown, *Lord of Beasts: The Saga of Buffalo Jones* (Tucson: University of Arizona Press, 1961), pp. 120-141, 238. See also Horace M. Albright and Frank J. Taylor, *"Oh, Ranger!"* (Palo Alto: Stanford University Press, 1928), p. 49.

39. Zane Grey, *Tales of Lonely Trails* (New York: Harper & Bros., 1922), pp. 57-168.

40. Will C. Barnes, "The Bison of House Rock Valley," *Nature Magazine* 10(October 1927):216-21. See also Charles C. Niehuis, "The Buffalo Hunt," *Arizona Highways* 21(February 1945):7-9.

41. Earl Y. Henderson, *The Havasupai Indian Agency, Arizona* (Lawrence, Kansas: Haskell Printing Department, 1928), p. 8. See also Henry F. Dobyns and Robert C. Euler, *The Havasupai People* (Phoenix: Indian Tribal Series, 1971), pp. 35-39; Douglas W. Schwartz, "The Havasupai 600 A.D.-1955 A.D.: A Short Culture History," *Plateau* 28(April 1956):84; Edwin D. McKee, "On Canyon Trails, Part II," *Grand Canyon Nature Notes* 8(September 1933):192.

42. *Coconino Sun*, January 14, 1910. See also Joseph Wampler, *Havasu Canyon: Gem of the Grand Canyon* (Berkeley, California: Howell-North Press, 1959), p. 99; and Stephen Hirst, *Life in a Narrow Place* (New York: David McKay, 1976), p. 75.

43. 57th Congress, 1st Session, H. of R. Report No. 2658, to accompany HR 11848, p. 3.

44. R. W. Birdseye, "Greatest Ladder in the World Built on the Cliff of Havasu Canyon," *Travel* 46(December 1925):33.

45. Henry F. Dobyns and Robert C. Euler, *The Hualapai People* (Phoenix: Indian Tribal Series, 1976), pp. 72-74.

46. Santa Fe, *A Special Exhibition of Paintings Featuring the Grand Canyon from the Santa Fe Collection of Art*, Visitors Center, Grand Canyon National Park, Winter 1975-1976.

47. Bruce Babbitt, *Color and Light: The Southwest Canvases of Louis Akin* (Flagstaff, Arizona: Northland Press, 1973).

48. Stephen T. Mather, *Proceedings of the National Parks Conference: Held in the Auditorium of the New National Museum, Washington, D.C., January 2, 3, 4, 5, and 6, 1917* (Washington, D.C.: Government Printing Office, 1917), pp. 7-9.

7

GRAND CANYON NATIONAL PARK: PERIOD OF ESTABLISHMENT

An Act of Congress established Grand Canyon National Park on February 26, 1919, and placed it under the administration of the National Park Service, an agency of the Department of the Interior that had been authorized only three years before. There had been national park rangers in the field for less than one year. Because the National Park Service was not ready to take over the administration of the new Grand Canyon National Park, the Forest Service continued to administer and protect it until August 15, 1919, when the first acting superintendent sent by the National Park Service, William Harrison Peters, arrived. The park was formally dedicated on April 30, 1920, in ceremonies at the Powell Memorial.[1]

The young National Park Service was faced in Grand Canyon with all the problems of moving into a new area and establishing the policies of administration, protection and management which would be appropriate to a great national park. There was considerable opposition at the outset from a few local interests, and there were inadequate finances, since congressional appropriations were meager. It was a challenging job, and yet, as the English visitor J. B. Priestly was to observe during those early years, not without compensation:

> Even to remember that the Grand Canyon is still there lifts up the heart. If I were an American, I should make my remembrance of it the final test of men, art, and policies. I should ask myself: Is this good enough to exist in the same country as the Canyon? How would I feel about this man, this kind of art, these political measures, if I were near that Rim? Every member or officer of the Federal Government ought to remind himself, with triumphant pride, that he is on the staff of the Grand Canyon.[2]
> What a possession for a country! And let me add, how well the country looks after it. The American does not boast enough about his National Parks. Their very existence is something to boast about. The finest pieces of landscape in North America, perhaps in the world, belong to the People and are theirs to enjoy. I take this to be something new in history. It marks a notable advance in civilization.[3]

The first director of the National Park Service was Stephen Tyng Mather, an energetic businessman who had made a fortune in borax, and a far-sighted conservationist who gave much of his life and his fortune to the cause of the national parks, fighting battles in Congress and generating the public support that was necessary to keep the parks safe from invasion by special interests. "He laid the foundation of the National Park Service, defining and establishing the policies under which its areas shall be developed and conserved unimpaired for future generations," says the memorial to Stephen Mather which stands at Mather Point on the South Rim of the Grand Canyon. Its words conclude with the simple statement, "There will never come an end to the good that he has done."

Mather's close associate throughout this period, and his successor from 1929 to 1933, was another Californian, Horace Marden Albright, a lawyer.[4] Albright had visited Grand Canyon on his honeymoon in 1915, and had worked with his friend, Senator Carl Hayden, in the efforts to create the park. His achievements in protecting the national parks and strengthening the National Park Service made him one of America's foremost conservationists.

Between 1919 and 1927, Grand Canyon National Park had six superintendents.

What was needed was an experienced superintendent who knew the area and would provide stability by serving for a considerable period. This man was Miner Raymond Tillotson, the park engineer, who had been at Grand Canyon since 1922. Born in Indiana in 1887, Tillotson graduated from Purdue University in 1908 with a degree in civil engineering, and worked for the Forest Service and then as construction engineer for the Standard Oil Company in San Francisco.[5] His son, Dean, suffered from a severe respiratory illness and could not stay in the damp climate, so when Tillotson was offered a position with the National Park Service in Yosemite and then at Grand Canyon, he accepted. Dean recovered in the high, dry air and his father served as superintendent from April, 1927 to the last day of 1938, when he was promoted to Regional Director of the National Park Service.

By the end of Superintendent

As first director of the National Park Service, Stephen Mather payed for many of the badly needed improvements in the early parks out of his own pocket. He is pictured here at Powell Memorial.

English visitor J. B. Priestly observed: "Even to remember that the Grand Canyon is still there lifts the heart." Photo courtesy of Kolb Studio

Tillotson's period of service in 1938, the main outlines of National Park Service administration at Grand Canyon could be seen clearly. The natural environment was being protected, and exploitative activities not in harmony with the national park were being ended. Patterns of use had been established for increasing numbers of visitors, and new facilities provided by the National Park Service and by the major concessioners, Fred Harvey on the South Rim and the Utah Parks Company on the North Rim. Scientific investigations of the area were encouraged and aided, and the results were communicated to visitors.

The superintendent was assisted by a clerical staff and a small ranger force. In 1920, funds permitted the hiring of only four park rangers to handle traffic, fire control and police work, and one checker for the entrance station. Through the next two decades, this number grew to about 10 permanent rangers and more or less the same number hired in addition for the summer season. In restrospect, the accomplishments of such a small force seem amazing.

The need of the National Park Service for buildings of many kinds was seen in 1919, and construction began as soon as funds were available on an administration building, residences, warehouse, mess hall, and a combination stable-garage and blacksmith shop. Another administration building was constructed in 1921 near El Tovar. This served until 1929, when a Park Headquarters was built in the new village area south of the railroad tracks.[6] The older building was enlarged and became the superintendent's residence. Ranger cabins were built at outlying points, serving as shelters for ranger patrols. In 1921, there were cabins at Rowe Well and Grandview on the South Rim, and at four points within the Canyon: Hermit Basin, Tram Camp at the mouth of Bright Angel Creek, Pipe Creek and Salt Creek. Pasture

Wash and Desert View Ranger Stations were built in 1925. On the North Rim, a ranger cabin, barn, warehouse and machinery shed were constructed at Bright Angel Point, and snowshoe cabins at Muav Saddle, Kanabownitz Spring and Greenland Seep in 1925.

In 1919, just 44,000 people visited Grand Canyon, mostly by rail. By 1926, the majority came by automobile. In 1929, more than 200,000 visitors came. During the Great Depression, travel decreased, but it began an upswing with improving conditions and passed 300,000 in 1937.

A few rough dirt roads led to Grand Canyon National Park when it was created in 1919. Three of these reached the South Rim, from Williams, Ashfork and Flagstaff. Of these, the second was virtually abandoned and the first was shortest and in the best condition. In 1921, Coconino County built a dirt road from Maine, Arizona, which was recommended over the others for three years or so after it was opened. As part of the agreement transferring the Bright Angel Trail from Coconino County to the National Park in 1928, the National Park Service promised to build a good highway to the Grand Canyon.[7] Constuction began immediately on the approach road from Williams, which became a paved thoroughfare within the next few years.

Trips from the east, through Cameron and Desert View, took place in the 1920's but a good approach road was begun only in 1932 and completely paved by 1937. This gave the South Rim two entrances.

The North Rim could be reached in 1919 by dirt road from Kanab, but was virtually inaccessible from the South Rim by automobile. The Lee's Ferry trip was not recommended, and the nearest river crossing downstream was at Searchlight, Nevada. The automobile trip from the South Rim to North Rim by that route crossed three states and was over 600 miles (950 km.) long. The direct air line distance is only ten miles (16 km.). In 1928,

the Navajo or Marble Canyon Bridge was completed near Lee's Ferry, although the road was still quite rough. This route was paved in 1938, reducing the distance from South Rim to North Rim to its present 215 road miles (346 km.). The approach road from Kanab, Utah was completely paved by 1939.

The National Park Service made efforts to complete a system of roads inside Grand Canyon National Park that would be paved and adequate for the increasing numbers of visitors coming by automobile.

The only paved road in 1919 was the Hermit Rim Road. It was opened to automobile traffic, but the caution which was felt about the dangerous new machines was reflected in the park speed limits: 20 miles per hour (32 k.p.h.) on straight stretches when no vehicle is nearer than 200 yards (180 m.), otherwise 12 miles per hour (19 k.p.h.), but when passing animals only 8 miles per hour (13 k.p.h.) and then the automobile must take the outside of the road.[8] The Hermit Rim Road was rebuilt by the National Park Service as the West Rim Drive. The South Entrance Road was paved in 1931 as part of a new Williams road. A new road to Desert View, the East Rim Drive, was completed in 1927. On the North Rim, the entrance road to Bright Angel Point was the only road until 1924, when forest roads were extended to Point Sublime and Cape Royal. A drive to Cape Royal and Point Imperial was paved in 1932. The entrance road was paved at the same time, but the Point Sublime road remained primitive.

The National Park Service developed the cross-canyon Kaibab Trail, the River Trail, and Clear Creek Trail and acquired the Bright Angel Trail during this period, completing the present system of maintained trails within the Canyon. The old Kaibab Trail led from Indian Gardens across the Tonto Platform to The Tipoff, thence down into the Inner Gorge at the cable, and continued up Bright Angel Canyon to the North Rim. In 1921 this

trail was improved, the Inner Gorge section reconstructed, and the old cable superseded by a new "swinging" suspension bridge with a span of 420 feet (128 m.) supported by two steel cables, 56 feet (17 m.) above low water.[9] A picture taken during construction shows the cables being carried down into the Canyon along the trail, each end rolled up and carried by a mule, with the center section supported by fifteen men at intervals. In crossing the completed bridge, it was necessary to dismount and lead the mules across one at a time. In 1923, a windstorm almost destroyed the bridge, but it was restored.

The Bright Angel Trail was the center of Ralph H. Cameron's attempts to dominate development at Grand Canyon.[10] Even though the trail belonged to Coconino County, it was controlled by Cameron, whose political career had advanced him from Coconino

County Supervisor to Territorial Delegate. In 1920, the Harding landslide swept him into a U.S. Senate seat. At about the same time, the Supreme Court declared several of Cameron's obstructing mining claims invalid, but he had his cronies file others covering some of the same ground. His enmity to both the Forest Service and National Park Service was evident in his actions as senator; in 1922, for example, he managed to have the money for operating Grand Canyon National Park removed from the appropriations for the Department of the Interior. Grand Canyon also had defenders in Congress like Representative Louis C. Cramton of Michigan, who said "The Grand Canyon belongs to the world. Man may attend and preserve but must not monopolize nor exploit, and no private use can be permitted to mar the superior use of all."[11] Cramton read into the Congressional Record many of the facts about Cameron's

special interests and activities at Grand Canyon. But Cameron seemed firmly entrenched.

In 1924 Coconino County was offered a proposal to sell the Bright Angel Trail to the National Park Service, but Cameron was adamantly opposed, and the voters rejected it. The Park Service then decided to bypass the Bright Angel Trail entirely, and began work on the new Kaibab Trail as an alternate route from rim to rim. The South Rim section from Yaki Point down to the Tipoff at the Inner Gorge was completed in 1925. Two years later, the North Rim section down Roaring Springs Canyon was completed to replace the old head of the trail in upper Bright Angel Canyon.

With the erection of a rigid suspension bridge in 1928 to replace the old swinging bridge, the cross-canyon Kaibab Trail was finished to high standards of pack animal construction. The new bridge was 440 ft. (134 m.) long, 78 ft. (24 m.) above low water, supported by eight main steel cables, each 550 ft. (168 m.) long, 1½ in. (3.8 cm.) in diameter and weighing 2,320 lb. (1052 kg.), plus two wind cables. Since these cables could not be loaded on mules, 42 Havasupai Indians were hired to station themselves at intervals, lift the cable to their shoulders and proceed down the trail like a gigantic centipede. The old bridge remained in place during construction, and the old wire cable was used as a "high line." During summer, most work was done at night by floodlight. The completed bridge had a tunnel at one end, and could carry loaded pack mules nose to tail for its whole length.

Meanwhile, court cases were in progress to remove Cameron's "caretaker" from Indian Gardens on the Bright Angel Trail, where travelers were finding offensive conditions. Threatened with contempt proceedings for refusing to vacate his invalid claims, Cameron backed down and allowed the National

One of the events which typified the period of establishment at Grand Canyon National Park was the building of the Kaibab Bridge. Built in 1928, the rigid suspension bridge spans the Colorado River at the foot of the South Kaibab Trail. Construction presented difficulties, as does most work in the Canyon. During the intense heat of summer, most work was carried out at night under floodlight. The main cables for the bridge were carried by Havasupai Indians who hoisted the cables to their shoulders and headed down the seven mile trail.

Park Service to take possession of the land at Indian Gardens. When rangers moved in, they found what appeared to be an illegal distilling operation (this was during prohibition). The grounds were thoroughly cleaned up, a vast amount of cans and debris removed, sanitary facilities provided, the trail relocated out of the stream, and the spring restored to provide safe drinking water.

Cameron launched an investigation of the Departments of Agriculture and Interior in an attempt to regain the initiative, but in 1926 still more of his mining claims were invalidated, and he lost his campaign for re-election.

The county finally agreed to exchange the Bright Angel Trail for a government pledge to build a $100,000 access road to the Grand Canyon in 1928. The National Park Service relocated and reconstructed the upper section of the trail in 1931, built a caretaker's cabin at Indian Gardens, and constructed four trailside shelters. The lower section was reconstructed in 1939.

Congress revised the boundaries of Grand Canyon National Park in 1927.[12] The north boundary was extended to include a representative area of the Kaibab forest. Smaller additions to the south made possible the construction of a road within the park to Desert View, and certain isolated sections were removed from the park. The effect of the change was to add 51 square miles (142 sq. km.) giving a total area of 1009 square miles (2613 sq. km.) within the national park.

A new Grand Canyon National Monument was proclaimed by President Herbert C. Hoover on December 22, 1932.[13] This was an area of over 300 square miles (800 sq. km.) adjoining the national park on the west, and extending 40 miles (64 km.) along the Colorado River. The Canyon in this section is of great geological interest. It is possible at Toroweap viewpoint to look almost straight down on the river, almost 3,000 feet (900 m.) below. There is an extinct volcano, Vulcan's Throne, and the remains of an ancient lava flow that came down into the Grand Canyon, dammed the river and formed a lake for a time. The national monument was administered by the superintendent of the national park, and was in most respects an extension of the park.

Civilian Conservation Corps camps were located in Grand Canyon National Park beginning in 1933 as part of an effort to relieve depression unemployment. They built a trail from Phantom Ranch to Clear Creek, where hikers could see Cheyava Falls and fish in the stream. At Phantom Ranch they built a campground, planted many trees, and constructed a swimming pool that was enjoyed by many weary travelers in the heat of the Inner Gorge. The River Trail, connecting the foot of Bright Angel Trail with the Kaibab Trail near the bridge, was blasted into the solid rock of the Inner Gorge for most of the distance of two miles (3 km.). Finished in 1936, it replaced the longer Tonto Trail as a route between the two major South Rim trails. Two trails on the North Rim, the Powell Saddle Trail out to the Powell Plateau, and the Thunder River Trail down to the falls in the Tapeats Creek drainage, were constructed by 1939.

A commercial activity that does not harmonize with the purpose of national parks is the grazing of cattle and sheep, which destroy vegetation and compete with wildlife. The National Park Service did not put an end to grazing at Grand Canyon abruptly, but sought to limit it by granting permits and building fences. Cattle still invaded the area of heavy visitor use around Grand Canyon Village in spite of the drift fence. A fence along the southern national park boundary was constructed by the C.C.C. in the 1930's, and the North Rim boundary fence followed in 1938. The number of cattle allowed by permit was reduced, and the grazing season shortened, so that eventually grazing could be ended in the park.

A classic example of a mistake in wildlife management came to a crisis in the Kaibab forest in the 1920's.[14] Deer were protected, but years of persecution had almost eliminated mountain lions. As a result, the deer herd increased from an estimated 4,000 in 1906 to about 100,000 in 1924. In addition, about 10,000 cattle and 5,000 sheep were permitted in the national forest, not to mention numbers of domestic and wild horses. The deer ate every green thing they could reach, and the forest took on the appearance of a carefully clipped city park. During the severe winter of 1924-1925, thousands of deer died of starvation.

Some steps were taken to remedy the problem, such as the famous deer drive of 1924, in which a Flagstaff man received permission to drive from 3,000 to 8,000 deer in a herd from the North Rim to the South Rim by way of the Nankoweap and Tanner trails. A line of 125 men was formed on the North Rim to drive the deer to the head of the trail. Armed with noisemakers, they moved forward. A storm broke, some lost their way, and when they reached the chosen point, all the deer were behind them. Another attempt was not made.

Fawns were captured and taken to other areas to start new herds. Some were flown across to the South Rim, where they took readily to being fed by hand and became a nuisance. By 1930 there were 120 "tame" deer in the herd, and later artificial feeding was stopped. In 1924, limited deer hunting was first permitted in Kaibab National Forest, but not in Grand Canyon National Park. Still, government hunters were paid to shoot predatory animals in the park until 1927. Rangers continued to shoot any predators they encountered until 1931, when all such measures were stopped. Unfortunately, these animals were still poisoned and shot outside the park. The National Park Service wants to

restore the balance of nature within the park by protecting all native wildlife. Destructive species that have been introduced, such as feral burros, are a threat to native plants and animals such as the desert bighorn sheep.

Artificial feeding and the provision of water sources for wildlife continued through the 1920's and early 1930's, but was gradually abandoned. Water "tanks" (ponds) were constructed along the South Rim, and a large lake was created in Grand Canyon National Monument for wildlife, but the dam gave way.

Another attempt to outdo Mother Nature was the 1925 introduction of pronghorn antelope fawns on the Tonto Platform. They increased from an original group of nine to a herd of 30 only through artificial feeding, and when that was stopped in 1936, they gradually died out.

Trout were planted in tributaries of the Colorado River in Grand Canyon, beginning in 1923. A fish hatchery was located at Roaring Springs, but the fish were hampered by high mineral content of the waters and flash floods that swept

Civilian Conservation Corp camp 818 along Bright Angel Creek. Working during the summer on the North Rim, they would move into the Inner Canyon during the winter to do much needed trail work.

Mail call was always welcome considering the isolation of the Inner Canyon.

down streambeds, carrying the fish into the river or leaving them high and dry.

From the beginning, the National Park Service regarded as one of its most important activities the education of visitors about the natural wonders they had come to see. It is appropriate that at Grand Canyon, the first money for educational services was given by a group of visitors who had come for the dedication of the national park, and felt the need for such services. This was the Brooklyn Daily Eagle Tour, and their gift of almost $2,000 was used in 1921 to open an "information room" at park headquarters where a library and collections of flowers, minerals and photographs were begun.[15] A ranger was usually stationed in this room. In 1922, a daily lecture illustrated with slides at El Tovar was begun by I. I. Harrison, a National Park Service ranger. Within two years, he had spoken before 60,000 people.

The first man hired specifically for summer work as a ranger-naturalist was Glen E. Sturdevant, a graduate of the University of Arizona in geology, who began giving campfire lectures and guiding nature walks in July, 1925. In the next year, Sturdevant was hired on a permanent basis, and became the first Park Naturalist of Grand Canyon National Park in 1927. He began the issue of a monthly bulletin, *Grand Canyon Nature Notes*, and made many additions to the study collections.

A fine observation station and museum was erected at Yavapai Point in 1928 through a grant by the Laura Spelman Rockefeller Foundation. This museum, emphasizing geology, had fixed binoculars pointed at important locations in the Canyon, and was a place where talks were given on the formation of Grand Canyon.

On February 20, 1929, while returning from a reconnaissance and collecting trip in the western part of the national park, Glen Sturdevant and two other men tried to cross the Colorado River in a boat above Horn Creek Rapids. The boat was caught in the rapids and Sturdevant and Park Ranger Fred Johnson were drowned.[16] Chief Ranger James P. Brooks was the survivor.

Edwin D. McKee became park naturalist in 1929 and served until 1940. Under his leadership, the interpretive program expanded to include auto caravans as well as campfire, lodge and museum talks and nature walks on both rims. McKee often conducted geology classes on field trips to the bottom of the Canyon with an overnight stay at Phantom Ranch. The first edition of his *Ancient Landscapes of the Grand Canyon Region*, a popular description of the geological history of northern Arizona and southern Utah, appeared in 1931.[17] He has also published technical studies of the various formations in the Grand Canyon and the surrounding country. Other geologists continued to study the strata and fossils. Among these were Charles W. Gilmore of the United States National Museum and David White of the Carnegie Institution, who made studies of the footprints and plant impressions in the Hermit shale.[18]

In 1932, the Grand Canyon Natural History Association was founded to further visitor understanding and enjoyment of the scenic, scientific and historical values of Grand Canyon National Park, and to cooperate with the National Park Service. It was primarily sponsored and operated by the naturalists, and recognized as an essential operating organization. The Association took over publication of *Nature Notes*, which ceased in 1935. In its place, a series of natural history bulletins on specific subjects having to do with the Grand Canyon was started. The first of these, "Mammals of the Grand Canyon Region," by Vernon Bailey, was printed

A group from the Brooklyn Daily Eagle dedicates the Nava-Hopi Road along the Little Colorado River Gorge. Courtesy of the Michael Harrison Western Research Center

in 1935. There followed bulletins on history and exploration, trees, birds, geology, plants, prehistoric Indians, amphibians and reptiles.

Ground sloth remains many thousands of years old were discovered in Rampart and Muav Caves in 1936 by Willis Evans of the National Park Service.[19] That part of western Grand Canyon was then in Lake Mead National Recreation Area, although it has since been added to the park. Edward T. Schenk, Senior Geological Foreman with the Park Service, made test excavations, finding bones, hair, dung, and plant materials. He sent samples to Dr. Chester Stock of the California Institute of Technology, who had been working with similar remains from Gypsum Cave, Nevada. A fascinating picture of life in the Grand Canyon during Ice Age times began to emerge in reports by J. D. Laudermilk, P. A. Munz, and Robert W. Wilson. A steel gate was installed to protect the cave deposits. Further excavations were made by Paul S. Martin between 1969 and 1976. Unfortunately, someone broke open the gate in 1976, the deposits caught fire, and much of the priceless paleontological record was lost.

Indian ruins had been noticed in the Grand Canyon by early river explorers, and others had been found along the rims. The park naturalist kept records of all these sites and soon there were over 300 known. Emil W. Haury and Harold S. Gladwin of Gila Pueblo, Globe, Arizona surveyed an area south of the South Rim in 1930, finding more than 100 ruins.[20] One of these, Tusayan Ruin, was excavated by Haury, supported by the gift of Mr. and Mrs. Gladwin. Two years later a small archaeological museum was built nearby through the generosity of Mrs. Winifred MacCurdy of Pasadena. Here visitors can see exhibits concerning the Indians and be guided through the ruins by a ranger-naturalist. Edward T. Hall, Jr., surveyed the Walhalla Glades area on the

North Rim, and found concentrated evidence of Anasazi agriculture and water control structures.[21]

Two biological surveys received nationwide publicity in the 1930's. The first was the ascent of Shiva Temple.[22] Harold E. Anthony of the American Museum of Natural History was interested in the existence of two "islands in the sky," Shiva Temple and Wotan's Throne, wooded mesas within the Grand Canyon which are separated from both rims. Scientists had long observed that the hot desert depths of the Grand Canyon are a climatic barrier which prevent the movement of many small animals from one rim to the other, and that some animals have developed different forms on the North Rim and South Rim. The best known example of this is the tassel-eared squirrel, of which the South Rim form (Abert) has a gray tail and white underparts, while the North Rim form (Kaibab) has a white tail and dark

underparts. Anthony thought that smaller mammals on Shiva Temple and Wotan's Throne might have been isolated and undisturbed for thousands of years. In 1937, he led an expedition to make a study of the life on these formations, to see if any variant forms existed. Shiva Temple was climbed first.

Superintendent Tillotson and Park Naturalist McKee accompanied the expedition. Supplies were dropped by parachute. Anthony stayed on Shiva for 10 days, collecting specimens of mice, chipmunks, squirrels and rabbits. He discovered deer antlers, indicating that the larger mammals sometimes ascend Shiva, and Pueblo Indian pottery, tools and ruins, about 800 years old. As to the major purpose of the expedition, differences between the rodents on Shiva and those on the North Rim were minor, and no more marked than in regions where such separation does not exist. This was hardly enough to satisfy an eager public encouraged by newspaper accounts that, perhaps recalling Sir Arthur Conan Doyle's *Lost World*, had even suggested that the scientists were looking for live dinosaurs. In the meantime, Wotan's Throne had been scaled with great difficulty by five other members of the party including George B. Andrews.[23] Indian ruins were also seen on Wotan, but no careful study of the wildlife was made.

Rumors of the band of tiny horses, trapped in a remote section of the Grand Canyon by a landslide and reduced over the years to the size of dogs by inbreeding and starvation, often reached park headquarters. In fact, "little horses from the Grand Canyon" were exhibited in sideshows and given publicity in national magazines and radio programs.[24] In 1938, Edwin McKee, Assistant Chief Ranger Warren Hamilton, and Park Ranger Bert Lauzon were sent on an expedition to check on the truth of the rumors. They went down into Havasu Canyon and hired as guides two Havasupai Indians familiar with the area from which the little horses were supposed to have come. The Havasupais assured the rangers that there were little horses that belonged to their own ancestors, and showed them three they had captured. These were simply Indian ponies stunted from poor desert grazing. The shortest one measured 48 inches (1.22 m.) tall at the shoulder and weighed about 300 pounds (135 kg.). In a careful search through the region, the rangers found other stunted wild horses, but none smaller than those captured by the Havasupais. They concluded that the canyon blocked off by landslides in which pygmy horses were supposed to have evolved was a myth, and that the small horses were normal results of the environment and were not confined to any one limited area. Later, Park Service officials stated that they had information that the very tiny horses exhibited as "Grand Canyon" little horses were actually Shetland ponies raised on a ranch where they were stunted for this purpose.

Artists continued to receive inspiration from the Grand Canyon scene in the 1920's and 1930's. Many painters were active, Carl Hoerman and Louis H. Sharp, for example, but the one most closely identified with Grand Canyon was Gunnar Mauritz Widforss, often called "the Painter of the National Parks."[25] Born in Sweden in 1879, he studied art at Stockholm. He made trips to the United States in 1905 and 1921. On the second trip, he saw the scenery of the West and did not return to Europe. While painting in Yosemite, he met Stephen T. Mather, who urged him to work in the national parks and became his patron. Of all the national parks, Widforss loved the Grand Canyon best. He spent most of the latter part of his life along the rims and in the Canyon, painting it in its various moods. He always liked to be on the North Rim in the fall to catch the beautiful shades of the aspen leaves. He became an American citizen in 1929, and after his death in 1934

his body was put to rest in the cemetery at Grand Canyon.

Without doubt the best-known musical portrait of the Grand Canyon is Ferde Grofe's "Grand Canyon Suite." This tone poem with its reflections of sunrise, sunset, the storm, the Painted Desert and the mules "On the Trail" was written and first performed in 1931, after a visit to the Canyon that deeply impressed the composer. "I saw color, but I 'heard' it, too,"[26] he later reflected.

In this period, the South Rim saw the further development of Grand Canyon Village. In a community of people within a national park, the National Park Service serves many of the functions of city government. In a sense, the superintendent is the "mayor," the park engineer's office is the planning commission, and the rangers are the police and fire departments. The National Park Service encouraged the people of Grand Canyon Village to form a community with as many aspects of town life as possible in such an isolated location. They laid out a new village area south of the tracks in 1927, and provided a plan for further growth to progress away from the rim, so as not to intrude upon the natural scene of the Canyon itself.

The almost total lack of permanent surface water at the Grand Canyon was the most pressing problem in the development of the area. Beginning in 1901, all water was hauled in railroad tank cars over distances of 60 to 120 miles (100 to 200 km.). M. R. Tillotson, when park engineer, conceived the idea of a "recycling" plant for reclaiming waste water, which could be used for non-potable purposes and thus relieve part of the demand on the "imported" supply. The well-designed plant began operating on May 29, 1926, and continues to be regarded as an excellent example, far ahead of its time, of effective conservation of a precious resource.[27] Reclaimed water was pumped through a

completely separate pipe system and used in steam locomotives, in boilers and as cooling water in the power plant, to flush toilets, and to irrigate lawns and landscaping.

Meanwhile, little more than two miles away and 3200 feet (975 m.) down in the Canyon, the waters of Garden Creek were spilling almost unused from Indian Gardens. The Santa Fe Railroad conducted a survey to determine whether this water could be pumped up to the rim. In 1931 a contract was awarded and construction began. First a cable tramway was built down to Indian Gardens to transport men and materials, and then 2½ miles (3½ km.) of six-inch (15 cm.) pipe were laid. A three-unit pumping plant built at Indian Gardens raised the water to the rim in one stage. The environmental impact was kept to a minimum by burying as much of the pipeline as possible, building the pump house of native materials, and removing the cableway when the job was completed. Power for the pumping station was produced by a steam generating plant which had been built by the railroad in 1926 to replace the older power plant. Water trains were stopped in 1932, as the new pipeline was adequate, but in more recent years demand would again exceed supply.

The scarcity of surface water and increasing visitation necessitated the building of a pipeline from Indian Gardens in 1931.

94

Noted conservationists John Muir and
John Burroughs (third and fifth in line) on a winter
trip down the Bright Angel.

"The Lion of the Argonne," French general
Gourand and his staff.

President William Howard Taft on a 1909
visit.

Crown Prince Olav of Norway, at left, on a
hike to Cedar Ridge.

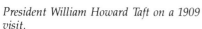

T. R. Roosevelt, on mule, and John Hance.

As one of the main scenic attractions in the
United States, the Grand Canyon has attracted
millions. More than 3 million visited in 1976
alone. Along with those from all walks of life
have come the famous.

His Majesty, Shah of Iran, watching Hopi dancers from the roof of Hopi House.

The Duke and Duchess of Windsor, 1959

General Dwight D. Eisenhower.

New York's Mayor Laguardia being instructed on the art of mule wrangling.

Prince Feisel of Saudi Arabia during his 1952 visit.

Fred Harvey, established at Grand Canyon for 15 years when the national park was created, was given a contract in 1920 as the principal concessioner on the South Rim. Phantom Ranch was built by Fred Harvey in 1922 as an overnight stop for riders on the muleback trips down the Bright Angel Trail and across the new swinging bridge. On the site of the old Rust and Roosevelt camps, Phantom Ranch was designed by Mary Jane Colter who named it after Phantom Creek, a tributary of Bright Angel Creek. The new "dude ranch" consisted of a large stone dining hall and several stone-and-wood cabins. All materials except native stone had to be packed in on muleback. When the Kaibab Trail was constructed, parties made the return trip that way, and a barn and guide's house were placed at the head of the trail. Housekeeping cabins, a delicatessen that later became a cafeteria, and a laundry plant were built near the South Rim campground, starting in 1926. The Desert View Watchtower, designed by the inimitable Mary Jane Colter, was erected at the end of the East Rim Drive in 1932.[28] This was a structure inspired by Indian ruins, built of native stone around a steel framework. The interior was decorated by Hopi Indian artists with replicas of ancient petroglyphs and kiva paintings. As remarkable as is the Watchtower, the new Bright Angel Lodge was Mary Jane Colter's masterpiece. A structure of stone and logs, its features included one fireplace constructed out of all the different types of rocks in the Grand Canyon in proper sequence. It replaced the unsightly main buildings of old Bright Angel Camp in 1935. Despite enlarged facilities, Fred Harvey received a taste of things to come when in 1938 it became necessary for visitors to make reservations during the summer season for lodgings and places on the muleback trips.

In 1921 the Babbitt Brothers Trading Company opened a general store east of the Fred Harvey garage, which was replaced by a building across the street from the site of Park Headquarters in 1925.

Tourist development on the North Rim began only shortly before the establishment of the national park. W. W. Wylie, who had operated camps in Yellowstone, opened the Wylie Way Camp on the North Rim in 1917.[29]

Transportation to the North Rim by auto stage from Lund, Bryce, and Zion in Utah, and trips out to Cape Royal were offered by the Parry Brothers, Gronway and Chauncey. Muleback trips into the Canyon were sold by Altus F. Jensen.

At the urging of Stephen Mather, the Union Pacific Railroad began to foster developments at Bryce, Zion, and the North Rim.[30] In 1923 they formed a subsidiary, the Utah Parks Company, which bought the McKee, Parry, and Jensen interests. The National Park Service designated this company as North Rim concessioner in 1927. They offered daily bus service, operated the muleback trips, and began the development of first-class accommodations on the North Rim. Grand Canyon Lodge was completed in 1928. A handsome building directly on the rim near Bright Angel Point, its exterior of Kaibab limestone seems to rise out of the cliff on which it stands. The lodge was provided with 120 cabins. North Rim Inn, with cafeteria and cabins, was located at the new campground. Water, almost as much a problem on the North Rim as on the South Rim, had been obtained from small springs on or just below the rim. In 1928 the Union Pacific Railroad installed a powerhouse and pumping plant on Bright Angel Creek near Roaring Springs, a dependable supply of water. Here electricity generated by the creek was used to pump water 3870 ft. (1180 m.) upward to the North Rim.[31] Fire destroyed the interior of Grand Canyon Lodge in 1932. Rebuilding began in 1936, and there was an attempt to keep the road plowed all winter so construction could continue. It proved to be even snowier than usual, and personnel had to be evacuated by snow tractor or down the Kaibab Trail.

A post office operated intermittently at Grand Canyon Lodge under various names such as Kaibab, Kaibab Forest, and North Rim, Arizona.

The Colorado River in the Grand Canyon began to be affected by water reclamation projects during this period. Dams for flood control, irrigation, and power generation had been suggested. The 1922 Colorado River Compact set Lee's Ferry as divider between the Upper and Lower Basins. Each basin was entitled to use a portion of the Colorado's annual flow. A U.S. Geological Survey trip down the Colorado River was organized to make a detailed map, taking elevations and locating damsites along the river.[32] Claude H. Birdseye headed the expedition. They ran the Grand Canyon section in 1923 with Emery Kolb as chief boatman. The boats were of the light Galloway-Stone type. This expedition established the custom of measuring river distances from Lee's Ferry and naming features such as creeks after these mileages.

Grand Canyon Lodge stands in ruin after being gutted by fire in 1932. Reconstruction began four years later.

The Desert View Watchtower was designed by Mary Jane Colter. She also designed Lookout Studio, Hermits Rest, and the current Bright Angel Lodge.

A river gauger was stationed by the Geological Survey at the mouth of Bright Angel Creek in 1923 to measure the flow and silt content of the Colorado River and to provide flood warnings for the lower river basin. He was provided with a cabin, a river level recorder and a cable car from which to measure and take samples. The Boulder Canyon Project Act of 1928 authorized Hoover Dam in Black Canyon, the "head of navigation" on the Colorado reached by Ives almost 75 years before. The dam was completed in 1936, forming Lake Mead, a reservoir that extended into the lower end of Grand Canyon and drowned some rapids, including Separation Rapids of the Powell expedition. Hoover Dam was the first in the canyons. Lake Mead National Recreational Area, established on October 13, 1936, included a large section of the western Grand Canyon from the boundary of Grand Canyon National Monument to the Grand Wash Cliffs, and was placed under the administration of the National Park Service.

Meanwhile, a few more parties attempted river trips through Grand Canyon. Clyde Eddy, in 1927, sought pure adventure.[33] In three Powell-type boats, he went down the river with eight college-age boys, a dog, and a bear cub. Eddy was a journalist, lecturer and a member of the Explorer's Club. He partly repeated his trip later the same year with the Pathe-Bray commercial motion picture expedition, which he accompanied from Lee's Ferry to Hermit Creek.

The next attempt on the river was made in October, 1928, when Mr. and Mrs. Glen R. Hyde decided to spend their honeymoon running the Colorado in a scow with sweep oars at each end.[34] They made the trip from Green River, Utah to Bright Angel Creek in 26 days. At that point they ascended to the South Rim, where they talked to Emery Kolb. He found they were making Brown's mistake in not wearing life preservers. He offered them his own, but they refused. They returned to the river, continued their journey, and were never seen again. When they were long overdue, an Army airplane was sent from March Air Base to search, and a boat was sighted in the lower Granite Gorge. Emery Kolb then rode in the airplane and identified the boat. Emery and Ellsworth Kolb and Chief Ranger Brooks repaired an old boat at the mouth of Diamond Creek and floated downstream 14 miles (23 km.) to the Hydes' boat, which they found dry, undamaged and empty, held by its own rope which had caught in the rocks. There was Mrs. Hyde's diary, with the last date recorded, December 1, 1928. Search uncovered no further clues as to the manner of the Hydes' deaths, but Emery Kolb surmised that Mrs. Hyde, holding the boat's rope while her husband scouted a rapid, was swept into the current, that her husband then tried to rescue her and both were drowned.

Clyde Eddy's third river trip was made in 1934 with Russell G. Frazier and others including Bus and Alton Hatch. This party erected a memorial plaque at Separation Rapid to the three men who left the first Powell expedition. It was the first to terminate its trip at the new Boulder (Hoover) Dam.

The only man ever to run the Colorado River through the canyons alone was Haldane ("Buzz") Holmstrom, a service station attendant from Coquille, Oregon.[35] He made his boat himself, a 15-foot (4.6 m.) craft of Galloway-Stone type, starting with a Port Orford Cedar tree that he sawed into boards. He drove to

Green River, Wyoming, with his boat in October, 1937, and seven weeks later arrived at Boulder Dam. "I know I have got more out of this trip by being alone than if I was with a party," he wrote in his diary on his last night in Grand Canyon, "as I have more time, especially at night, to listen and look and think and wonder about the grandeur that surrounds me..." He reflected on his trip down the wild river:

> I find I have already had my reward, in the doing of the thing. The stars, the cliffs and canyons, the roar of the rapids, the moon, the uncertainty and worry, the relief when through each one...the campfires at night...the real respect and friendship of the rivermen I met....
> This may be my last camp where the roar of the rapids is echoed from the cliffs around and I can look at the stars and moon only through a narrow slit in the earth.
> The river and canyons have been kind to me.[36]

The first recorded airplane flight over the Grand Canyon was made in a DeHaviland bomber by Lieutenants R. O. Searle and E. D. Jones of the U. S. Army Air Service at an altitude of 10,000 to 14,000 feet (3000 to 4300 m.) on February 24, 1919.[37] On the following day, Lieutenant Charles Rugh piloted the airplane down into the Canyon in the section north of the Hualapai Indian Reservation, descending about 2000 feet (600 m.) below the rim. His passenger, Lewis Lewyn, the official photographer for the Gulf-to-Pacific squadron, took both motion and still pictures. In the summer of 1922, Ellsworth Kolb hired R. V. Thomas, a barnstorming World War I flyer, to make a landing in the Canyon on Turtle Head (Plateau Point), a promontory of the near-level Tonto Platform.[38] Rangers cleared a runway 90 feet (27 m.) wide and 400 feet (120 m.) long. Thomas made two

landings and, what is more remarkable, two successful flights out of the Canyon from that point, 3200 feet (975 m.) below the rim. An airport for scenic flights through the Grand Canyon was developed near Red Butte, 16 miles (26 km.) south of the South Rim, and beginning in 1931 was operated by Grand Canyon Airlines. Landings were also made in V. T. (DeMotte) Park on the North Rim and at times an airplane was stationed there.

The Havasupai Indians found their small reservation completely surrounded by the new national park in 1919.[39] Since they were used to grazing their stock, particularly horses, over a sector outside the reservation, the Superintendent immediately granted grazing permits

covering 150,000 acres (60,700 ha.) so that this use could continue. The Havasupais also grazed about 200 cattle in the canyons southwest of their village and on the Hualapai Reservation. Thus the Indians used a much larger area than would be indicated by the size of their reservation.

Leslie Spier of the American Museum of Natural History was in Havasu Canyon during 1918, 1919 and 1920, studying the way of life of the Indians.[40] Many of the Havasupais talked to him about their customs and traditions, but his principal informant was Sinyella. His anthropological report, the classic work on the Havasupai, was published in 1928.

Along with most other American

Indians, the Havasupais were granted U.S. citizenship in 1924, but this produced no immediate changes for them. The day school was still operating, but not at capacity. In 1927, for example, there were only 9 children in grades 1-3. The others, about 50, were being educated in boarding schools far from home.

Mining was revived in the Havasu area by W. I. Johnson's Arizona Lead and Zinc Company, which worked in Carbonate Canyon below Havasu Falls, but also had tunnels near the Colorado River. Considerable development took place without adequate financial returns, and finally an engineer's report stated there were no significant mineral deposits. In 1938 a new graded road was built to Hualapai Hilltop from a point near Peach Springs.

A considerable number of Havasupais found employment in Grand Canyon Village both with Fred Harvey and the National Park Service, which recognized their special status within the park. Men worked mainly on construction jobs, while women became maids, kitchen helpers, and laundresses. Many Indians lived in a camp near Grand Canyon Village; a 160-acre (65 ha.) plot was designated for them in 1926. But without medical attention, proper housing, or adequate water, the camp was a rural slum. In the mid-1930's, the National Park Service provided new cabins, and the Bureau of Indian Affairs made arrangements with the resident physician to give medical care. Later, the older shacks were torn down, and Havasupai children began to attend the Grand Canyon school.[41] When a heavy snowstorm isolated the Havasu Canyon village for several weeks in the winter of 1933, the National Park Service sent in 16 mules loaded with food and other supplies.

This period of the establishment of Grand Canyon National Park was one in which some threats to the administration

R. V. Thomas, a barnstorming, World War I flyer, made the first landing in the Grand Canyon.

of the Canyon as a place of natural splendor belonging to all the people had been turned aside, and a good foundation laid for the future. In 1938, the National Park Service could look back proudly on solid accomplishments.

1. U. S. Department of the Interior, National Park Service, Grand Canyon National Park, *Superintendent's Annual Reports*, 1920-1953. Hereinafter referred to as *Annual Reports*. Grand Canyon National Park Library.
2. John Boynton Priestley, *Midnight on the Desert* (New York: Harper & Brothers, 1937), p. 285.
3. John Boynton Priestley, "Grand Canyon, Notes on an American Journey," *Harper's Magazine* 170(February-March 1935):399.
4. Donald C. Swain, *Wilderness Defender: Horace M. Albright and Conservation* (Chicago: University of Chicago Press, 1970).
5. Miner Raymond Tillotson, letter, December 29, 1923.
6. U. S. Department of the Interior, National Park Service, Grand Canyon National Park, *Formal Opening: New Administration Building, Grand Canyon National Park, Grand Canyon, Arizona, Saturday, April 6th, 1929.*
7. *Annual Reports*, 1929.
8. *Ibid.*, 1920.
9. "Bridges: Kaibab Suspension," File No. 650-04, Grand Canyon National Park Museum.
10. Douglas Hillman Strong, "The Man Who 'Owned' Grand Canyon," *American West* 6(September 1969):33-40. See also Shankland, pp. 225-42.
11. *Congressional Record*, 68th Congress, 1st Session, Vol. 65, Part 4, March 3, 1924, p. 3490.
12. HR 9916, 69th Congress, H 2-25-27, 44 Stat. 1238.
13. Presidential Proclamation No. 2022, 12-22-32, 47 Stat. 2547, P. & O. 204.
14. John P. Russo, *The Kaibab North Deer Herd: Its History, Problems, and Management* (Phoenix: State of Arizona Game and Fish Department, 1964).
15. *Annual Reports*, 1921.
16. P. T. Reilly, "How Deadly is Big Red?" *Utah Historical Quarterly* 37(Spring 1969):244-60. See also "Glen Ernest Sturdevant," Grand Canyon Nature Notes 3(February 1929).
17. Edwin Dinwiddie McKee, *Ancient Landscapes of the Grand Canyon Region* (Flagstaff, Arizona: Northland Press, 1931).
18. Charles W. Gilmore, "Fossil Footprints from the Grand Canyon," *Smithsonian Miscellaneous Collections*, Vol. 77, No. 9, 1926. See also David White, *Flora of the Hermit Shale, Grand Canyon, Arizona* (Washington, D.C.: Carnegie Institution, Publication No. 405, December 1929).
19. J. D. Laudermilk and P. A. Munz, "Plants in the Dung of Nothrotherium from Rampart and Muav Caves, Arizona," in *Studies on Cenozoic Vertebrates of Western North America*, by Robert W. Wilson, *et. al.* (Washington, D.C.: Carnegie Institution, Contributions to Paleontology, Publication No. 487, 1938), pp. 271-81. See also Robert W. Wilson, "Preliminary Study of the Fauna of Rampart Cave, Arizona," in *Studies of Cenozoic Vertebrates of Western North America and of Fossil Primates*, by Arthur B. Drescher, *et. al.* (Washington, D.C.: Carnegie Institution, Contributions to Paleontology, Publication No. 530, 1942), pp. 169-85.
20. Douglas W. Schwartz, "A Historical Analysis and Synthesis of Grand Canyon Archaeology," *American Antiquity* 31(April 1966):474. See also Emil W. Haury, *Kivas of the Tusayan Ruin, Grand Canyon, Arizona* (Globe, Arizona: Gila Pueblo, Medallion Papers, No. 9, 1932).
21. Edward T. Hall, Jr., *Archaeological Survey of Walhalla Glades* (Flagstaff, Arizona: Museum of Northern Arizona, Bulletin No. 20, June 1942).
22. Harold E. Anthony, "The Facts about Shiva: The Real Story of One of the Most Popular Scientific Adventures in Recent Years," *Natural History* 40(December 1937):708-21,775-76.
23. George B. Andrews, "Scaling Wotan's Throne: An Exciting Feat in which Shiva's Sister 'Sky Island' Yields to the Skillful Rock Climbers of the Patterson Grand Canyon Expedition," *Natural History* 40(December 1937):722-24,776.
24. H. G. Franse, "Vest Pocket Horses," *Arizona Highways* 14(October 1938):18-19.
25. William Belknap and Frances Spencer Belknap, *Gunnar Widforss: Painter of Grand Canyon* (Flagstaff, Arizona: Museum of Northern Arizona and Northland Press, 1969).
26. Ferde Grofe, "Story of the Grand Canyon Suite," *Arizona Highways* 14(December 1938):6-9.
27. Edmund C. Garthe and Wilfred C. Gilbert, "Wastewater Reuse at the Grand Canyon," Journal, Water Pollution Control Federation (September 1968). See also Louise M. Hinchliffe, *Water Use at Grand Canyon: A History* (Report, Grand Canyon National Park, May 1976).
28. Mary E. J. Colter, *Manual for Drivers and Guides Descriptive of the Indian Watchtower at Desert View and its Relation, Architecturally, to the Prehistoric Ruins of the Southwest* (Grand Canyon: Fred Harvey, 1933).
29. Angus M. Woodbury, "A History of Southern Utah and its National Parks," *Utah Historical Quarterly* 12(July-October 1944):203.
30. Robert Shankland, *Steve Mather of the National Parks* (New York: Alfred A. Knopf, 1970), pp. 137-41.
31. Miner Raymond Tillotson, "A Water Supply for the North Rim of the Grand Canyon," State of Arizona *State Board of Health Bulletin* 50(July 1929):35-37.
32. Claude H. Birdseye and Raymond C. Moore, "A Boat Voyage through the Grand Canyon of the Colorado," *Geographical Review* 14(April 1924):177-96. See also Claude H. Birdseye, "Exploration in the Grand Canyon," *Reclamation Era* 28(August 1938):170-71; and Ellsworth L. Kolb, "River Running 1921: The Diary of E. L. Kolb," ed. by W. L. Rusho, *Utah Historical Quarterly* 37(Spring 1969):269-83; and the following works of Lewis R. Freeman: *The Colorado River: Yesterday, Today, and Tomorrow* (New York: Dodd, Mead, 1923), *Down the Grand Canyon* (London: William Heinemann, 1924), and "Surveying the Grand Canyon of the Colorado," *National Geographic Magazine* 45(May 1924):471-530,547-48.
33. Clyde Eddy, *Down the World's Most Dangerous River* (New York: Frederick A. Stokes, 1929).
34. Emery C. Kolb, personal interview, July 31, 1962.
35. "He Shot the Colorado Alone," *Saturday Evening Post* 210(February 26, 1938).
36. Haldane Holmstrom, "Down the Colorado," MS journal in Otis Marston, ed., "Some Colorado River Journals and Diaries," p. 70, Grand Canyon National Park Library.
37. Los Angeles *Examiner*, February 25, 1919, and associated newspaper clippings, Grand Canyon National Park Museum, catalog Nos. 19371-89, case No. 87.
38. *Annual Reports*, 1922.
39. Henry F. Dobyns and Robert C. Euler, *The Havasupai People* (Phoenix: Indian Tribal Series, 1971), pp. 40-48. See also Stephen Hirst, *Life in a Narrow Place* (New York: David McKay, 1976), pp. 132, 202-04.
40. Leslie Spier, *Havasupai Ethnography* (New York: American Museum of Natural History, Anthropological Papers, Vol. 29, No. 3, 1928), p. 83.
41. "Havasupai Indians," File No. A9431, Grand Canyon National Park Museum.

8

GRAND CANYON NATIONAL PARK: PERIOD OF EXPANSION

A crisis of growth affected almost every kind of human activity at Grand Canyon National Park after the Second World War when the Canyon felt the effect of the economic boom. Increasing waves of visitors arrived almost every year.

In 1944, only 65,000 visitors came, and many of these were servicemen on trips arranged for their units. Bus trips within the park were discontinued. Most of the concessioner's facilities except El Tovar were closed. No trains ran from Williams. Many rangers and other employees volunteered for service or were drafted, and work was done by a skeleton crew.

After the war, increasing waves of visitors arrived almost every year, including foreign visitors, now a major component among the travelers to the Canyon. In 1956 the number rose above 1,000,000 annually, and facilities in the park were overloaded. Reservations were required throughout the summer, and traffic and parking were congested. In 1969, there were over 2,000,000, while the Vietnam crisis caused the government to cut appropriations for staff and facilities. Visitation reached 2,700,000 in 1972, but declined in the next two years to the 1969 level due to fuel shortage and rising costs brought about by the Middle East conflict. When that crisis seemed to be over, numbers shot up again, passing 3,000,000 in 1976. In one year, travel figures doubled on the North Rim alone. By this time, policy makers for the national parks were giving consideration to limiting, rather than constantly increasing, visitor facilities.

The importance of the tourist industry to northern Arizona became apparent in the postwar period, and new roads were built. By the early 1960's it became possible to drive between Grand Canyon and points in the Indian country to

the east by direct paved roads.

The growing flood of automobiles that almost inundated the park, and Grand Canyon Village in particular, made studies necessary for new patterns of traffic and visitor use. The National Park Service relocated the south entrance road in 1954 to provide visitors with a view of the Canyon from Mather Point before they reached the village with its confusion of roads, and to make it possible for

through traffic to avoid the village entirely. Concern over possible development of the south approach road frontage into a string of hamburger stands, billboards and subdivisions prompted Senator Carl Hayden to introduce a bill to protect scenic values along the road within Kaibab National Forest. The bill passed and was signed by President Harry S. Truman in July, 1951.[1] Developments have appeared south of the park on private land that was not affected by the law.

In the 1950's the National Park Service decided that new public and private facilities should be located in an area away from the Canyon rim and about a mile east of the older village on the new entrance road. At the same time, it was evident that facilities in national parks across the country were inadequate. In 1956 Congress authorized a ten-year program of construction, known as "Mission 66" because it was designed to provide enough visitor facilities by 1966. At Grand Canyon, Mission 66 projects centered around the new village area. The first unit, completed in 1957, was a

South Entrance Station, 1948

Mather Campground, 1952

Visitor Center, with information desk, museum exhibits, library, study collection, audiovisual room, workshop and offices for the naturalists. A new wing was added in 1966 to house administrative offices and the structure became Park Headquarters. Mather Campground was located in the new area in 1961. Near the Visitor Center, an amphitheater was built for campfire programs. Roads were relocated, parking areas and campgrounds enlarged, and viewpoints rebuilt with Mission 66 funds. By 1966, it was clear that the increase in use of the national parks was more rapid than the provision of new facilities. In that respect, Mission 66 failed, although it had provided many necessary improvements.

The virtual impossibility of providing everything motoring tourists wanted, combined with a desire to protect the natural scene and preserve the very things people came to see, caused the National Park Service to alter its policy, limiting and controlling access in some areas. The West Rim Drive, for example, was closed to private vehicles again during the busy season, beginning in 1974. Instead, free buses were made available there and within Grand Canyon Village on a regular schedule.[2] These were operated by Fred Harvey under a government contract, and helped reduce traffic congestion.

While automobile travel remained the predominant means of reaching Grand Canyon, air travel developed rapidly. A modern airport facility was completed near Rain Tank ten miles (16 km.) south of Grand Canyon Village in 1965, outside the national park, and several commercial airlines offered service. Not long afterward, this airport had become the third busiest in Arizona. An era of travel came to an end in 1968 when the Santa Fe Railroad discontinued passenger service to Grand Canyon. Some of the tracks near the station in the village were removed and replaced by parking lots.

The chief responsibility for meeting the challenge of expanding numbers lay with the National Park Service staff. During the Second World War and for several years afterwards, Harold Child Bryant, who had done much to establish interpretation and education as activities of the National Park Service, was superintendent of Grand Canyon National Park. He acted in that capacity for 14 years, longer than any other individual.

By 1972, the history of federal land decisions had produced a patchwork of jurisdictions over the Grand Canyon. Grand Canyon National Park and Monument occupied the central section, and the National Park Service also administered the western section, as part of Lake Mead National Recreation Area. The Forest Service controlled part of the Canyon north of the river near Kanab Creek, while the Bureau of Land Management administered the west rim

The Canyon Shuttle began service in 1974 to decrease auto congestion and pollution in Grand Canyon Village.

In a span of just over thirty years, travel to the Grand Canyon had gone from the day long stage ride from Flagstaff to scenic airplane rides over the Canyon. Americans in ever increasing numbers came to see the Grand Canyon of the Colorado. Foreign visitors, at first a small minority, became a major component among travelers to the Canyon. Many came by train, but as time went on, the Canyon became easily accessible by bus, car, and airplane.

As was the case in other American towns, Grand Canyon Village grew up around the railroad station.

In 1937, this Ford Tri-motor flew the Canyon
on a regular basis.

of Marble Canyon. Three Indian
Reservations extended into the Canyon: the
Navajos east of the Colorado and north of
the Little Colorado, the Hualapais south
of the river in the western Canyon, and the
Havasupais in a tiny enclave completely
surrounded by the national park. A
passenger on a boat trip down the river at
that time might have passed through
seven administrative areas. In addition,
a few pieces of private land, mostly mining
claims, were scattered through
the Canyon.

Government and conservation groups
urged several times that as much of the
Grand Canyon as possible be placed
inside the national park and protected as a
unit. This proved to be politically
impossible while proposals to build
dams in Grand Canyon were the center of a
national controversy, described later in
this chapter. But after the decision not to
build the dams had been made, park
enlargement was again considered. At the
urging of Stewart L. Udall, Secretary of
the Interior, President Lyndon B. Johnson
created Marble Canyon National
Monument on his last day in office,
January 20, 1969. The new monument
included the area between the rims from
the national park upstream to the mouth
of the Paria River just below Lee's Ferry.

Plans for a more comprehensive
enlargement of the national park were
begun by the Park Service and members of
Congress, most notably Senator Barry
Goldwater of Arizona. The Sierra Club
and other conservation groups supported
the expansion, but a conflict over Indian
land rights soon surfaced. After
generations in which Indians generally had
lost their land, often without adequate
compensation, Congress wished to be
fair to the tribes involved. The Hualapais
posed no major issue regarding the bill for
park enlargement; their land, all south of
the river, was left out of the park. The
Navajos were asked to make a decision;
the area inside the Canyon on the

periphery of their reservation would be included in the new park area only if their Tribal Council agreed. The Havasupais found themselves the center of the major controversy on the bill; since their 500-acre reservation was not adequate for them, they requested the addition to it of the land where they grazed their animals on the plateaus under special permit. The area included thousands of acres of Grand Canyon National Park and Monument. The bill as finally approved gave the Havasupais about 185,000 acres (75,000 ha.) in all, including the Great Thumb and other plateau lands above the rim, and Havasu Canyon itself down to Beaver Falls. In addition, about 95,000 acres (38,500 ha.) inside the national park was designated "Havasupai Use Lands" for traditional purposes, under a plan to be worked out by the tribe and the National Park Service. Except for tribal small business enterprises, all mining, logging, and industrial development were forbidden by the bill on Havasupai lands, which "shall remain forever wild and no uses shall be permitted . . . which detract from the existing scenic and natural values."[3]

The act "to further protect the outstanding scenic, natural, and scientific values of the Grand Canyon by enlarging the Grand Canyon National Park" was signed into law by President Gerald R. Ford on January 3, 1975. It almost doubled the size of the park, to 1,892 square miles (4,901 sq. km.), and included all of the interior of the Canyon, with the exception of the Indian Reservations as noted, from the Paria River to the Grand Wash Cliffs, and a few segments of the surrounding plateaus. It also provided for examination of some adjacent lands for possible later inclusion in the park. It states "that the entire Grand Canyon, . . . including tributary side canyons and surrounding plateaus, is a natural feature of national and international significance. Congress recognizes the need for, and in this Act provides for, the further

protection and interpretation of the Grand Canyon in accordance with its true significance."[4]

The Wilderness Act of 1964 required that every roadless area of more than 5,000 acres (2,000 ha.) in the national parks be reviewed for possible designation as a wilderness area. The law defined a wilderness area as "an area where the earth and its community of life are untrammeled by man, where man himself is a visitor who does not remain."[5] Since most of the land in Grand Canyon National Park seemed to meet this definition, the National Park Service prepared and held hearings on a wilderness plan, which was ready in 1973. But the park expansion outdated this plan. The Enlargement Act was amended on June 10, 1975 to require a wilderness study for the larger park. That report, still in tentative form at this writing, will

probably designate more than 80% of park lands as wilderness, with another 10% to be considered for addition to wilderness. Major areas excluded are the developed South Rim from Hermit's Rest to Desert View, the roads and developments on the North Rim, the corridor along the Kaibab and Bright Angel Trail with pipelines and power lines, and an area south of the Grand Wash Cliffs where there is subdivided land. Probably to be added to the wilderness area are the Havasupai Use Lands, with the concurrence of the Tribal Council, where traditional Indian use does not conflict with wilderness values, and some private lands that may be purchased by the Park Service. Proposals have been made to limit river trips to oar-powered boats, allowing the river to be included in the wilderness. It seems certain that most of Grand Canyon National Park will be designated as

The 8,000 ft. elevations on the North Rim can produce an annual snowfall exceeding 200".

wilderness by Congress within our lifetime.

Historically, most of the park has been administered as wilderness since the national park was established, and even before that. In the period from 1939 to the present, the ranger force continued its dual function in protecting the visitors and protecting the national park itself. The staff to do this adequately was available in the 1950's and early 1960's, but since then, cutbacks have reduced Park Service personnel while public use has continued to escalate. Winter ski patrols and snow-cat patrols were initiated to keep watch on the North Rim during its long closed season. A full-time ranger was stationed in Grand Canyon National Monument. The huge area added to the national park had at this writing made only one new position available to the Park Service: a ranger stationed at Meadview in the western Grand Canyon.

Rescues of people isolated or injured in the Canyon are one aspect of the rangers' work. There are many of these every year, and only a few examples may be mentioned. One of the more spectacular incidents involved an air accident. Three men of the Army Air Corps parachuted into the Grand Canyon at night on June 20, 1944, when their B-24 bomber developed engine trouble.[6] Unaware of their location, they were surprised to see lights on the Canyon rim pass them by and disappear above their heads. They fell onto the Tonto Platform four miles (6 km.) south of Point Sublime, and found a small spring of water. Three days later they were sighted and supplied by air drop, but it was not until June 30 that a route was found to bring them out.

Another airplane accident at Grand Canyon was one of commercial aviation's worst disasters up to that time. Near noon on a reasonably clear day, June 30, 1956, two airliners on eastward flights from Los Angeles collided over the Canyon and fell into the gorge near the river,

killing all 128 persons aboard.[7] The planes were a Trans-World Airlines Constellation and a United Airlines DC-7. The points of impact were on Temple and Chuar Buttes near the confluence of the Colorado and Little Colorado rivers. The bodies of the victims were removed by helicopter and many were buried in Grand Canyon cemetery, where a memorial stands.

Hikers and climbers in the Canyon are a source of concern to rangers. Those going off maintained trails must register. Hikers sometimes take old trails, and there are a few who make a hobby of hiking into little-known parts of the Canyon. One is Harvey Butchart, a former mathematics professor at Northern Arizona University, who has gone into almost every nook and cranny of the Canyon.[8] Another is Colin Fletcher, who in 1963 packed from Havasu Canyon to the head of the Nankoweap Trail and wrote a popular book about his experiences.[9]

Increasing numbers of people are seeking out more remote places for hiking, backpacking, and camping. By the early 1970's, they had produced a virtual explosion of use at Grand Canyon. Trails that had been almost abandoned were suddenly being hiked almost every day in the summer season, and their now more beaten paths could be seen easily from the rims. Established trails and camps were overcrowded. On some summer nights at Phantom Ranch, 800 to 1,000 campers occupied a campground that could comfortably accommodate 75 at most. Regulations became a necessity. Beginning in 1971, permits and reservations were required for overnight camping inside the Canyon. About 70,000 of these are issued each year. Specialized activities like cave exploration have also increased, and are controlled by a permit system.

Similar crowding existed in automobile campgrounds. After a decade or so of attempting to accommodate everyone who wanted to camp, by

opening "overflow campgrounds" and parking areas, it became necessary to limit campers to existing spaces on a first come, first served basis. From 1973 to 1975, a computerized reservation system including Mather Campground was tried nationally, and although it was not continued, reservations were still accepted at Mather only.

A necessary response to expanding human activities at Grand Canyon was the provison of increased supplies of water and energy. The Santa Fe Railway Company gave its electric power

generation, steam heat, and water supply facilities to the National Park Service in 1954. Commercial power was provided by the Arizona Public Service Company in 1955. A power line to Indian Gardens was installed with the aid of helicopters in 1959. Three new water tanks tripled South Rim storage facilities, but the water supply from Indian Gardens soon proved inadequate to keep the tanks filled. In 1960, the old method of bringing in water in railroad tank cars had to be started again. So it was decided to bring water from Roaring Springs below the North Rim all

Helicopter ferrying equipment into the Canyon during the construction of the pipeline.

the way down Bright Angel Canyon, across the river on a new suspension bridge, and up to the pumping station at Indian Gardens by gravity flow. Construction began in 1965, using helicopters to transport workmen and equipment. Early in December, 1966, when the project was near completion, a disastrous flood swept down Bright Angel Canyon, heavily damaging the pipeline and North Kaibab Trail. Congress provided new appropriations, and the contractors, Elling Halvorson, Inc. and Lents, Inc. of Seattle, began work again. In spite of the construction of even larger storage tanks, severe water shortage was experienced as the pipeline was delayed, and campgrounds had to be closed briefly. In 1970, the project was completed, and has provided an adequate water supply, except for brief interruptions of service due to rockslides and corrosion.

Much of the rangers' time is spent enforcing laws and park regulations for the protection of visitors, traffic regulations in particular requiring much time and expense. Most rangers would rather be helping people in that friendly manner that has come to be associated with the National Park Service uniform. One way to make this personal contact possible was the reestablishment of horseback patrols, particularly in campgrounds.

Forest fires in Grand Canyon National Park are fought by trained crews assisted by lookouts, radio, and air patrols. There have been few large fires in recent years. The largest, the Saddle Mountain blaze of 1960, destroyed about 9000 acres, mostly in the Kaibab National Forest but including 300 acres of Park Land. A large brush fire spread across an area on the Tonto Platform near Indian Gardens in 1968.

Wildlife management in recent years has involved the release within the park of wild turkeys and prairie dogs and the removal of destructive wild burros. The Kaibab squirrel, with its unusual

coloration, is rare and limited to a small forest area north of Grand Canyon. In 1964, an open season on the Kaibab squirrel was at first announced and then withdrawn by Arizona game officials in the face of protests. With the assistance of Clyde Harden, who had been photographing these squirrels, the park naturalist edited a film, "Tassel-Eared Squirrels of the Grand Canyon," in 1964. Later the Kaibab squirrel was placed on the government's official list of Rare or Endangered Species, and thus protected. Since the animal is completely dependent on Ponderosa pines, the Forest Service is trying to determine whether the current logging of these trees in the Kaibab forest will have an adverse effect on its population.[10]

Louis Schellbach, who first came to Grand Canyon as a seasonal ranger-naturalist in 1933, served as Chief Park Naturalist from 1941 to 1957, and told the story of the Grand Canyon at Yavapai Point in a fascinating way that enriched the understanding of thousands of visitors.[11]

The old wooden school building became the naturalists' workshop in 1940, and the priceless study collections

were located there until the move to the new Visitor Center in 1957. Manpower shortages during the war cut interpretive activities to the minimum. Guided auto caravans ceased and did not resume due to traffic problems. As more naturalists could be hired in the postwar period and on through the 1960's, new activities began: innovations were a man stationed at Mather Point to contact visitors during their first view of the Grand Canyon, a geology talk at Cape Royal, guided nature hikes within the Canyon along the Kaibab and Hermit trails, and a guided walk to observe and photograph the sunset from Grandeur Point. Campfire talks were given at each automobile campground in the park. Trailside and roadside exhibits such as the Colorado River exhibit at the foot of Bright Angel Trail, interpretive signs, and self-guiding nature trails using signs or leaflets proved useful and popular. Every year a larger percentage of visitors attended one or more talks, hikes, museums or exhibits.

By 1970, however, the program was under severe strains. The very popularity of naturalist talks and hikes meant that the crowds who showed up for them were so large as to threaten the personal, "face-to-face" character of those Park Service activities. But at the same time, budget cuts were reducing staff. Interpretive and educational services suffered. The Naturalist Workshop was eliminated, museum space was reduced, and the famous Yavapai geology talks were no longer given daily. Fewer nature walks and other activities were offered for visitors. But some new services designed to reach greater numbers of the public began. In 1972, the Grand Canyon Natural History Association began local radio broadcasts to give general park information to visitors on their car radios, and two years later commenced frequent publication of a newspaper of information and current activities that was distributed free to visitors at entrance

stations and elsewhere.

Several national programs of the National Park Service had components at Grand Canyon. One of the most important of these was the National Park Service Academy's Horace M. Albright Training Center, located south of Grand Canyon Village.[12] This "graduate school for rangers," designed for men and women who have already passed the Civil Service Examination and are ready for assignment to any National Park Service area, was dedicated in 1963. New rangers learn the history, philosophy, and goals of the National Park Service, the skills needed in operating the parks, and the art of helping people to enjoy and understand their national parks. Later they may return for in-service training. Personnel from other countries that are developing their own park systems often attend the Training Center.

The increasing demand for accommodations was felt by the concessioners. On the South Rim, Fred Harvey moved into the new village area by opening a motel, Yavapai Lodge, a trailer camp, and a camper service building. Fred Harvey also expanded in the traditional village area by building Thunderbird and Kachina Lodges between Bright Angel Lodge and El Tovar in 1968 and 1971, and

adding two-story units to the Motor Lodge. A historic tradition ended in 1971, as Fred Harvey's women employees were given new uniforms to replace the famed ruffled black-and-white "Harvey Girl" costumes that had been standard since early railroad days.

A shopping center was opened in the new village area in 1971, with quarters for Valley National Bank and a supermarket-sized Babbitt's General Store. The Post Office moved there in 1975.

On the North Rim, the Utah Parks Company added a service station and a grocery store. But in 1973, they donated all their facilities to the National Park Service and ceased operations. Another company, T.W.A. Services, was granted the concession.

Church services have long been held at Grand Canyon Village, and in summer on the North Rim.[13]

Separate religious denominations would not be encouraged to build churches on national park land, due to the constitutional principle of the separation of church and state, but a building to be used for worship by all faiths was often proposed. In 1952, the Shrine of the Ages Chapel Corporation was formed by representatives of the various religious groups. An article appeared in *Arizona Highways* magazine three years later, showing full-color architect's renditions of a large kiva-shaped structure of stone and glass to be built near the rim.[14] Many people favored having a place of worship at Grand Canyon, but many others objected to the intrusion on the Canyon rim of another large structure that would be visible from many viewpoints, even across the Canyon. As expected financial support failed to come, plans were scaled down. Ground was broken for a more modest structure between the Visitor Center and Pioneer cemetery in 1967. The Shrine of the Ages was transferred to the National Park Service in 1975, and was kept available to religious groups for

worship.

The importance of the human history of the Grand Canyon, and the historic structures connected with it, received recognition. An historic district in Grand Canyon Village was designated in 1975 to include the area from Verkamp's and the Superintendent's Residence on the east to Kolbs' Studio on the west, and from the rim across the railroad tracks to Apache Street, with its residences dating from the park's period of establishment. Many buildings at Grand Canyon have been placed on the National Historic Register, such as El Tovar, Buckey O'Neill's Lodge, the Railroad Station, and the Water Reclamation Plant, in addition to those already mentioned in Grand Canyon Village. Others elsewhere in the park include Toroweap Ranger Station, Tusayan Museum, and the Grandview Mine. When El Tovar was reconstructed, care was taken to preserve its historic character.

Mining is a problem for a national park, since it disfigures the landscape with excavations, buildings, and piles of waste, and usually requires access over park lands. Although mining and prospecting were forbidden within Grand Canyon National Park by a law enacted in 1931, there are a number of claims remaining from the years before the park was set aside. These are acquired as money becomes available.

Dan Hogan built a tourist lodge on his Orphan Mine claim in 1936, which he called the "Grand Canyon Trading Post." After he sold the place, it became in succession the Kachina Lodge, "Rogers' Place" in 1949 when it was owned by Will Rogers, Jr., and finally Grand Canyon Inn. With the advent of the atomic age, the Orphan became the only active mine in Grand Canyon National Park. In 1951, the Geological Survey discovered that the lode was rich in uranium. Three years later the mine was put into production by the Golden Crown Mining Company, afterwards the Western Gold and Uranium Company. A cableway was erected down to the entrance. Later, a 1,500-foot (457 m.) elevator shaft was sunk. Ore was sent out of the park to be processed near Tuba City. The noisy mine, a disturbing sight from nearby Powell Memorial Point, and laden ore trucks on park roads, annoyed many visitors. Then the company proposed to build a huge terraced hotel down the side of the Canyon on the mine property.[15] An agreement formalized by an act of Congress was concluded between the Park Service and the mining company in 1962, allowing uranium to be mined under national park land until 1987. In return, the land will revert to the park. Under the terms of the agreement, the tramway was removed. The mine suspended operations in 1966, and the Inn was closed.

One of the mines in the western Grand Canyon before the park was extended into that area had an unusual product: bat guano, to be used as fertilizer, taken out of Bat Cave. This strange mine operated in the 1940's and 1950's.[16] At one time, the guano was brought out by wheelbarrows and loaded into mine cars on a steep track leading down to the river bank, where a donkey-engine powered a drum cable to pull the car up to the cave. The men wore face masks, and emerged in the afternoon absolutely black from guano dust, which they washed off in the river. Later a suction hose was used to fill a barge that was then towed across Lake Mead. The last operators built a tram across the Canyon from the south side, but the mine closed down after the news media reported a discovery by scientists that bats and their droppings can transmit rabies.

The threat that dams might be built in the Grand Canyon produced one of the most exciting controversies over conservation in the twentieth-century United States. The river surveys of the 1920's had located many potential damsites in Grand Canyon, and even before Hoover Dam was authorized, some Arizona leaders were advocating a dam at Bridge Canyon, not far above Separation Rapid, to divert water to their own state. Glen Canyon had long been recommended for a storage reservoir, and in 1946 the Bureau of Reclamation located the damsite above Lee's Ferry. In 1948, the states of the Upper Colorado River Basin recommended the Colorado River Storage Project, including dams in Glen Canyon and Echo Park. Echo Park Dam aroused the opposition of many conservation groups because it would have flooded much of Dinosaur National Monument.[17] The debate raged through the early 1950's. Conservationists kept Echo Park Dam out of the bill as finally passed in 1956, which authorized dams at Flaming Gorge on the Green River, along with Glen Canyon and two others. Too late, conservationists realized that Glen Canyon Dam would flood an area larger and as spectacular as Dinosaur, with many historic and prehistoric sites. When the gates of Glen Canyon Dam closed in 1964, the historical period of the Colorado as a wild river within Grand Canyon was ended. From then on, the volume of the river depended on decisions of the Bureau of Reclamation regarding power generation and the need for transfer of water to the Lower Basin. Because silt from upstream settles out in Lake Powell, the river in Grand Canyon became clearer. Occasionally when little rain falls in the immediate area, the Colorado, the "Red River" of the explorers, turns blue-green. While boat trips are still made and the rapids are still there (although changing in size and character), the days of spring flood and the untamed river are gone.

With Glen Canyon Dam authorized, pressures increased for dams in the Grand Canyon itself. A bill authorizing Bridge Canyon Dam passed the Senate as early as 1950, only to be defeated in the House. Both the State of Arizona and the City of Los Angeles pressed for dams at Bridge Canyon and Marble Canyon. The Los Angeles proposal included plans for a

A replica of an Indian pueblo, Hopi House is included in the historic district established in 1975.

"Congestion at Babbitt's Store, 1976"

tunnel 42 miles (68 km.) long underneath the Kaibab Plateau from Marble Canyon to Kanab Creek, with some facilities located in the national park, through which almost all the flow of the Colorado would have been diverted for power generation.[18] The Bureau of Reclamation, however, asserted its paramount rights to develop the river, and in 1963 presented the Pacific Southwest Water Plan, including dams at Marble Canyon and Bridge Canyon, the latter subsequently renamed "Hualapai Dam." These dams were not intended to produce water for irrigation, but to generate power which could be sold to finance other parts of the water plan. Marble Canyon Dam would have flooded most of Marble Canyon, but would not have been inside Grand Canyon National Park as it then existed. Bridge Canyon (Hualapai) Dam would have flooded the entire length of the national monument, extended 13 miles (21 km.) into the national park, and also into the lower end of Havasu Canyon. Both dams and reservoirs would be within the enlarged park as it now exists. Environmentalists opposed both dams, especially Bridge Canyon, feeling that if they could not protect the Grand Canyon, then no other national park or natural treasure in America could be considered safe from invasions of similar kinds. The fight against the Grand Canyon dams included many conservation groups, but leadership was assumed by the Sierra Club and its Executive Director, David Brower.[19] In June, 1966, the Sierra Club placed full-page advertisements in the nation's largest newspapers, headlined "Now Only You Can Save Grand Canyon From Being Flooded . . . For Profit."[20] The case for public opposition to the dams was epitomized in one sentence from the advertisement: "This time it's the Grand Canyon they want to flood. *The Grand Canyon.*" People responded by writing an unprecedented number of letters to their representatives. Bureau of Reclamation protests that the reservoirs would not be visible from the usual viewpoints in the national park as it then existed, and would improve public access by boat, were shouted down by a new Sierra Club advertisement that asked, "Should we also flood the Sistine Chapel so tourists can get nearer the ceiling?"[21] Meanwhile, the Internal Revenue Service had acted to take away the Sierra Club's tax-exempt status on the grounds that it was engaging in a major attempt to influence legislation. To many people, this action seemed heavy-handed, and the result was probably a further strengthening of the opposition to the dams. In 1967, the Secretary of the Interior abandoned his support of the dams, and in the following year, Congress refused to approve their construction, and placed a moratorium on the Federal Power Commission's right to sanction dams, or even studies for dams, in the Grand Canyon. In this decision, Congress was responding to the evident will of the great majority of the American people that the Grand Canyon should be preserved in all its unaltered natural beauty.

Boat trips down the Colorado River became more numerous, and commercial river runners made their appearance. First of these in Grand Canyon was Norman D. Nevills, who completed his first traverse in 1938, using a wider version of the Galloway-Stone cataract boats. With him were the first women to make the trip, botanist Elzada U. Clover and Lois Jotter.[22] Nevills founded "Nevills Expeditions," and boated the Grand Canyon almost yearly until his death in an airplane crash in 1949. Among Nevills' passengers was Barry Goldwater, who made his first trip in 1940.[23] Another "river rat," as they liked to call themselves, was Katie Lee, the singer, collector of cowboy and folk songs, and composer, who celebrated the oar-powered trips by writing and recording a series of *Folk Songs of the Colorado River*.[26] On Nevills' 1941 trip, Alexander "Zee" Grant piloted a kayak,

or cloth-covered foldboat, through the Canyon. Nevills' successors, James P. Rigg, Jr., and J. Frank Wright, renamed the business "Mexican Hat Expeditions, Inc." Other pilots included Don Harris, Bert Loper, who drowned in the river in 1949 while making a run at the age of 79, Pat T. Reilly, Harry Aleson and the famous Mrs. Georgia White, whose widely publicized commercial trips used inflated neoprene rafts.

Ed A. Hudson and Otis "Dock" Marston pioneered the use of power boats in the Grand Canyon. Their first downriver run, in Hudson's *Esmeralda*, occurred in 1949. Marston repeated with his own boat in 1950, as Hudson lost the *Esmeralda* and was airlifted out. Upstream attempts were made from Lake Mead with no success until jet-propelled boats invented in New Zealand by William Hamilton were tried. The feat of running the Canyon's river upstream was accomplished by Marston in 1960.[25]

Running the Colorado River without a boat is certainly some sort of record. This was done in 1955 by two young men, William K. Beer and John Daggett, who swam it, rapids and all, from Lee's Ferry to Lake Mead, wearing life jackets.[26]

Before 1949, fewer than 100 people had gone down the Canyon's river by boat. By 1964, the number was about 900, and the Park Service had begun to require advance permission and qualification of guides. But in 1967 alone, more than 2,000 made the trip, and the increase in numbers soon became incredible, reaching over 16,400 in 1972. In that year, an outbreak of dysentery, probably a result of overcrowding, served as a warning signal. Camping on narrow beaches along the river produced problems of waste disposal and insect concentrations, motor noise became an irritant, and the impact on the natural ecosystems was severe. Campfires sometimes escaped, consuming riverbank vegetation. Trampling destroyed plants and accelerated erosion. A number of

visitors broke park regulations by feeding wild animals and birds, taking artifacts from archaeological sites, and committing other acts of vandalism. The Park Service concluded that some limitation on river trip numbers was necessary until studies could be completed and further steps taken. At this writing, the number of people who take the river trips is limited to about 14,000 annually. A National Park Service Research Study Team headed by Dr. R. Roy Johnson has completed a study of human impacts on the Colorado River ecosystems in the Grand Canyon.[27]

The historic Powell Expedition was commemorated in many ways as 1969, its centennial year, arrived.[28] The U.S. Post Office issued a stamp and medals were struck. Several centennial trips along the Colorado River marked the event. Grand Canyon National Park passed its own 50th birthday in 1969, so a double celebration was held on August 16, the 100th anniversary of Powell's arrival at Bright Angel Creek, in ceremonies at Powell Memorial Point, with many present who had made contributions to Grand Canyon and Colorado River history.

An epoch on the Colorado River passed in 1974, when Emery Kolb made his last trip in Grand Canyon at the age of 93 as a passenger in Dock Marston's boat, from the Little Colorado River to Crystal Rapid.

This has been an eventful generation for the Havasupai.[29] Although sheer geography still allows a degree of isolation, these Indian people have become acutely aware of the world around them, and their tribal land base has expanded. The Havasupai Tribe organized itself under a constitution in 1939. Their governing body is a tribal council of seven, with staggered two-year terms, elected each December. The 1940's saw some advances, with a tractor purchased and electric generators installed. But the 1950's were the difficult days of "termination," when the federal

The boats used on the second Powell Expedition, 1871.

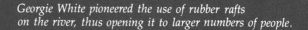

Georgie White pioneered the use of rubber rafts on the river, thus opening it to larger numbers of people.

Traversing the Colorado river through the Grand Canyon still presents many of the same challenges encountered by Powell and his men on their first expedition. Thousands have come year after year to rediscover the Canyon after it was opened to commercial use by river runners like Norman Nevills and Georgie White. Many have been attracted by the challenge and the promise of adventure, but have come away from the experience with the knowledge that the muddy thread of the Colorado runs not only through the Canyon but through their lives.

"Zee" Grant's Escalante, *the first kayak to go through the Canyon.*

Norman Nevills, the first to run commercial trips through the Canyon.

The first powerboat run through the Canyon was achieved by Ed Hudson's Esmeralda.

Otis "Doc" Marston ran the river in 1963 in a one-man Sportyak.

An oar powered trip enjoying a quiet stretch of water. Photo by David C. Ochsner

government was trying to get itself "out of the Indian business." The day school was closed, and the children had to be sent 350 miles (560 km.) away to a boarding school. The electric power often failed. Families were encouraged to relocate in urban areas, as in the Colorado River Reservation far from Havasu Canyon, but few did. The Public Health Service, which took over responsibility for Indian health in 1955, found many diseases rampant among the Havasupais. The clinic provided for the Hualapais and Havasupais at Peach Springs was too far away for any except the most serious cases; sometimes a "medic" visited the Havasupai Village, and later on, a helicopter ambulance service was provided. In spite of a poor health record, Havasupai population increased from the 1906 low of 166 to 239 in 1947 and 425 in 1973. Helicopters pierced the Canyon's isolation; tractors, construction equipment, and even buildings like the quonset hut chapel, provided by the Episcopal Church in 1948, were flown in.

The situation of the Havasupais improved through the 1960's. The day school reopened for the first two grades in 1964, and had been extended up to the fifth grade a decade later. Some programs of the Office of Economic Opportunity benefited the Havasupais: a Head Start program for pre-school children and a Community Action Program in 1966, both of which came under Havasupai leadership. The War on Poverty made surplus food available. The Bureau of Indian Affairs provided a number of prefabricated ranch-style homes, although there were complaints about their poor construction. New diesel generators on Long Mesa provided electricity. Friends of the Havasupais in Santa Monica, California raised money for a community building. Although Indians were allowed to vote in Arizona in 1948, the first election with a precinct located in the Havasupai village

occurred in 1968.

Tourism is probably the best economic hope for the Havasupais, although many of them worry about the ever-increasing numbers of outsiders, now over 10,000 per year. Proposals to build a tramway into the village from the rim have been discouraged by the Tribal Council,[30] largely because income for many of the men comes from fees they receive as guides,

and for the riding and pack horses that bring visitors down the trail from Hualapai Hilltop. The Havasupai Development Enterprise has encouraged tourism by building a lodge and a restaurant. Genuine isolation remains; Supai Post Office is inaccessible by road or rail, and is the only one left in the U.S. that regularly receives its mail by pack train.

In a case before the Indian Claims Commission first filed in 1951, the

Havasupai Tribe was awarded $1,240,000 for the land that had been taken from them in the past by the government with inadequate compensation. The tribe accepted this by a vote of 52 to 10 in an election held in 1969, and a portion of the money was distributed, $651.35 to each Havasupai. The rest of the money could be spent by the tribe for projects approved by the Bureau of Indian Affairs. If some people had thought that payment closed the books on Havasupai land claims, however, they were wrong. When the Grand Canyon National Park Enlargement Bill was being debated in Congress, the Havasupais gained the support of Arizona's delegation to return a large area of land to the tribe, and this was included in the bill, as described above.

The Hualapais also adopted a tribal constitution, and incorporated.[31] The

Supai as it looks today. Courtesy of Robert C. Euler

land case against the Santa Fe Railroad was settled in the Hualapais' favor. Children attended school in the Hualapai Public School District. In 1968, the Indian Claims Commission awarded the tribe almost $3,000,000 for the lost lands of their aboriginal territory outside the reservation, and the tribal council began developing plans to use the money. Programs initiated by the Johnson administration provided a community center and improved housing. The tribe opened an Indian doll factory at Peach Springs, and began development of tourism. The Hualapais also operate commercial boat trips on the Colorado River.

Artists continue to find the Grand Canyon environment congenial to their work. The National Park Service has hosted important exhibits in the Visitor Center. Beginning in 1972, Grand Canyon National Park cooperated with the Artists-in-residence program of the National Endowment for the Arts by providing facilities for visiting artists.

The 1970's saw increasing cultural enrichment at Grand Canyon. The Western Opera Theatre has included Grand Canyon in its performing tours, and the Utah Symphony gave concerts. The Russian poet, Yevgeny Yevtushenko, visited the Canyon in 1972 and responded in a poem, "Who are you, Grand Canyon?" including these lines:

A sixhundredmillionyear thing,
Something of the very beginning,
Something of the end...[32]

That scientific research can find a rich source of data in the national parks generally, and in Grand Canyon in particular, has become increasingly evident in recent years. Archaeologists have found the Canyon to be dotted with thousands of sites of many different types.[33] Douglas W. Schwartz worked on Havasupai prehistory and began surveys in the Shinumo, Nankoweap, and Unkar areas. His 1967 Unkar Delta digs were the first to use helicopters as the major means of access, and revealed much about the ecological relationships of the early inhabitants.[34] Realizing the value of archaeological investigation, along with the growing importance of modern Indian tribes, the National Park Service appointed as anthropologist at Grand Canyon, Robert C. Euler, a man who had already devoted much of his career to the archaeology, ethnology, and history of this area. Recent projects include the start of a computerized survey of all site locations in the national park, with a complete photographic record of each one. The enlargement of the park has added perhaps a half million acres (200,000 ha.) that need to be investigated archaeologically. And mysteries still remain. In excavating Stanton's cave in 1969-1970, Euler found 60 twig figurines, and radiocarbon dating gave them expected ages around 4000-5000 years.[35] Deeper, changes in animal and plant remains indicated a climate change for the warmer around 11,500 years ago (the end of the Ice Age). Below this was a layer of Pleistocene animal and plant material "in fantastic quantities," including bones of an extinct mountain goat and a giant vulture. Still deeper, at an age of more than 37,000 years ago and resting on bedrock, was a layer of driftwood! Since the cave entrance is 140 feet (43 m.) above the river, how can one explain the driftwood? Erosion studies near Lava Falls have indicated that the Grand Canyon has only deepened by about 50 feet (15 m.) since a lava dam blocked the river there a *million* years ago.

Topographical knowledge of Grand

Researchers working to assess the impacts that river running has had on the canyon.

Canyon has also increased. The U.S. Geological Survey remapped the Grand Canyon on standard scale in the 1960's. Since 1971, Bradford Washburn has been preparing the first really large-scale map of the most visited section of Grand Canyon, using laser beams to measure distances, helicopters for transport to difficult locations, and aerial photography.

Grand Canyon entered the Space Age in 1964, when the American astronauts being trained for the first landing on the moon descended to the bottom of the Canyon as part of their training program. They were taught geological skills which they might need on the moon. Later, Russian astronauts visiting the United States were given the same opportunity. As the world's greatest geological exhibit, the Grand Canyon was perfectly suited for this purpose. And since the Grand Canyon is the most popular national park for foreign visitors, it could be a fine location for a model interpretive program that would make lasting impressions all over the world.

The story is not yet ended. People have come and gone in the Grand Canyon, but the scene today is largely the same as it was when the Indian placed his votive figurine within the limestone cave; when the Spaniard gazed in amazement into its depths, and when the American explorer launched his frail boats into the darkening rapids. This is because the American people have decided that it is best this way; that human beings should have the unmarred majesty of the Grand Canyon to see, to marvel at, to study, and to attempt to comprehend. Most of the earth may bear the marks of human activities, but the Grand Canyon was not made by hands, and is beyond human powers of description. Past generations with their plans have come and gone here. They have found the Grand Canyon a barrier, a challenge, a prison, a grave, a scientific textbook and a religious shrine. They have left it much as it was. The Grand Canyon, which represents the earth's long past, belongs to the earth, and to the future generations who come to dwell, even briefly, in the house of stone and light.

1. S 109, 7-12-51, 65 Stat. 118, 82nd Congress.
2. R. D. Butcher, "At Grand Canyon You Can Leave the Driving to Them," *National Parks and Conservation Magazine* 49(May 1975):4-5. See also "Around Grand Canyon by Bus," *Sunset* 152(April 1974):57.
3. Public Law 93-620, 93rd Congress, S 1296, 1-3-75, 88 Stat. 2089-94, Sec. 10 (b) (7). See also "Indians and the Canyon," *Time* 104(August 12, 1974):65.
4. *Ibid.*, Sec. 2. See also I. R. Webster, "Arizona's Lost Hundred: Proposed Expansion of the Park," *National Parks and Conservation Magazine* 48(March 1974):4-8.
5. U. S. Department of the Interior, National Park Service, *Draft Environmental Statement DES 76-28: Proposed Wilderness Classification for Grand Canyon National Park*, 1976, I-1,3.
6. U. S. Department of the Interior, National Park Service, Grand Canyon National Park, *Superintendent's Monthly Reports*, 1938-1967. Hereinafter referred to as *Monthly Reports.* Bound annually and accessioned in Grand Canyon National Park Library. July, 1944.
7. *Monthly Reports*, July, 1956. See also Mary H. Cadwalader, "Air Mystery is Solved," *Life* 42(April 29, 1957):151-64; and "A Perilous Searching Operation," *Life* 41(July 16, 1956):19-25.
8. Articles by J. Harvey Butchart: "Backpacking on the Colorado," *Appalachia*, n.s., 26(December 1960):176-82; "Backpacking Grand Canyon Trails," *Summit* 10(June 1964):12-15,18; "The Lower Gorge of the Little Colorado," *Arizona Highways* 41(September 1965):34-42; "Grand Canyon's Remote Upper Corner," *Summit* 14(March 1968):23-28; "Wotan's Throne," *Summit* 11(September 1965):8-11.
9. Colin Fletcher, *The Man Who Walked Through Time* (New York: Alfred A. Knopf, 1967).
10. Zeke Scher, "Prisoner in Peril," Denver Post, *Empire Magazine* 28(February 20, 1977): 12-17 and cover. See also Ann Sutton and Myron Sutton, "Arizona's Tassel-Eared Clowns," *Arizona Highways* 31(June 1955):38-39.
11. Washington, D.C., *National Park Courier* (December 1971). See also Louis Schellbach, "Grand Canyon: Nature's Story of Creation," *National Geographic Magazine* 107(May 1955):589-629.
12. W. Cone, "Preparing the Park Ranger for His Job: Horace M. Albright Training Center," *Parks and Recreation* 4(December 1969):30-31,34,46.
13. Fred Doidge, personal interview, June 9, 1976. Rev. Doidge has assembled much documentation on Church History at Grand Canyon.
14. Ken Park, "Shrine of the Ages: Proposed Chapel at Scenic Shrine Will Be Place of Worship for All Men," *Arizona Highways* 31(August 1955):8-15.
15. "Bizarre Hotel Proposed for Grand Canyon Rim," *National Parks Magazine* 35(September 1961):16.
16. P. T. Reilly, letter, February 23, 1977.
17. Roderick Nash, "Conservation and the Colorado," in *The Grand Colorado: The Story of a River and its Canyons*, ed. by T. H. Watkins (Palo Alto, California: American West Publishing Co., 1969), pp. 263-67.
18. Anthony Wayne Smith, "Campaign for the Grand Canyon," *National Parks Magazine* 36(April 1962):12-15.
19. Roderick Nash, *Grand Canyon of the Living Colorado* (New York: Ballantine Books, 1970), pp. 99-107. See also Richard Reinhardt, "The Case of the Hard-Nosed Conservationists," *American West* 4(February 1967):52-54,85-92; Francois Leydet, *Time and the River Flowing: Grand Canyon* (San Francisco: Sierra Club, 1964); and John McPhee, *Encounters with the Archdruid* (New York: Ballantine Books, 1971), pp. 135-215.
20. Nash, *Grand Canyon of the Living Colorado*, pp. 132-33.
21. *Ibid.*, pp. 138-39.
22. Roderick Peattie, ed., *The Inverted Mountains: Canyons of the West* (New York: Vanguard Press, 1948), pp. 183-84, 187-207.
23. By Barry M. Goldwater: "An Odyssey of the Green and Colorado," *Arizona Highways* 17(January 1941):7-13,30-37; *Delightful Journey Down the Green and Colorado Rivers* (Tempe, Arizona: Arizona Historical Foundation, 1970).
24. Katie Lee, "Folk Songs of the Colorado River," Folkways Records, Album No. FH 5333. (New York: Folkways Records and Service Corp., 1964).
25. William Belknap, Jr., "Shooting Rapids in Reverse! Jet Boats Climb the Colorado's Torrent through the Grand Canyon," *National Geographic Magazine* 121(April 1962):552-65.
26. Bill Beer, "We Swam the Colorado," *Collier's* 136(August 5, 1955):19-21.
27. R. Roy Johnson, *et. al.*, "Man's Impact on the Colorado River in the Grand Canyon," *National Parks and Conservation Magazine* 51(March 1977):13-16.

The Grand Canyon from Yaki Point. This photo courtesy of David C. Ochsner also appears on the cover.

28. Jerrold G. Widdison, "John Wesley Powell;" David Toll, "The Powell Expedition of the Green and Colorado Rivers;" and "1919—Grand Canyon National Park—1969: A Tribute to the National Park Service;" all in *Arizona Highways* 45(March 1969). See also Buzz Belknap, *Powell Centennial Grand Canyon River Guide* (Salt Lake City: Canyonlands Press, 1969), and Joseph Judge, "Retracing John Wesley Powell's Historic Voyage down the Grand Canyon," *National Geographic Magazine* 135(May 1969):668-713.

29. John Buchanan, "Misery in Shangri-La," photography by Alexander G. Zaphiris, Denver *Post, Empire Magazine* (November 23, 1969):14-19. Dr. Zaphiris has written a perceptive, frank report on the Havasupai that unfortunately has not been published. Many of his observations are contained in this article. See also John I. Griffin, *Today with the Havasupai Indians* (Phoenix: Indian Tribal Series, 1972); Jay Johnston, "Indian Shangri-La of the Grand Canyon," *National Geographic Magazine* 137(March 1970):354-73; Terry Eiler and Lyntha Eiler, "Head Start in the Grand Canyon," *Saturday Review* 55(July 22, 1972):34-37; Stephen Hirst, *Life in a Narrow Place* (New York: David McKay, 1976), pp. vi, 4-12, 206-63; and Henry F. Dobyns and Robert C. Euler, *The Havasupai People* (Phoenix: Indian Tribal Series, 1971), pp. 40-67.

30. Juan Sinyella, "Havasupai Traditions," ed. by J. Donald Hughes, *Southwest Folklore* 1(Spring 1977):50.

31. Henry F. Dobyns and Robert C. Euler, *The Hualapai People* (Phoenix: Indian Tribal Series, 1976), pp. 84-97.

32. Yevgeny Yevtushenko, "Who are You, Grand Canyon?" quoted in *Southern Sierra* (Los Angeles: Sierra Club, May 1976).

33. Douglas W. Schwartz, "A Historical Analysis and Synthesis of Grand Canyon Archaeology," *American Antiquity* 31(April 1966):474-82. See also C. S. Wilder, "Archaeological Survey of the Great Thumb Area, Grand Canyon National Park," *Plateau* 17(October 1944):17-26; Richard A. Thompson, *Prehistoric Settlement in the Grand Canyon National Monument* (Cedar City, Utah: Southern Utah State College, Faculty Research Series, No. 1, 1970); and W. W. Taylor, *The Pueblo Ecology Study: Hail and Farewell and a Brief Survey through the Grand Canyon of the Colorado River* (Flagstaff, Arizona: Museum of Northern Arizona, Bulletin No. 30, 1958).

34. George E. Stuart and Gene S. Stuart, *Discovering Man's Past in the Americas*, 2nd Ed. (Washington, D.C.: National Geographic Society, 1973), pp. 31, 113, 124-27.

35. *Ibid.*, pp. 122-23, and Robert C. Euler, personal interview, June 7, 1976.

FURTHER READING

I. Bibliography and Reference:

Farquhar, Francis P. *The Books of the Colorado River and the Grand Canyon: A Selective Bibliography.* Los Angles: Glen Dawson, 1953.

Granger, Byrd H. *Will C. Barnes' Arizona Place Names.* Tucson: University of Arizona Press, 1960, pp. 135-59

U. S. Department of the Interior, National Park Service. *Report of the Director of the National Park Service to the Secretary of the Interior for the Fiscal Year Ended June 30, 1921, and the Travel Season 1921.* Washington D.C.: Government Printing Office, 1921, pp. 342-47.

II. General:

Corle, Edwin. *Listen, Bright Angel.* New York: Duell, Sloan & Pearce, 1946.

Crampton, C. Gregory. *Land of Living Rock: The Grand Canyon and the High Plateaus: Arizona, Utah, Nevada.* New York: Alfred A. Knopf, 1972.

Hughes, J. Donald. *The Story of Man at Grand Canyon.* Grand Canyon, Arizona: Grand Canyon Natural History Association, Bulletin #14, 1967.

Krutch, Joseph Wood. *Grand Canyon, Today and All Its Yesterdays.* New York: William Sloane Associates, 1958. New edition: *Grand Canyon.* New York: Doubleday, 1962.

Peattie, Roderick, ed. *The Inverted Mountains: Canyons of the West.* New York: Vanguard Press, 1948.

Wallace, Robert. *The Grand Canyon (The American Wilderness).* New York: Time-Life Books, 1972.

Woodbury, Angus M. "A History of Southern Utah and its National Parks." *Utah Historical Quarterly,* (July-October, 1944): 110-223. Revised edition printed separately by the Utah State Historical Society, 1950.

III. The Natural Environment:

Breed, William J., and Evelyn C. Roat, eds. *Geology of the Grand Canyon.* Flagstaff, Arizona: Museum of Northern Arizona and Grand Canyon Natural History Association, 1974.

Hoffmeister, Donald F. *Mammals of Grand Canyon.* Urbana, Illinois: University of Illinois Press, 1971.

Price, L. Greer. *Grand Canyon: The Story Behind the Scenery.* Las Vegas, Nevada: KC Publications, 1991.

Sutton, Ann and Myron Sutton. *The Wilderness World of the Grand Canyon.* New York: J. B. Lippincott, 1970.

U.S. Department of the Interior Geological Survey. *Plan and Profile of Colorado River from Lees Ferry, Arizona, to Black Canyon, Arizona-Nevada, and Virgin River, Nevada.* Washington, D.C.: Government Printing Office, 1924.

IV. American Indians:

A. General

Collier, John. *On the Gleaming Way: Navajos, Eastern Pueblos, Zunis, Hopis, Apaches, and Their Land; and their Meanings to the World.* Denver: Sage Books, 1962.

B. Prehistoric Indians:

Euler, Robert C. "The Canyon Dwellers". *American West,* 4(May 1967):22-27, 67-71.

_____. "Willow Figurines from Arizona." *Natural History,* Vol. 75, No. 3(March 1966): 62-67.

Muench, David and Donald G. Pike. *Anasazi: Ancient People of the Rock.* Palo Alto, California: American West Publishing Company, 1974.

Mule riders by the Colorado River during the early 1900's.

Schwartz, Douglas W. "A Historical Analysis and Synthesis of Grand Canyon Archaeology." *American Antiquity,* 31(April, 1966):469-484.

Wormington, Hannah Marie. *Prehistoric Indians of the Southwest.* Denver: Denver Museum of Natural History, Popular Series No. 7, Third Edition, 1956.

C. Pueblo Indians:

Beaglehole, Ernest. *Notes on Hopi Economic Life.* New Haven: Yale University Publications in Anthropology, No. 15, 1937.

Roediger, Virginia. *Ceremonial Costumes of the Pueblo Indians.* Berkeley: University of California Press, 1961.

Stewart, Guy R. "Conservation in Pueblo Agriculture." *Scientific Monthly,* (1940): 201-20, 329-40.

_____, and Maurice Donnelly. "Soil and Water Economy in the Pueblo Southwest." *Scientific Monthly* 56(1943):31-44, 134-44.

Talayesva, Don. *Sun Chief: The Autobiography of a Hopi Indian.* Ed. by Leo W. Simmons. New Haven, Connecticut: Yale University Press, 1942.

D. Paiutes:

Euler, Robert C. *The Paiute People.* Phoenix, Arizona: Indian Tribal Series, 1972.

E. Navajos:

Gorman, Carl N. "Navajo Vision of Earth and Man." *Indian Historian,* (Winter, 1973): 19-22.

Kluckhohn, Clyde and Dorothea Leighton. *The Navajo.* Cambridge, Massachusetts: Harvard University Press, 1946.

Underhill, Ruth Murray. *The Navajos.* Norman, Oklahoma: University of Oklahoma Press, 1956.

Yazzie, Ethelou, ed. *Navajo History,* Volume 1. Many Farms, Arizona: Navajo Community College Press, 1971.

F. Hualapais:

Dobyns, Henry F. and Robert C. Euler. *The Hualapai People.* Phoenix, Arizona: Indian Tribal Series, 1976.

Kroeber, Alfred Louis, ed. "Walapai Ethnography." *Memoirs of the American Anthropological Association,* 42, Contributions from the Laboratory of Anthropology, I 1935.

United States Senate. United States 74th Congress, 2nd Session, Senate Document 273: *Walapai Papers, Historical Reports, Documents, and Extracts from Publications Relating to the Walapai Indians of Arizona.* Washington, D.C.: Government Printing Office, 1936

G. Havasupais:

Buchanan, John, photography by Alexander G. Zaphiris. "Misery in Shangri-La" *Denver Post, Empire Magazine,* November 23, 1969, pp. 14-19.

Cushing, Frank Hamilton. *The Nation of the Willows.* Atlantic Monthly 50 (September-October 1882):362-74, 541-59. Reprinted, with foreword by Robert C. Euler, Flagstaff, Arizona: Northland Press, 1965.

Dobyns, Henry F. and Robert C. Euler. *The Havasupai People.* Phoenix, Arizona: Indian Tribal Series, 1971.

Hirst, Stephen. *Life in a Narrow Place.* New York: David McKay, 1976.

McKee, Barbara, Edwin D. McKee, and Joyce Herold. *Havasupai Indian Baskets and Their Makers: 1930-1940.* Flagstaff, Arizona: Northland Press, 1974.

Sinyella, Juan. "Havasupai Traditions," ed. by J. Donald Hughes. *Southwest Folklore* 1(Spring 1977):35-52.

For years, Hopi dancers like Jason Quohongva performed nightly at Hopi House. Courtesy of the Michael Harrison Western Research Center

Smithson, Carma Lee. *The Havasupai Woman*. Salt Lake City: University of Utah, Department of Anthropology, Anthropological Papers 38(April 1959).

Smithson, Carma Lee and Robert C. Euler. *Havasupai Religion and Mythology*. Salt Lake City: University of Utah, Anthropological Papers, No. 68, 1964.

Spier, Leslie. *Havasupai Ethnography*. New York: Anthropological Papers of the American Museum of Natural History, Vol. 29, No. 3, 1928.

V. Spanish Explorations:

Bolton, Herbert E. *Coronado on the Turquoise Trail: Knight of Pueblos and Plains*. Albuquerque: University of New Mexico Press, 1949.

Bolton, Herbert E. *Pageant in the Wilderness: The Story of the Escalante Expedition to the Interior Basin, 1776. Including the Diary and Itinerary of Father Escalante Translated and Annotated*. Salt Lake City, Utah: Utah State Historical Society, 1950.

Garces, Francisco. *On the Trail of a Spanish Pioneer: The Diary and Itinerary of Francisco Garces (Missionary Priest)*. 2 Volumes. Tr. and Ed. by Elliott Coues. New York: Francis P. Harper, 1900.

_____, *A Record of Travels in Arizona and California, 1775-1776*. Trans. and ed. by John Galvin. San Francisco: John Howell, 1967.

Hammond, George P. and Agapito Rey, trs. *Narratives of the Coronado Expedition, 1540-42*. Albuquerque: University of New Mexico Press, 1940.

Winship, George Parker. "The Coronado Expedition, 1540-1542." *Fourteenth Annual Report of the Bureau of Ethnology*. Washington: Government Printing Office, 1896, pp. 329-613.

VI. American Explorations:

Darrah, William Culp. *Powell of the Colorado*. Princeton: Princeton University Press, 1951.

Dellenbaugh, Frederick S. *A Canyon Voyage: The Narrative of the Second Powell Expedition down the Green-Colorado River from Wyoming, and the Explorations on Land, in the Years 1871 and 1872*. New Haven: Yale University Press, 1926.

Dutton, Clarence E. *Tertiary History of the Grand Canon District, with Atlas*. Washington: Government Printing Office, 1882.

Favour, Alpheus H. *Old Bill Williams: Mountain Man*. Norman: University of Oklahoma Press, 1962.

Hillers, Jack. *"Photographed All the Best Scenery": Jack Hillers' Diary of the Powell Expeditions, 1871-1875*, ed. by Don D. Fowler. Salt Lake City, Utah: University of Utah Press, 1972.

Horan, James D. *Timothy O'Sullivan, America's Forgotten Photographer*. New York: Bonanza Books, 1966.

Ives, Joseph Christmas. *Report upon the Colorado River of the West: Explored in 1857 and 1858*. Washington: Government Printing Office, 1861.

Pattie, James Ohio. *The Personal Narrative of James O. Pattie*, the 1831 Edition Unabridged, ed. by William H. Goetzmann. Philadelphia: J. B. Lippincott, 1962.

Powell, John Wesley. *Exploration of the Colorado River of the West and its Tributaries*. Washington: Government Printing Office, 1875.

Powell, W. Clement. "Journal of W. C. Powell, April 21, 1871-December 7, 1872." *Utah Historical Quarterly*, 16-17 (1948-1949), 253-478.

Reilly, P. T. "How Deadly is Big Red?" *Utah Historical Quarterly* 37(Spring 1969): 244-60.

Stanton, Robert Brewster. *Colorado River Controversies*, edited by James M. Chalfant. New York: Dodd, Mead & Co., 1932.

Powell with Tau-Gu, chief of the Paiutes.

Stegner, Wallace. *Beyond the Hundredth Meridian: John Wesley Powell and the Second Opening of the West.* Boston: Houghton Mifflin Co., 1953.

_____, *Clarence Edward Dutton, an Appraisal.* Salt Lake City: University of Utah Press, 1936.

Thompson, Almon Harris. "Diary of Almon Harris Thompson, Geographer, Explorations of the Colorado River of the West and Its Tributaries, 1871-1875." Gregory, Herbert E., ed. *Utah Historical Quarterly,* 7(January-July, 1939):3-138.

Weinstein, Robert A. and Roger Olmsted. "Image Makers of the Colorado Canyons." *The American West* 4(May 1967):28-39.

Wheeler, George M. *Report upon United States Geographical Surveys West of the One Hundredth Meridian...I: Geographical Report,* Washington, D.C.: Government Printing Office, 1889.

Wilkins, Thurman. *Thomas Moran: Artist of the Mountains.* Norman, Oklahoma: University of Oklahoma Press, 1966.

Woodward, Arthur. *Feud on the Colorado.* Los Angeles: Westernlore Press, 1955.

VII. The Frontier:

Bass, William G. *The Grand Canyon in Poem and Picture.* Wickenburg, Arizona: William G. Bass, n. d. (c. 1975?)

Brooks, Juanita. *John Doyle Lee: Zealot–Pioneer Builder–Scapegoat.* Glendale, California: Arthur H. Clark, 1962.

Burroughs, John. "The Divine Abyss," in *The Writings of John Burroughs,* Vol. 14, *Time and Change,* pp. 39-70. Boston: Houghton Mifflin Company, 1912.

Chapman, H. H. "Mining Claims in the Grand Canyon." *American Forestry* 23(April 1917):225-27.

Garrison, Lemuel A. ("Lon"). "John Hance: Guide, Trail Builder, Miner and Windjammer of the Grand Canyon." *Arizona Highways* 25(June, 1949):4-11.

Higgins, C. A. *Titan of Chasms, the Grand Canyon of Arizona.* Chicago: Rand McNally, 1913.

James, George Wharton. *The Grand Canyon of Arizona: How to See It.* Boston: Little, Brown, 1910.

_____. *In and Around the Grand Canyon.* Boston: Little, Brown & Company, 1900.

Lockwood, Frank C. *More Arizona Characters.* Tucson: University of Arizona, General Bulletin No. 6, 1943.

Muir, John. "The Grand Cañon of the Colorado." *Century Magazine,* 65(November, 1902):107-116.

Murbarger, Nell. "Trail-Blazer of Grand Canyon." *The Desert Magazine,* 21(October, 1958):5-9.

Nims, Franklin A. *The Photographer and the River, 1889-1890: the Colorado Cañon Diary of Franklin A. Nims with the Brown-Stanton Railroad Survey Expedition,* ed. by Dwight L. Smith. Santa Fe: Stagecoach Press, 1967.

Rusho, W. L. and C. Gregory Crampton. *Desert River Crossing: Historic Lee's Ferry on the Colorado River.* Salt Lake City, Utah: Peregrine Smith, 1975.

Stanton, Robert Brewster. *Down the Colorado.* Edited and with an introduction by Dwight L. Smith. Norman: University of Oklahoma Press, 1965.

Strong, Douglas Hillman. "The Man Who Owned Grand Canyon." *American West,* 6(September, 1969):33-40.

Walker, Dale L. *Death Was the Black Horse: The Story of Rough Rider Buckey O'Neill.* Austin, Texas: Madrona Press, 1975.

The Orphan Mine.

Watson, Editha L. "Tuba City." *Arizona Highways* 27(August 1951):2-7.
Wittick, Thomas. "1883 Expedition to the Grand Canyon: Pioneer Photographer Ben Wittick Views the Marvels of the Colorado." *American West,* 10(March, 1973):38-47.

VIII. Forest Reserve and National Monument:
Babbitt, Bruce. *Color and Light: The Southwest Canvases of Louis Akin.* Flagstaff, Arizona: Northland Press, 1973.
Baker, Pearl. *Trail on the Water.* Boulder, Colorado: Pruett Press, 1970.
Barnes, Will C. "The Bison of House Rock Valley." *Nature Magazine,* 10(October, 1927):216-221.
Easton, Robert and Mackenzie Brown. *Lord of Beasts: The Saga of Buffalo Jones.* Tucson, Arizona: University of Arizona Press, 1961.
Garrison, Lon. "A Camera and a Dream." *Arizona Highways,* 29(January, 1953):30-35.
Grey, Zane. "Roping Lions in the Grand Canyons," in *Tales of Lonely Trails.* New York: Harper & Bros., 1922, pp. 57-168.
Henderson, James David. *"Meals by Fred Harvey,"* a Phenomenon of the American West. Fort Worth: Texas Christian University Press, 1969.
Kolb, Ellsworth L. *Through the Grand Canyon from Wyoming to Mexico.* New York: The MacMillan Company, 1914.
_____, and Emery C. Kolb. "Experiences in the Grand Canyon." *National Geographic Magazine* 26(August, 1914):99-184.
Matthews, John. "The Grand Canyon Caper." *Arizona Highways* 53(August 1977):36-41.
Roosevelt, Theodore. *A Book-lover's Holidays in the Open.* New York: Charles Scribner's Sons, 1916.
Shankland, Robert. *Steve Mather of the National Parks.* New York: Alfred A. Knopf, 1951.
Stone, Julius Frederick. *Canyon Country: The Romance of a Drop of Water and a Grain of Sand.* New York: G. P. Putnam's Sons, 1932.

IX. The National Park: Establishment:
Albright, Horace M. and Frank J. Taylor. *"Oh, Ranger!" A book about the National Parks.* Palo Alto, California: Stanford University Press, 1928.
Belknap, William and Frances Spencer Belknap. *Gunnar Widforss: Painter of Grand Canyon.* Flagstaff, Arizona: Museum of Northern Arizona and Northland Press, 1969.
Birdseye, Claude H. and Raymond C. Moore. "A Boat Voyage Through the Grand Canyon of the Colorado." *Geographical Review* 14(April, 1924):177-96.
Eddy, Clyde. *Down the World's Most Dangerous River.* New York: Frederick A. Stokes, 1929.
Freeman, Lewis R. "Surveying the Grand Canyon of the Colorado." *National Geographic Magazine,* 45(May, 1924):471-530, 547-48.
Grofe, Ferde. "Story of the Grand Canyon Suite." *Arizona Highways* 14(December, 1938):6-9.
Ise, John. *Our National Park Policy: A Critical History.* Baltimore, Maryland: Johns Hopkins Press, 1961.
Priestley, J. B. "Grand Canyon, Notes on an American Journey." *Harper's Magazine* 170 (February-March, 1935):269-276, 399-406.
Smith, Dama Margaret. *I Married a Ranger.* Stanford, California: Stanford University Press, 1930.

Emery Kolb with the camera used to record their historic trip.

Strong, Douglas Hillman. *The Conservationists*. Menlo Park, California: Addison-Wesley, 1971.

Swain, Donald C. *Wilderness Defender, Horace M. Albright and Conservation*. Chicago: University of Chicago Press, 1970.

Tillotson, Miner Raymond. *Grand Canyon Country*. Stanford, California: Stanford University Press, 1929.

X. The National Park: Expansion:

Fletcher, Colin. *The Man Who Walked Through Time*. New York: Alfred A. Knopf, 1967.

McPhee, John. *Encounters with the Archdruid*. New York: Farrar, Strauss and Giroux, 1971.

Leydet, Francois. *Time and the River Flowing: Grand Canyon*. San Francisco: Sierra Club, 1964.

Nash, Roderick, ed. *Grand Canyon of the Living Colorado*. San Francisco: Sierra Club, 1970.

Reinhardt, Richard. "The Case of the Hard-Nosed Conservationists." *The American West*, 4(February, 1967):52-54, 85-92.

Udall, Stewart L. *The Quiet Crisis*. New York: Holt, Rinehart and Winston, 1963.

Superintendents of Grand Canyon National Park

William Harrison Peters, 1919-1920 (Acting)
DeWitt L. Reaburn, 1920-1921
John Roberts White, 1921-1922 (Acting)
Walter Wilson Crosby, 1922-1924
George C. Bolton, 1923 (Acting)
John Ross Eakin, 1924-1927
Miner Raymond Tillotson, 1927-1938
Harold Child Bryant, 1939-1940 (Acting)
James V. Lloyd, 1940 (Acting)
Frank Alvah Kittredge, 1940-1941
Harold Child Bryant, 1941-1954
Preston P. Patraw, 1954-1955
John S. McLaughlin, 1955-1964
Howard B. Stricklin, 1964-1969
Robert R. Lovegren, 1969-1972
Merle E. Stitt, 1972-1980
Richard W. Marks, 1980-1988
John H. Davis, 1989-1991
Robert S. Chandler, 1991-1993
Boyd Evison, 1994
Robert L. Arnberger, 1994-

From Lipan Point. Photo courtesy of David C. Ochsner.

A trail party nears the head of the Bright Angel Trail.

INDEX

A

Abert, John James, 27
Abert squirrel, 27, 93
agave, 9, 14
agriculture, 3, 5, 9-11, 14, 21, 46, 55, 123
airplanes, 52, 99-100, 104-106, 108, 110
airport, 100, 104
Akin, Louis, 78, 80, 82, 126
Alarcón, Hernando de, 17, 20
Alaska, 3
Albright, Horace Marden, 66, 82-83, 85, 126-27
Albright, H. M., Training Center, 111
Aleson, Harry, 114
Alter, J. Cecil, 41
American Indians, see Indians
American Legion, 78
American Museum of Natural History, 78, 82, 93, 100
amphibians, 76, 93
Anasazi, 9-11, 93, 122. See also Pueblo Indians
Andrews, George B., 93, 101
animals, 5, 6, 9, 12, 14, 44, 46-47, 50, 59, 66, 70, 76, 87, 90-91, 93, 110, 114, 118
Anita, 57, 60, 62
antelope, see pronghorn
Anthony, Harold E., 93, 101
anthropologists, 30, 118
Antilia, 17
Antiquities Act, 66, 82
Anza, Juan Bautista de, 21
Apaches, 15, 29, 122; Mescalero, 29
Apache Street, 111
Arabia, Saudi, 96
archaeologists, 9-11, 72, 76, 93, 112, 114, 118, 122-23
Arizona, 3, 9, 14, 23, 25, 27-29, 50, 60, 66, 76, 78, 93, 104, 112, 117, 123-24; Legislature, 60; northern, 29, 43-44, 65, 76, 92, 103; northwestern, 76; place names, 122; population, 43; statehood, 66, 76
Arizona, University of, 92
Arizona Air-Tight Stoves, 54
Arizona Highways, 111
Arizona Lead and Zinc Co., 100
Arizona Public Service Co., 108
Arizona State Game and Fish Commission, 77, 110
Arizona Strip, 76
Arizona Territory, 29, 43, 54, 76; delegate, 88
Armijo, Antonio, 23
Arthur, Chester A., 29-30

art, artists, 6, 10, 28, 36, 38-39, 44, 70, 78-82, 94, 97, 118, 125-26
asbestos, 3, 47, 50, 52
Ashfork, 50, 57, 87
Ashley, William Henry, 25, 27-28, 39
Ashley Falls, 25
Ashurst, Henry Fountain, 47, 66
Ashurst, William, 47
aspen, 5, 94
astronauts, 120
Athapascan languages, 15
Atlantic and Pacific Railroad, 44, 57, 59-60, 62
Aubrey, Francis Xavier, 29
Aubrey Cliffs, 29
Austin, William E., 62-63, 82
automobiles, 3, 53, 55, 70-71, 87, 92, 103, 108, 110
Awatovi, 20
Ayer, Edward Everett, Mr. and Mrs., 48-49

B

Babbit, Bruce, 83, 126
Babbitt, C. J., 68
Babbitt Brothers Trading Co., 70, 97
Babbitt's General Store, 111, 113
backpacking, 108
Bailey, Paul, 41
Bailey, Vernon, 92
Baker, Charles, 31
Baker, Pearl, 126
Baldwin, Percy M., 23
Barnes, Will C., 63, 83, 122, 126
barranca, 37
Bartlett, Katharine, 23
Basketmakers, 9-10
baskets, 9, 14, 123
Bass, Ada Diefendorf, 50, 53
Bass, Edith, 50, 53
Bass, Hazel, 50
Bass, Mabel, 50
Bass, William G., 50, 125
Bass, William Wallace, 50-53, 57, 63, 75, 125
Bass Camp, 50, 53, 62
Bass limestone, 50
Bass Station, 50
Bass Tomb, 53
Bass Trail, 50, 72, 75
Bat Cave, 112
Beaglehole, Ernest, 15, 123
Beal, Merrill D., Jr., 7, 122
Beale, Edward Fitzgerald, 28-29
Beaman, E. O., 36

Beamer, Ben, 47
bear, 99
beaver, 5, 25, 60
Beaver Falls, 107
Beckman, W. C., 47
Beer, William K., 114, 120
Belknap, Buzz, 121
Belknap, Frances Spencer, 101, 126
Belknap, William, 55, 101, 126
Belknap, William, Jr., 120
bells, 70, 78
Berry, John, 54
Berry, Martha Thompson, 54-55
Berry, Peter D., 54-55, 63, 68, 71
Berry, Peter D., Mrs., 54
Berry, Ralph, 54-55
Berry, Ray W., 55, 63
Berry Ranch (Belknap Ranch), 55
Berry Saloon, 54
Best, James S., 47
Betatakin, 11
bicycles, 57
Big Canyon (Cañon), 28-30, 37
bighorn sheep, 5, 9, 33, 35, 91
Big Jim, 52, 55, 77
Big Springs, 43
Bill Williams Mountain, 25, 44
biologists, 59, 93
birds, 5-6, 10, 93, 114
Birdseye, Claude H., 97, 99, 101, 126
Birdseye, R. W., 83
Bishop, Francis M., 36
bison, 25, 77, 126
Black Canyon, 28, 99, 122
Black Skunk Mining Claim, 48
blazingstar, 14
boats, 3, 25, 27-28, 32-38, 44, 47, 59-60, 72, 75, 99-100, 106-107, 112, 114, 118, 120
bobcats, 77
Bolton, George C., 127
Bolton, Herbert E., 23, 124
borax, 85
Bosque Redondo, 29
Boston, 44, 50
Boston Conservatory of Music, 50
botanists, 59, 114
Boucher, Louis D., 53-54, 72
Boucher Canyon, 54
Boulder Canyon Project Act, 99
Boulder Dam, 99-100
Bourke, John Gregory, 30
Bradley, George, 33, 35
Brady, Matthew, 38
Brahma Temple, 39

Breed, William J., 122
Bridal Veil (Havasu) Falls, 47
Bridge Canyon Dam, 112-13. See also Hualapai Dam
bridges: "swinging," 88, 97; Kaibab, 88-90; Navajo (Marble Canyon), 44-45, 87; water pipeline, 110
Bright Angel Camp, 67, 70, 97
Bright Angel Canyon, 75, 87, 110
Bright Angel Creek, 35, 47, 72, 75-77, 87, 91, 97, 99, 114
Bright Angel Hotel, 50, 56-57, 67-68, 70, 72, 82
Bright Angel Lodge, 50, 57, 68, 97, 111
Bright Angel Point, 77, 87, 97
Bright Angel quadrangle, 75
Bright Angel Tavern, 68
Bright Angel Trail, 48, 54, 57-58, 65, 67-68, 70, 72-74, 87-88, 90, 95, 97, 107, 110
Brooklyn Daily Eagle Tour, 92
Brooks, James P., 92, 99
Brooks, Juanita, 125
Brower, David, 113, 127
Brown, n., 53
Brown, Frank Mason, 59, 99
Brown, James S., 43
Brown, Mackenzie, 83, 126
Bryant, Harold Child, 63, 104, 127
Bryce Canyon, 97
Bucareli, Puerto de, 37
Bucareli y Ursua, Antonio Maria, 21
Buchanan, John, 121, 123
Buckskin Mountains, 43
buffaloes, 25, 77, 126
Bufkin, Donald, 82
Buggeln, Martin, 50, 67-68
burros, 6, 46-47, 52-54, 75, 91, 110
Burro Spring, 76
Burroughs, John, 57-58, 63, 95, 125
buses, 97, 103-106
Butchart, J. Harvey, 63, 108, 120
Butcher, R. D., 120
Butler, Howard Russell, 82

C

Cabeza de Vaca, Álvar Núñez, 17, 23
cables, cableways, 44, 52, 70, 76-77, 88, 94, 99, 112, 117
Cable Trail, 76
Cadwalader, Mary H., 120
California, 9, 21-23, 25, 27-29, 31, 59, 72, 76, 85, 117, 124
California, Gulf of, 3, 35, 60
California Institute of Technology, 93
Callville, 30

camels, 28
Cameron, 53, 87
Cameron, Bert, 63, 82
Cameron, Niles, 54, 68
Cameron, Ralph H., 54, 67-68, 88, 90, 125
Cameron Hotel, 68
Camp, Charles L., 39
Campbell, Ian, 82
campfires, 92, 104, 110, 114
campgrounds, 55, 57, 71, 97, 103-104, 108, 110, 114
Camp Mojave, 38
Camp Verde, 50
Canaan Cooperative Stock Co., 43
Canada, 15, 25, 54, 59
Cañonita, 36
Cañon Maid, 44
Canyon Copper Co., 55
Canyon de Chelly, 29
Canyon Diablo, 60
Canyon Shuttle, 104
Cape Royal, 75, 87, 97
Captain Burro, 50, 57
Carbonate Canyon, 100
Cárdenas, García López de, 19-20, 37, 70
Cardenas Hotel, 70
Carnegie Institution, 92
Carson, Christopher "Kit," 25, 29, 39
Casanova, Frank E., 41
Castañeda, Pedro de, 17, 20, 23, 37
Castillo, 17
Cataract Canyon (Colorado River), 25, 27, 59, 72
Cataract Creek, 12, 21, 50. *See also* Havasu Creek
Catholic Church, Roman, 16-23
Catlin, George, 82
cattalo, 77
cattle, 5, 14, 21, 43-44, 70-71, 77, 90, 100
cattlemen, *see* stockmen, grazing
caves, 9-10, 50, 52, 54, 77, 93, 108, 118, 120
cedar, 99
Cedar City, 43
Cedar Ranch, 57
Cedar Ridge, 95
Cemetery, Pioneer, 53, 72, 94, 108, 111
Chaco Canyon, 11
Chakwaina, 23
Chalfant, James M., 41
Chapman, H. H., 125
Chapman, Thomas M., 70-71
Chávez, Angelico, 23

Cheyava Falls, 72, 90
Chicago, 33, 48, 54, 62
China, 39
chipmunks, 93
Chuar Butte, 108
Chuarrumpeak, 35
chuckwalla, 6
churches, 111
Cíbola, 17, 19-20
Civil War, 29, 38, 44, 50
Clear Creek Canyon, 72
Clear Creek Trail, 87, 90
Clemens, n., 72
cliffrose, 14
climate, 3, 5, 11, 43, 59, 118
climbers, 19, 108
Clover, Elzada U., 114
Coal Canyon, 20
Coconino County, 44, 60, 68, 87-88, 90
Coconino Cycling Club, 57
Coconino National Forest, 66
Coconino Plateau, 5, 11
Coconino sandstone, 76
Cody, William "Buffalo Bill," 43
Cogswell, Raymond A., 72
Cohonina, 9, 11
Colburn, J. E., 38
Collier, John, 122
Cologne, 33
Colorado, boat, 44
Colorado, State of, 23, 25, 31, 33, 44, 54, 59, 70
Colorado City, 31
Colorado River, *passim*; bibliography, 122; description, 3; explorations, Spanish, 19-23, America, 25-38, 44, 59-60, 97, 99, 114, 118; illustrations, 19, 26-27, 31, 34, 36-38, 45, 74, 77, 79-80, 89, 99, 115-16, 118, 122, 127; names, 20-21, 23; reclamation projects, 97- 99, 112-14; *see also* river trips, bridges, drownings
Colorado River Basins, Upper and Lower, 97, 112
Colorado River Compact, 44, 97
Colorado River Indian Reservation, 117
Colorado River Storage Project, 112
Colorado Springs, 31
Colter, Mary Elizabeth Jane, 70, 97, 101
Colton, Harold S., 15, 62-63
Columbian Exposition, 54
Columbus Point, 54
concessioners, 66, 97, 103
Cone, W., 120
conservation, conservationists, 11, 57, 65-66, 85, 94, 106, 112-14, 123, 127

copper, 3, 10, 12, 17, 47, 50, 53-55, 62
Coquille, 99
Corle, Edwin, 122
corn, Indian, *see* maize
Coronado, Francisco Vásquez de, 16-17, 19-20, 23, 124
Cortez, Hernando, 17
cotton, 10
cottonwoods, 5, 31, 77
Coues, Elliott, 23, 30, 41, 124
Coupe, James, Mr. and Mrs., 63
Covey, Cyclone, 23
Cowan's Ferry, 50
Coyote Mine, 48
coyotes, 77
Crampton, C. Gregory, 1, 41, 62, 122, 125
Cramton, Louis C., 88
Creer, Leland Hargrave, 62
Crook, George, 29-30
Crookham, George, 32
Crosby, Walter Wilson, 127
Crossing of the Fathers, 22-23
Crozier, S., 47
Crystal Rapid, 72, 114
Cuba, 55, 62
Cushing, Frank Hamilton, 30, 41, 123

D

Daggett, John, 114
Daingerfield, Elliott, 82
dams, 3, 5-6, 28, 53, 97, 99, 106, 112-14
dancers, 10, 12, 14, 46, 70, 123
Darby, 47
Darby, John T., 62
Darrah, William Culp, 41, 124
Davis, Daniel E., 15
Dean, Emma, 32
deer, 5-6, 9, 14, 33, 35, 46, 66, 71, 90, 93
Defiance, 74
DeHaviland bomber, 100
Delaware River, 28
Dellenbaugh, Frederick S., 36, 82, 124
Del Rio, 29, 70
DeMotte, Harvey C., 36
DeMotte Park, 37, 43, 100
Denver, Colorado Canyon, and Pacific Railroad Co., 59
Depression, Great, 87, 90
Desert Culture, 9
Desert View, 19-20, 87-88, 90, 98, 107; Watchtower, 97-98
Deubendorff, Seymour S., 72
Diamond Creek, 14, 28-29, 32, 38, 44, 99

Diamond Creek Hotel, 46
Díaz, Melchior, 20
Diefendorf, Ada, 50
Dineh, 15
Dinosaur National Monument, 112
dinosaurs, 33, 93
Dirty Devil River, 33, 35
Disaster Falls, 33
Dobyns, Henry F., 15, 41, 62, 83, 101, 121, 123
Dockstader, Frederick J., 23
dogs, 9, 77, 93, 99
Doidge, Fred, 120
Domínguez, Francisco Atanasio, 22-23
Dorantes, 17
Douglas fir, 12, 70
Dowling, William, 63
Doyle, Al, 70-71
Doyle, Arthur Conan, 93
Drescher, Arthur B., 101
Dripping Springs, 53-54
Drought, Great, 11
drownings, 27, 33, 44, 54, 59, 92
Dunn, Bill, 33, 35
Dutton, Clarence Edward, 38-39, 41, 75-76, 124-25

E

eagles, 14, 46, 77
Eakin, John Ross, 127
Easton, Robert, 83, 126
East Rim Drive, 87, 97
Echo Park Dam, 112
ecology, ecologists, 1, 5-7, 11, 46-47, 59, 118
Eddy, Clyde, 99, 101, 126
education (National Park Service), 92, 104, 110
Egloffstein, F. W. von, 27-29
Eiler, Lyntha, 121
Eiler, Terry, 121
Eiseman, Fred B., Jr., 15
Eisenhower, Dwight D., 96
elk, 25
El Tovar, 67-70, 72, 77, 87, 92, 103, 111
Emett, James S., 44, 77
Emma Dean, 33, 35-36, 44
Endangered Species, 110
engineers, 59, 85, 94, 100
England, 38
English people, 32-33, 43-44, 85, 96
English language, 77
entrance stations, 103, 110-11
environmentalists, 1, 112-14. *See also* conservationists

Episcopal Church, 117
erosion, 3, 5, 11, 28, 114
Escalante, Silvestre Vélez de, 22-23, 124
Escalante, 115
Esmeralda, 114, 116
Estéban, 17, 23
ethnologists, 30, 32, 100, 118, 122-24
Euler, Robert C., 1, 7, 15, 41, 62, 83, 101, 117-18, 121-23
Evans, Richard T., 75, 82
Evans, Willis, 93
Ewing, Henry P., 46
Explorer, 26, 28
explorers, American, 3, 24-41, 120, 124; Indian, 3, 9; Spanish, 16-23, 124
Explorers' Club, 99

F

Farlee, J. H., 46
Farlee Hotel, 46
Farmer, Malcolm F., 15
farming, 9, 11, 46, 55. *See also* agriculture
Farquhar, Francis P., 41, 122
Favour, Alpheus H., 41, 124
Feisal, Prince, 96
fences, 90
Fennemore, James, 36
Ferguson, Robert, 63
Field Museum, 48
figurines, clay, 9; twig, 6, 9, 118, 122
fireplaces, 70, 97
fires, firefighters, 11, 71, 87, 93, 97, 110, 114
fish, 6, 33, 35, 90-91
Flagstaff, 44, 46, 48-50, 54-55, 57-58, 60, 62-63, 65, 68, 70-71, 77, 82, 87, 90, 105
Flagstaff and Grand Railroad Co., 60
Flaming Gorge Dam, 112
Flavell, George F., 60, 63
Fletcher, Colin, 108, 120, 127
Flint, Timothy, 39
floods, 78, 91, 97, 99, 110, 112
Florida, 17
Folk Songs of the Colorado River, 114
Ford, Gerald R., 107
Ford Tri-motor, 106
Forest Reserve, 64-83
Fort Defiance, 28-29
Fort Leavenworth, 50
Fort Mojave, 38, 46
Fort Mojave Indian School, 46
Fort Sumner, 29

Fort Yuma, 28, 35
fossils, 72, 76, 92-93, 118
Fowler, Don D., 124
France, 52, 57, 95
Franciscans, 17, 20-22
Frankfurt, Germany, 76
Franse, H. G., 101
Frazier, Russell G., 99
Fredericksburg, 33
Fred Harvey, 50, 55, 67, 82, 97, 100, 104, 111, 126
Freeman, Lewis R., 101, 126
Fremont, John Charles, 27, 29, 41
French-Canadians, 25, 54
frog, 14
Frome, Michael, 63
frontier, 3, 25, 36, 38, 42-63, 125-26
Fruita, 41
fruit trees, 70, 77
Fryxell, Fritiof Melvin, 82
Fuchs, James R., 63
fur traders, 25-27. *See also* trappers

G

Gale, Ed I., 63
Galeras, Juan, 19
Galloway, Nathaniel T. "Than," 60, 63, 72, 97, 114
Galvin, John, 23, 124
Game Reserve, 66, 77
game wardens, 71, 77
Garcés, Francisco Tomás Hermenegildo, 21-23, 37, 124
Garden Creek, 94
Garland, Hamlin, 62
Garrison, Lemuel A. "Lon," 62-63, 82, 125-26
Garthe, Edmund C., 101
General Grant National Park, 65
General Jesup, 28
geographers, 35-37
geology, geologists, 3, 7, 28, 32-33, 35-39, 72, 76, 90, 92-93, 110-11, 120, 122, 124
Georgetown Loop, 59
Georgia, 33
Germany, 57, 76
Gettysburg, 33
Ghost Dance, 46
Gila Pueblo, 93
Gila River, 22, 25
Gilbert, Grove Karl, 38-39
Gilbert, Wilfred C., 101
Gilliland, R., 48
Gilmore, Charles W., 92, 101

Giralda, 20, 23
Gladwin, Harold S., Mr. and Mrs., 93
Glen, 99
Glen Canyon, 22, 31
Glen Canyon Dam, 6, 112
Globe, 93
Goetzmann, William H., 41, 124
gold, 6, 17, 27, 46, 50, 53
Golden Crown Mining Co., 111
goldfish, 54
gold rush, 27, 46
Goldwater, Barry M., 106, 114, 120
Goodfellow, Joseph, 31
Goodman, Frank, 33
Goodnight Ranch, 77
Gorman, Carl N., 123
Gourand, Gen., 95
Grand Canyon, *passim.,* as barrier, 3, 17, 19-22, 25, 28, 43, 75-76, 93, 120; descriptions, 3, 6, 19-22, 25, 28, 30-31, 33, 35, 38-39, 52, 57-59, 66, 85, 100; environment, 1-6, 9; name, 21-22, 28, 37-38; place names, 39, 76; as prison, 34-35, 52, 120; as scenery, 6, 21, 28, 30, 66, 103; travel to, 87, 103
Grand Canyon Airlines, 100
Grand Canyon Cattle Co., 44
Grand Canyon Forest Reserve, 60, 62, 66, 77, 126
Grand Canyon Game Reserve, 66, 71, 77
Grand Canyon Inn, 111-12
Grand Canyon Lodge, 97
Grand Canyon Mine, 47
Grand Canyon National Forest, 66
Grand Canyon National Monument, (1908), 66, 76, 78, 126; (1932), 90-91, 99, 104, 107-108, 113
Grand Canyon National Park, *passim,* 53, 65, 67, 85-121, 126-27; creation, 66; dedication, 85, 92; enlargement, 1, 90, 106-107, 118; fiftieth anniversary, 114; travel figures, 87, 103; wilderness study, 107-108
Grand Canyon Natural History Association, 1, 15, 92, 110, 122
Grand Canyon Nature Notes, 92
Grand Canyon Railway Co., 62
Grand Canyon Series, 39
Grand Canyon Stage Line, 58
Grand Canyon Suite, 94, 126
Grand Canyon Trading Post, 111
Grand Canyon Transportation Co., 76
Grand Canyon Village, 50, 53, 62, 67, 70-72, 77-78, 87, 90, 94, 100, 103-105
Grandeur Point, 110
Grand Falls, 28

Grand Gulch Mine, 47
Grand River, 23, 30-31, 33, 72
Grandview, 62, 66, 68, 71, 87
Grandview Cave, 63
Grand View Hotel, 54-55, 63, 68
Grandview Mine, 111. *See* Last Chance Mine
Grandview Monocline, 20
Grandview Point, 47, 54
Grandview Trail, 12, 54
Grand Wash Cliffs, 3, 44, 47, 60, 99, 107
Granger, Byrd H., 63, 122
Granite Gorge, Lower, 99
Grant, Alexander "Zee," 114-15
Grant, Blanche M., 39
grapes, 50, 54
graphite, 54
Gray Mountain, 20
grazing, 43-44, 46, 65-66, 71, 78, 90, 100, 107
Great Basin, 14
Great Canyon, 37
Great Thumb, 107
Greeks, 10
Green River, 23, 25, 30-31, 33, 36, 72, 112, 124
Green River, Utah, 47, 59, 72, 99
Green River, Wyoming, 60, 72-73, 100
Greenland (Walhalla Plateau), 43
Greenland Seep, 87
Gregory, Herbert E., 125
Grey, Zane, 77, 83, 126
Griffin, John I., 121
Grofe, Ferde, 94, 101, 126
Guadalupe Hidalgo, Treaty of, 27
guidebooks, 44, 59
Gulf-to-Pacific Squadron, 100
Guzmán, Nuño de, 17
Gypsum Cave, 93

H

Hackberry, 46
Hague, Donald V., 41
Hakatai Canyon, 52
Hall, Andy, 33, 35
Hall, Edward T., 15, 93, 101
Halvorson, Elling, Inc., 110
Hamblin, Jacob, 30, 35, 41, 44
Hamel, P. W., 38
Hamilton, Ed, 55
Hamilton, Warren, 93
Hamilton, William, 114
Hammond, George P., 124
Hampton, John W., 79
Hance, Frances, 63

Hance, George, 50
Hance, John, 42, 47-50, 65, 95, 125
Hance Mines, 72
Hance Ranch, 50, 54, 57, 62, 67
Hance Rapid, 72
Hance Trail, New, 49, 57, 72; Old, 47, 49
Hansbrough, Peter M., 59
Harden, Clyde, 110
Harding, Warren G., 88
Harper, S. S., 59
Harris, Don, 114
Harrison, Benjamin, 65
Harrison, I. I., 92
Harrison, Michael, Western Research Center, 92, 123
Harvey, Fred. *See* Fred Harvey
Harvey Girls, 111
Hatch, Alton, 99
Hatch, Bus, 99
Hatcher, John, 25
Hattan, Andy, 36
Haury, Emil W., 93, 101
Havasu Canyon, 5, 11-12, 14, 21, 28-30, 46-47, 50, 77, 93, 100, 107-108, 113, 117
Havasu Creek, 21, 50, 53
Havasu Falls, 12, 47, 78, 100
Havasupai Development Enterprise, 117
Havasupai Indian Reservation, 29-30; enlargement, 46, 107
Havasupai Indians, 3, 11-14, 19, 21-22, 28-30, 37, 44, 46-47, 50, 52-53, 55, 57, 66, 68, 77-78, 88-89, 93, 100, 106-107, 114, 117-18, 123-24; painting, 79
Havasupai Point, 50
Havasupai School, 46, 78, 100, 117
Havasupai Tribal Council, 107, 114, 117
Havasupai Use Lands, 107
Havasupai Village, 117
Hawkes Brothers, 54
Hawkins, Billy, 33, 35
hawks, 77
Hay, John, 82
Hayden, Carl, 38, 66, 85, 103
Hayes, Rutherford B., 29
Hearst, William Randolph, 55, 66
helicopters, 108, 110, 117-18, 120
hematite, 11
Henderson, Earl Y., 83
Henderson, James David, 82, 126
Hermit Basin, 53, 55, 70, 87
Hermit Camp, 70
Hermit Canyon, 53, 70
Hermit Creek, 99
Hermit Creek Rapid, 72

Hermit Rim Road, 70, 87
hermits, 48, 53-54
Hermit shale, 76, 92
Hermit's Rest, 70, 107
Hermit Trail, 70
Herold, Joyce, 123
Hichi-hichi, 29
Hickock, James Butler "Wild Bill," 50
Hickock, Lorenzo Butler "Tame Bill,"50
Higgins, C. A., 62, 125
Highland Mary Mine, 55
hikers, 19, 47-49, 108-109
Hillers, John K. "Jack," 36, 41, 124
Hinchliffe, Louise M., 1, 82, 101
Hindu Amphitheater, 39
Hirst, Stephen, 41, 62, 83, 101, 121, 123
historic district, 111
Hoerman, Carl, 94
Hoffman, W. J., 38
Hoffmeister, Donald F., 122
Hogaboom, Winfield C., 70-71
Hogan, Daniel L., 55, 62-63, 111
Holland, 76
Holmes, Burton, 59, 63
Holmes, William Henry, 5, 39-40, 82
Holmstrom, Haldane "Buzz," 99-101
Holy Grail Temple, 53
Hoover, Herbert C., 90
Hoover Dam, 28, 99, 112
Hopi House, 70, 96, 123
Hopi Indians, 10-12, 14, 17, 19-23, 25, 29-30, 36-37, 44, 70, 78, 96-97, 122-23
Hopi Point, 47, 71
Horan, James D., 124
Horn Creek Rapids, 92
horses, 3, 14, 17-18, 20-21, 23, 25, 31-32, 39, 43-44, 47, 50, 52-54, 57-58, 65-66, 70-71, 75, 77, 90, 100, 110, 117
horses, little, 93-94
Horseshoe Mesa, 12, 54
Horsethief Tank, 55
Horsethief Trail, 53
hotels, 46-47, 49-50, 57, 66-68, 70-71, 111-12
Hot Springs National Park, 82
House Rock Valley, 43, 77, 126
Howland, Oramel, 33, 35
Howland, Seneca, 33, 35
Hoyt, T. C., 77
Hualapai Canyon, 46
Hualapai Dam (Bridge Canyon Dam), 112-13
Hualapai Hilltop, 100, 117
Hualapai Indian Reservation, 29, 46, 100, 106

Hualapai Indians, 11, 14, 21-22, 29-30, 46-47, 78, 117-18, 123
Hualapai Public School District, 118
Hualapai Tribal Council, 78, 117-18
Hudson, Ed A., 114, 116
Hughes, J. Donald, 15, 62, 111, 121-23
Hughes, Johnson, 1
Hughes, Vannelia B., 1
Hull, Philip, 49
Hull, William, 49
Hull Park, 55
Hull Ranch, 49
Hummel, J. H., 72
hunting, hunters, 6, 9, 11, 14-15, 33, 43, 49, 66-67, 77
Hyde, Glen R., Mr. and Mrs., 99

I

Ice Age, 93, 118
Illinois Normal University, 33
Illinois River, 32
Illinois State Natural History Society, 32-33
Illinois Wesleyan University, 33
India, 39
Indiana, 50, 85
Indian Gardens, 5, 14, 54, 67-68, 76-77, 87-88, 90, 94, 108, 110
Indian reservations, 78, 106-107. *See also* names of tribes
Indians, American, 3, 5-6, 9-15, 17, 19-21, 25, 29-33, 35, 37, 46-48, 50, 70, 78, 93, 97, 103, 117-18, 120, 122-24; crafts, 68, 70; exploration, 3, 9. Prehistoric, ruins, *see* archaeologists. *See also* names of tribes
Indian trails, 12, 20, 39, 50, 53-54, 68
Inner Canyon, 14, 91
Inner Gorge, 5, 33, 35, 87-88, 90
insects, 114
International Congress of Geologists, 39
interpretation, 92, 104, 107, 110
Iowa, 25
Iran, 96
irrigation, 5, 10, 14, 21, 37, 77, 94, 97, 113
Ise, John, 126
Ives, Joseph Christmas, 26-28, 30, 33, 37-38, 41, 99, 124
Ivins, A. W., 44

J

Jackson, William Henry, 59
Jacob Lake, 30, 47
James, George Wharton, 51, 59, 62-63, 125

Jensen, Altus F., 97
Jesuits, 21
Johnny, 58
Johnson, Frank, 44
Johnson, Fred, 92
Johnson, George Alonzo, 28
Johnson, Jerry, 44
Johnson, Lyndon B., 106, 118
Johnson, Price, 44
Johnson, R. Roy, 114, 120
Johnson, Warren Marshall, 44, 59, 62
Johnson, W. I., 100
Johnston, Jay, 121
Jones, Charles Jesse "Buffalo," 77, 126
Jones, Duncan, 63
Jones, E. D., 100
Jones, S. V., 36
Jotter, Lois, 114
Judd, Neil Merton, 76, 82
Judge, Joseph, 121
Julien, Denis, 25, 27
juniper, 5, 9, 14, 20-21

K

Kachina Lodge, 111
kachinas, 9, 12, 23
Kaibab, 14
Kaibab, Arizona, 97
Kaibab Bridge, 88-90
Kaibab deer herd, 6, 90
Kaibab forest, 43, 90, 110
Kaibab Forest, Arizona, 97
Kaibabits Paiutes, 14, 35, 78
Kaibab Land and Cattle Co., 43-44
Kaibab limestone, 5, 97
Kaibab National Forest, 66, 90, 103, 110
Kaibab Plateau, 5, 14, 30, 36, 44, 47, 77, 113
Kaibab squirrel, 59, 93, 110
Kaibab Trail, 62, 70, 76, 87-90, 97, 107, 109, 110
Kanab, 36, 43-44, 71, 75-76, 87
Kanab Creek, 36, 46-47, 104, 113
Kanabownitz Spring, 87
Kanab Plateau, 47
Kansas, 31, 50
kayak, 114
Kayenta, 10-11
Keithley, Ralph, 63
Kelly, Charles, 41, 62
Kelly, Isabel T., 15
Kendrick Peak, 75
Kenosha, 31
King, John A., 72

Kingman, 29, 46, 78
Kino, Eusebio Francisco, 21
Kittredge, Frank Alvah, 127
Kitty Clyde's Sister, 33
kivas, 10, 97, 111
Kluckhohn, Clyde, 15, 123
Kolb, Ellsworth L., 72-74, 82, 99, 100-101, 126
Kolb, Emery C., 63, 72-74, 82, 97, 99, 101, 114, 126
Kolb Studio, 65, 67, 72, 74, 85, 111
Krishna Shrine, 76
Kroeber, Alfred Louis, 15, 123
Krutch, Joseph Wood, 7, 63, 122

L

ladders, 11, 21, 28, 47, 78
LaGuardia, Fiorello H., 96
Lake Mead, 99, 112, 114
Lake Mead National Recreation Area, 93, 99, 104
Lake Powell, 112
Lange, Arthur L., 15
Lantier, Felix, 47
lasers, 120
Last Chance Mine, 54-55, 111
Latter-day Saints, 27, 30, 35, 43-44, 47, 53, 76
Laudermilk, J. D., 93, 101
Lauzon, Hubert R. "Bert," 72, 93
lava, 90, 118
Lava Falls, 118
lead, 47
Lee, Emma, 44
Lee, John Doyle, 44, 46, 50, 53, 125
Lee, Katie, 114, 120
Lee's Ferry, 3, 30, 35-36, 43-45, 47, 59, 72, 75-76, 87, 97, 106, 112, 114, 122
Leigh, William Robinson, 78-79, 82
Leighton, Dorothea, 15, 123
Lemmon, John Gill, 59, 63
Lents, Inc., 110
Leroux, Antoine, 25, 28
Leve-leve, 29
Lewyn, Lewis, 100
Leydet, Francois, 120, 127
library, 92, 104
life preservers, 59, 99, 114
life zones, 5, 59
limestone, 12, 120
Lincoln, Abraham, 29, 32
Lingenfelter, R. E., 41
Lippincott, Oliver, 70-71
Little, James A., 41
Little Colorado Mining District, 53

Little Colorado River, 7, 12, 20, 28-29, 33, 37, 43, 47, 53, 60, 76, 92, 106, 108, 114
Little Mamie Mine, 55
Little Springs, 57
lizards, 6
Lloyd, James V., 127
Lockwood, Frank C., 62, 125
Locomobile, 71
logging, 48, 107, 110. *See also* sawmill, timber
Lombard, Goode & Co., 62
Lonely Dell, 44
Long (Boucher) Canyon, 54
Long Mesa, 117
Long's Peak, 33
Lookout, The, 70
Loper, Albert "Bert," 72, 114, 126
Los Angeles, 70, 108, 112
Lost Orphan Mine, 55
Lost World, 93
Louisiana Purchase, 22
Lovegren, Robert R., 127
Lucky Strike Mine, 55
Lull, Richard Swann, 76, 82
Lummis, Charles Fletcher, 46, 62
Lund, 77, 97
Lynch, Pat, 48

M

McClure, C. H., 63
McClure, James, 54
MacCurdy, Winifred, 93
McGonigle, P. H., 54
McGregor, John, 15
McKee, Barbara, 123
McKee, Edwin D., 41, 63, 83, 92-93, 101, 123
McKee, Thomas H., Mr. and Mrs., 97
McLaughlin, John S., 127
McLean, Charles, 54
McMillan, T.F., 63
McNutt, Charles, 15
McPhee, John, 120, 127
Maid-of-the-Canyon, 33
Maine, Arizona, 87
maize, 5, 9, 14-15, 50
"Major Powelling," 60
mammals, 92, 122. *See also* animals
Manakaja, 77
Mancos River, 31
maps, 32, 36, 38, 72, 75-76, 97, 120
Marble Canyon, 3, 7, 22, 29, 33, 44, 59, 106, 113
Marble Canyon Bridge (Navajo

Bridge), 87
Marble Canyon Dam, 112-13
Marble Canyon National Monument, 106
March Air Base, 99
Maricopa Point, 55
Mars, 6
Marshall, E. J., 44
Marston, Otis "Dock," 63, 82, 101, 114, 116
Martin, Paul S., 93
Massachusetts Institute of Technology, 76
Mather, Stephen Tyng, 82-83, 85, 94, 97, 126
Mather, William, 32
Mather Campground, 103-104, 108
Mather Point, 85, 103, 110
Matthes, Francois Emile, 72, 75-76, 82, 126
Mattoon, W. R., 71
Meadview, 108
Melgosa, Pablo de, 19
melons, 14, 50, 54
Mendoza, Antonio de, 17, 19, 23
Meriwitica Creek, 14
Merriam, Clinton Hart, 59, 63
Mesa Verde, 11, 31
mesquite, 31
Methodists, 32
Metzger, D. G., 7
Mexican Hat Expeditions, 114
Mexican period, 14, 23, 25, 27
Mexican War, 27
Mexico, 3, 9-10, 17, 22-23, 29, 35, 59, 126
Mexico, Gulf of, 73
Mexico City, 17, 25
Miami University, 59
mice, 93
Miera y Pacheco, Bernardo, 22
Miles, Nelson A., 52
Miller, David, 72
Miller, David E., 41
Millionaire Mine, 48
Milton, John, 35
Milwaukee Public Museum, 76
miners, mines, mining, 6, 10, 44, 46-55, 59-60, 62, 65-66, 72-73, 78, 100, 107, 111-12, 125
mining claims, 47-48, 53-54, 67-68, 78, 88, 90, 106, 111
ministry, 32, 38
Mishongnovi, 11
missionaries, 21-22
Mission 66, 103-104

Mississippi River, 32, 76
Missouri, 54, 60
Moccasin Spring, 78
Moenave, 44
Moenkopi, 20-21, 43
Moenkopi Wash, 14, 20
Mohave County, 46, 76
Mohrland, 54
Mojave Desert, 9
Mojave Indians, 14, 25
Mollhausen, H. B., 28
Monett, Edward Regan, 72, 82
Monterey, 22
Montez, Ramon, 60
moon, 100, 120
Mooney, Daniel W., 47
Mooney, James, 62
Mooney Falls, 47, 78
Moore, Raymond C., 101, 126
Moqui Tanks, 57
Moran, Edward, 38
Moran, Peter, 38
Moran, Thomas, 37-39, 80-82, 125
Moran Point, 19-20, 38
Morgan, Dale L., 39
Mormons, *see* Latter-day Saints
Morrison formation, 33
Moslems, 17
motion pictures, 72, 74, 99, 100, 126
Motor Lodge, 111
mountain goat, 118
mountain lions, 77-78, 90, 126
Mountain Meadows, 44
mountain men, 25. *See* trappers
mountain sheep, *See* bighorn sheep
Mount Rainier, 76
Mount Trumbull, 43, 47
Muav Cave, 93
Muav (Powell) Saddle, 50, 87
Muench, David, 122
Muir, John, 46, 57, 62-63, 95, 125
mules, 23, 47, 50, 52-54, 58, 75-76, 88, 94-96, 100
mule trips, 58, 68, 70, 73-74, 95-97, 122
Munz, P. A., 93, 101
Murbarger, Nell, 63, 125
museums, 92-93, 104, 110
music, musicians, 6, 46, 50, 70, 126
Music Mountain, 47
Mystic Springs, 50

N

Nankoweap, 118
Nankoweap Trail, 39, 53, 90, 108
Naraguts, 44

Narváez, Pánfilo de, 17
Nash, Roderick, 120, 127
national forests, 66, 78, 90
National Historic Register, 111
national monuments, 66
national parks, 6, 57, 65-66, 85, 94, 103, 111, 122, 126-27
National Parks Paintings, First Exhibition of, 82
naturalists, 30, 32, 38, 46, 92-93, 104, 110
nature, balance of, 6, 91
nature walks, 92, 110
Nava-Hopi Road, 92
Navajo, Havasupai chief, 29-30, 46
Navajo Bridge, 44-45, 87
Navajo Falls, 29
Navajo Indian Reservation, 29, 106
Navajo Indians, 9, 11, 14-15, 28-30, 44, 55, 70, 77, 122-23
Navajo Tribal Council, 107
Needles, 72
Nellie Powell, 36,44
Nevada, 9, 46, 87
Nevills, Norman D., 114-15
Nevills Expeditions, 114
Newberry, John Strong, 28, 33, 38
Newberry Library, 22, 48
New Mexico, 9, 15, 20, 22, 25, 29, 70, 78
New Mexico Territory, 27, 29
New Spain, 17, 20-22
newspapers, 49, 93, 110, 113
New York, 31, 50, 55, 81-82, 96
New Zealand, 114
Niehuis, Charles C., 83
Nims, Franklin A., 59, 125
Niza, Marcos de, 17, 23
Noble, Levi F., 76, 82
No-Name, 33
North America, 3, 9, 85
Northeastern Pai, 14
Northern Arizona University, 108
North Rim, 5, 9, 20, 25, 30, 36, 38, 43, 47, 50, 52, 59, 66-67, 71, 75-77, 87-88, 90-91, 93-94, 97, 100, 103, 107-108, 110-11
North Rim, Arizona, 97
North Rim Inn, 97
Norway, 95
Number Seven, 47
Nutter, Preston, 44

O
Ochsner, David C., 12, 19, 33, 109, 116
Ohio, 54, 59
Ohio River, 32

Olav, Crown Prince of Norway, 95
Olmsted, Roger, 41, 125
Olsen, Robert W., Jr., 62
Oñate, Juan de, 20
O'Neill, William Owen "Buckey," 49, 55, 60, 62, 111, 125
O'Neill Butte, 62
On the Trail, 94
Oraibi, 11, 20, 78
Orderville, 43
Oregon, 99
ornithologists, 30
Orphan Lode Mining Claim, 55
Orphan Mine, 47, 55, 111-12, 125
O'Sullivan, Timothy H., 38, 124
overgrazing, 43, 46
Owens, James T. "Uncle Jim," 77-78
owls, 77
oxen, 50

P
Pacific Ocean, 9
Pacific Southwest Water Plan, 113
Pahlavi, Mohammed Reza, 96
Painted Desert, 20, 94
painters, paintings, *see* art, artists
Paiute Indian Reservation, 78
Paiute Indians, 11, 14, 22, 30, 35, 37, 44, 46, 78, 123-24
paleontology, 93. *See also* fossils
Palfrey, Carl F., 30, 41
Palmer, William J., 38, 44
Panthon, 60
Papago Indians, 21
parachutes, 93, 108
Paradise Lost, 35
Paria River, 33, 44, 106-107
Park, Ken, 120
Park Headquarters, 87, 92, 104
Park Naturalist, 92-93, 110
Parry, Chauncey, 97
Parry, Gronway, 97
Parshall, DeWitt, 82
Parsons, Sheldon, 82
Pasadena, 93
Pasture Wash, 87
Pathe-Bray Expedition, 99
Patraw, Preston P., 127
Pattie, James Ohio, 25, 28, 37, 39, 124
Pattie, Sylvester, 25
Peabody, Henry G., 59
peaches, 14, 44, 50, 54, 77
Peach Springs, 28-29, 44, 46, 57, 60, 100, 117-18
Peach Springs Canyon, 29

Peach Springs Wash, 44, 46
Peattie, Roderick, 41, 120, 122
Pendleton, Mark A., 62
Pershing, John J., 57
Peters, Dewitt C., 39, 41
Peters, William Harrison, 85, 127
petroglyphs, 9, 11, 79, 97
Peyraud, Frank C., 82
Phantom Creek, 97
Phantom Ranch, 70, 76-77, 90-92, 97, 108
Philadelphia, 28
photographers, 36, 38, 46, 52, 59, 72-74, 77, 92, 100, 110, 124-26
physicians, 78, 100
Pierce, Harrison, 44
Pierce's Ferry, 30, 44
Pike, Donald G., 122
Pima Indians, 21
Pima Point, 70
Pimería Alta, 21
Pinchot, Gifford, 57, 66
Pine Springs, 47
pinyon pines, 5, 9, 14, 20-21, 55
Pipe Creek, 54, 87
pipeline, water, 94, 110
Pipe Spring, 43
plants, 5-6, 9-10, 14, 47, 59, 76, 90, 92-93, 114, 118
Plateau Point, 100
Pleistocene, 118
Plymouth Rock, 3
Point Imperial, 3, 87
Point Sublime, 10, 47, 87, 108
Ponderosa pines, 14, 110
Popé, 20
Port Orford cedar, 99
pottery, 9-12, 14, 93
Potthast, Edward Henry, 82
Powell, Emma Dean, 32-33
Powell, John Wesley, 6, 24, 30, 32-41, 44, 59-60, 72, 76, 82, 99, 115, 124-25
Powell, Joseph, 32
Powell, Walter, 33
Powell, Walter Clement "Clem," 36, 124
Powell Centennial, 114
Powell Memorial Point, 72, 85, 112, 114
Powell Plateau, 77
Powell Saddle, 50
Powell Saddle Trail, 90
power generation, 70, 78, 94, 97, 108, 113
predators, 66, 71, 90

Prescott, 29, 50, 62
Prescott, William Hickling, 29, 41
Price, Virginia N., 62
Price, William Redwood, 29
Priehs, Tim, 1
Priestly, John Boynton, 85, 101, 126
pronghorns, 9, 46, 91
prospectors, 35, 43-44, 46-48, 52-54, 59, 75, 111
Prospect Valley, 47
Pueblo Indians, 9-11, 15, 17, 20, 47, 70, 76, 93, 122-24
Puerto de Bucareli, 21, 37
pumps, 94, 97, 110
Purdue University, 85

Q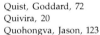
Quebec, 54
Quist, Goddard, 72
Quivira, 20
Quohongva, Jason, 123

R
rabbits, 5, 14, 93
radiocarbon, 9, 118
rafts, 30; inflated, 114-15
railroads, 6, 43-44, 46-47, 50, 55, 59-62, 66-68, 70-71, 78, 87, 94, 102-105, 108, 111; surveys, 38, 59-60
rain, rainfall, 3, 5, 10, 35, 57
Rain Tank, 104
Rampart Cave, 93
ranchers, 43-44, 50, 55
rangers, 85, 87, 90, 92, 94, 103, 108, 110-11, 126
rapids, 3, 25, 28, 31, 33, 35-36, 59-60, 72, 92, 99, 100, 120
Reaburn, DeWitt L., 127
reclamation, 3, 66, 97, 99, 112-14
recycling, 94
Red Butte, 9, 28, 100
Red Canyon Trail, 49
Red Horse, 68
Red River, 21, 25, 112
Redwall limestone, 9
Reilly, P. T., 1, 7, 15, 62, 101, 114, 120, 124
Reinhardt, Richard, 120, 127
religion, 6, 9-10, 39, 46, 111, 120, 124
reptiles, 76, 93
reservoirs, 91, 112-14
Rey, Agapito, 124
Rhine, 70
Richards, Henry C., 59
Richardson, Frank, 36
Richmond, William C., 60, 63

Ridenour, William, 47
Rigg, James P., Jr., 114
Riley, George, 46
Río Colorado, 21
Río Jabesua, 21
Ritschel, William, 82
River Trail, 76, 87, 90
river trips, 3, 25-38, 45-47, 59-60, 72, 93, 97, 99-100, 106-108, 112, 114, 118, 124-27
roads, 6, 71, 78, 87, 100, 103
Roaring Springs, 91, 97, 108
Roaring Springs Canyon, 88
Roat, Evelyn C., 122
Robidoux, Antoine, 25
Robidoux, Michel, 25
Rockefeller, Laura Spelman, Foundation, 92
Rocky Mountain Fur Co., 25
Rocky Mountain National Park, 82
Rocky Mountains, 33
Roediger, Virginia, 123
Rogers, Will, Jr., 111
Rogers' Place, 111
Rome, N.Y., 30
Roosevelt, Theodore "T. R.," 55, 62, 64-66, 77, 82, 95, 126
Roosevelt Camp, 77, 97
Rose, Frances Hance, 63
Rough Riders, 55, 62, 125
Rough Rim, 37
Rowe, Sanford H., 55, 57
Rowe Well, 55, 87
Rugh, Charles, 100
Rusho, W. L., 62, 101, 125
Russell, Charles S., 72
Russians, 118, 120
Russo, John P., 101
Rust, David D., 76-77, 83
Rust's Camp, 76, 97
Ryan, 47

S

Saddle Mountain, 110
St. George, 46; Temple, 43
St. Vrain, Ceran, 25
saloons, 50, 54
salt, 3, 12, 14, 20
Salt Creek, 87
Salt Lake City, 35, 71, 76
Salt River, 25
Salt Trail, 12, 20
San Andreas Fault, 76
San Carlos (Apache) Reservation, 50
San Diego, 59

sandstone, 31, 35, 70
Sandzen, Birger, 82
San Francisco, 21, 85
San Francisco Peaks, 44, 59, 71, 75
Sanger, Arthur Randall, 72, 82
San Juan Hill, 62
San Juan River, 31-32
San Luis Valley, 31
Santa Fe, 22-23
Santa Fe and Grand Canyon Railway Co., 62
Santa Fe Railroad, 53, 62, 67-68, 83, 94, 104-105, 108; land claims, 46, 78, 118; station, 67, 76, 111
Santa Maria Spring, 70
Santa Monica, 117
San Xavier del Bac, 21-22
Saunders, B. F., 44
Saussure, Raymond de, 15
sawmills, 43-44, 48, 50
Schellbach, Louis, 110, 120
Schenk, Edward T., 93
Scher, Zeke, 120
schools: Grand Canyon, 53, 100, 110; Havasupai, 46, 78, 100, 117; Hualapai, 46, 118; superintendent, 60
Schroeder, Albert H., 15
Schuchert, Charles, 76, 82
Schwartz, Douglas W., 15, 82-83, 101, 118, 121, 123
science, scientists, 32, 36, 38-41, 44, 59, 66, 72, 76, 87, 118, 120
Scottish, 33
Scott Ranch, 50
Searchlight, 87
Seargeant, Helen Humphreys, 62
Searle, R. O., 100
Seattle, 110
Seegmiller, Dan, 43
sele, 14
Sentinel Point, 72
Separation Rapid, 35, 99, 112
Sequoia National Park, 65
settlers, 43, 47, 50, 53, 65
Seville, 20
Shah of Iran, 96
shale, 35
Shankland, Robert, 82, 101, 126
Sharp, Louis H., 94
sheep, 5, 43, 54, 90
sheep, mountain, see bighorn sheep
Shelford, Victor E., 7
Sherbrooke, 54
sheriffs, 54, 60
Sherman, William Tecumseh, 33

Sherum, 29, 46
Shetland ponies, 94
Shiloh, Battle of, 32-33
Shinumo, 118
Shinumo Creek, 50
Shinumo quadrangle, 75-76
Shiva Temple, 39, 93
Shivwits, 14
Shoshonean languages, 14
Shrine of the Ages, 111
Sierra Club, 106, 113-14
silt, 3, 112
silver, 17, 47
Silver Bell Trail, 54
Silverton, 31
Simmons, Leo W., 15, 123
Sinyella, 100
Sinyella, Juan, 15, 121, 123
Sipapu, 12
Sistine Chapel, 114
Sitgreaves, Lorenzo, 28-29, 41
ski patrols, 108
sloths, ground, 93
smelters, 47, 55
Smith, Anthony Wayne, 120
Smith, Dama Margaret, 126
Smith, Dwight L., 62, 125
Smith, Jedediah, 25
Smithson, Carma Lee, 124
Smithsonian Institution, 33
Smoot, Reed, 66
Smythe, Donald, 63
snake dance, 10
snow, snowfall, 5, 25, 39, 49, 97, 107
snow-cats, 107-108
soldiers, 17, 19-20, 27-32, 36, 38, 57, 62, 95, 100, 103
Solomon Temple, 76
Sotomayor, Pedro de, 17
South Rim, 5, 9, 11, 14, 20, 25, 27, 43, 47, 50, 67, 72, 85, 87-88, 90-91, 93-94, 97, 99-100, 107, 111
Southwest Museum, 14, 78
Space Age, 120
Spanish, 3, 10, 14-23, 25, 37, 120, 124
Spanish-American War, 55
Spanish Trail, 23, 30
speed limits, 87
Spencer, Charles, 47
Spencer Canyon, 14, 29
Spier, Leslie, 15, 100-101, 124
springs, 12, 68, 77, 108
squash, 9, 14
squirrels, tassel-eared, 93, 110
stagecoaches, 44, 50, 57-58, 62, 67-68

stamps, postage, 6, 114
Standard Oil Co., 85
Stanton, Robert Brewster, 41, 47, 59-60, 62-63, 124-25
Stanton's Cave, 118
steamboats, 28
Stegner, Wallace, 41, 125
Stejneger, Leonhard, 63
Steward, John F., 36
Stewart, Guy R., 123
Stewart, Levi, 43
Stitt, Merle E., 127
Stock, Chester, 93
Stockholm, 94
stockmen, 44, 65, 70-71
Stone, Julius Frederick, 72, 82, 126
Stone boats, 97, 114
Story of Man at Grand Canyon, The, 1, 122
Stricklin, Howard B., 127
Strole, George, 31
Strong, Douglas Hillman, 82, 101, 125, 127
Stuart, Gene S., 121
Stuart, George E., 121
study collections, 92, 104, 110
Sturdevant, Glen E., 52, 63, 92
Sukwatama, 29
Sumner, Jack, 33, 35
sunrise, 94
sunset, 94, 110
Supai, see Havasupai
Supai Post Office, 77, 117
Superintendent, 85, 94, 100, 104, 127
Superintendent's Residence, 111
Sutton, Ann, 120, 122
Sutton, Myron, 120, 122
Swain, Donald C., 101, 127
Swaskagame, Sam, 78
Sweden, 94
Sweet Corn, 14
swimmers, 114
swimming pool 94
Swiss chateaux, 68
Switzerland, 76

T

Tadje, A. J., 72
Taft, William Howard, 95
Talayesva, Don, 15, 123
Tanner, Seth B., 53
Tanner's Crossing, 53
Tanner Trail, 12, 47, 53, 90
Taos, 78
Tapeats Creek, 90
Tau-Gu, 124

Taylor, Frank J., 83, 126
Taylor, W. W., 121
teachers, 36, 46, 53
Temple Butte, 108
Tennessee, 50
Texas, 29, 77
Thomas, R. V., 100
Thomas Flyer, 71
Thompson, Almon Harris, 36, 38, 125
Thompson, Martha, 54
Thompson, Richard A., 121
Thunderbird Lodge, 111
Thunder River Trail, 90
Thurber, J. Wilbur, 50, 57-58, 67, 82
Thwaites, Reuben Gold, 39
Tillotson, Dean, 85
Tillotson, Miner Raymond, 85, 93-94, 101, 127
timber, 5, 43, 46, 66
Timpanogotzis, 22
Tinker, Ben H., 63
Tinker, George H., 63
Tipoff, The, 87-88
Tisón River, 20
Titiev, Mischa, 15
Toledo Eight-horse, 70-71
Toll, David, 121
Tombstone, 60
Tonto Platform, 5, 54, 70, 76, 87, 91, 100, 108, 110
Tonto Trail, 90
Topocoba Canyon, 78
Topocoba Hilltop, 20
topographers, 33, 38, 72, 75-76, 118, 120
Toroweap, 90, 111
Totonteac, 17
Tourist, Arizona, 50
tourists, 44, 47, 49-60, 65, 67-68, 70-71, 97, 117. See also visitors
Tovar, Pedro de, 19, 70
Tower of Babel, 39
Tower of Seville, 29, 23
trails, 39, 47, 50, 54, 67-68, 70, 76, 87-88, 108. See also Indian trails
Training Center, 111
Tram Camp, 87
Trans-World Airlines, 108, 111
trappers, 5, 23, 25-28, 30, 33, 43, 60, 124
travertine, 12, 78
Trinidad, Colorado, 32, 70
trout, 91
Truman, Harry S, 103
Tuba City, 43, 53, 112, 126
Tucano, 17
Tucson, 21, 29

turkeys, 6, 9, 110
Turner, J. M. W., 38
turquoise, 10, 17
Turtle Head, 100
Tusayan, pueblos, 17, 19-20; ruin/museum, 11, 93, 111
T. W. A. Services, 111
twig figurines, see figurines
Tyrol, 21

U

Udall, Stewart L., 106, 127
Ufer, Walter, 80, 82
Uinkarets, 14
Uinta, 41
Uinta Indian Agency, 33
Uinta River, 25
Underhill, Ruth Murray, 15, 123
Union Pacific Railroad, 33, 97
United Airlines, 108
United Gold and Platinum Co., 78
United Order, 43
United States, 3, 11, 22, 27, 29, 43, 65, 85, 94; Army, 29, 31-33, 50, 99; Army Air Corps, 108; Army Air Service, 99-100; Army Corps of Engineers, 30; Bureau of American Ethnology, 30, 37, 76; Bureau of the Census, 43; Bureau of Indian Affairs, 46, 77, 100, 117; Bureau of Land Management, 104; Bureau of Reclamation, 112-14; Capitol, 38; Centennial, 44; citizenship, 94, 100; Civil Service Examination, 111; Civilian Conservation Corps, 90-91; Community Action Program, 117; Congress, 23, 33, 35, 38, 62, 66, 72, 76, 78, 85, 90, 106, 110, 112, 114; Congressional Record, 88;
United States (cont.):
Corps of Topographic Engineers, 27; department of Agriculture, 66, 90; Department of the Interior, 76, 85, 88, 90, 122; Division of Forestry, 66; Federal Power Commission, 114; Forest Service, 57, 66, 68, 70-72, 77, 85, 88, 104, 110; General Land Office, 65; Geographical Surveys, 38; Geological Survey, 35, 37-39, 72, 76, 97, 111, 120, 122; Head Start, 117; House of Representatives, 66, 78; Indian Claims Commission, 117-18; Internal Revenue Service, 114; National Endowment for the arts, 118; National Museum, 92, National Park Service, 7, 55, 66, 68, 85, 87-88, 90, 92-122, 127; Office of Economic Opportunity, 117; Post Office, 6, 44, 50, 52, 68, 97, 111, 114, 117; Public Health Service, 117; Secretary of

Agriculture, 77; Secretary of the Interior, 66, 72, 114; Senate, 66, 76, 78, 88, 123; Supreme Court, 66, 68, 82, 88; War Department, 28
Unkar Delta, 118
uranium, 3, 111-12
U.S. Rubber Co., 71
Utah, 9, 23, 29, 60, 72, 76-77, 87; and Arizona Strip, 76; southern, 29-30, 43, 92, 122
Utah Parks Co., 87, 97, 111
Utah Symphony, 118
Utah Territory, 27, 76
Utah Valley, 22, 27

V

Valley National Bank, 111
vanadium, 3
Van Dyke, Henry, 7
Vargas, Diego de, 20
Vasey's Paradise, 15
vegetables, 54, 70
Verkamp, John G., 70
Verkamp, Margaret M., 62-63, 82
Verkamp Studio, 70, 111
Vicksburg, 33
Virgin River, 25, 27, 35, 122
Vishnu quadrangle, 75
Vishnu Temple, 5, 39, 76
Visitor Center, 104, 110-11, 118
visitors, 1, 6, 44, 46, 65, 87, 90, 95-96, 103-104, 110; foreign, 103, 105, 120. See also tourists
volcanoes, 71, 90
V. T. Park, 43, 100
Vulcan's Throne, 90
vulture, giant, 118

W

Waesche, Hugh H., 63, 83
wagons, 43, 50, 57, 77-78
Walapai, see Hualapai
Walapai Indian Agency, 46
Walcott, Charles Doolittle, 39, 41
Walhalla Glades, 15, 93
Walhalla Plateau, 43, 76
Walker, Dale L., 125
Walker, Don D., 62
Wallace, Robert, 122
Walpi, 17
Wampler, Joseph, 62, 83
Washburn, Bradford, 120
Washington, D.C., 53, 60
Watchtower, 97-98
water, 3, 5, 7, 9, 11, 14, 20, 25, 33, 35, 37, 44, 46-47, 49-50, 57, 70-71, 75, 78,

90-91, 100, 108, 123
waterfalls, 32, 47
Water Reclamation Plant, 94, 111
water supply, Grand Canyon, 94, 97, 108
Watkins, T. H., 39, 120
Watkins, Trevor, 15
Watson, Editha L., 126
Wauba Yuma, 29
Weaver, Pauline, 25, 28
Webster, I. R., 120
Weinstein, Robert A., 41, 125
Welsh, 32
Wesley, John, 32
West, George A., 76
Western Gold and Uranium Co., 112
Western Opera Theatre, 118
West Rim Drive, 48, 70, 87, 104
Wheat, Joe Ben, 15
Wheeler, George M., 38, 41, 125
Whipple, Amiel Weeks, 28
White, David, 92, 101
White, Georgia, 114-15
White, James B., 30-32
White, James L., 28
White, John Roberts, 127
White Creek, 50
White River, 33
White Trail, 50
Whiting, Alfred F., 15, 62
Whittlesey, Charles F., 68
Wickenburg, 53
Widdison, Jerrold G., 121
Widforss, Gunnar Mauritz, 79, 94, 126
Wikatata, 37
Wilder, C. S., 121
wilderness, 3, 7, 50, 65, 107-108, 122
wildlife, see animals
Wilkins, Thurman, 41, 125
Willcox, E. S., 57
Williams, 25, 38, 44, 46, 50, 57, 60, 62, 72, 77, 87, 103
Williams, F. Ballard, 82
Williams, William Sherley "Old Bill," 25, 124
willows, 30, 122-23
Wilson, Robert W., 93, 101
Wilson, Woodrow, 66
Windsor, Duke and Duchess of, 96
Winship, George Parker, 23, 124
Winsor Castle Stock Growing Co., 43
Wisconsin, 31-32
Wittick, Ben, 46, 126
Wittick, Thomas, 62, 126
Wolfskill, William, 25

Woodbury, Angus M., 62, 82-83, 101, 122
Woodbury, Richard Benjamin, 15
Woods, G. K., 63
Woodward, Arthur, 41, 125
Woolley, E. B., "Hum," 72
Woolley, E. D. "Uncle Dee," 71, 76-77
Woolley, E. G., Jr., 71
Worcester, N. Y., 50
World Wars, I, 71, 78, 100; II, 103-104, 110
Wormington, Hannah Marie, 15, 123
Wotan's Throne, 76, 93
Wovoka, 46
Wright, J. Frank, 114
writers, 6, 36, 46, 57-60, 77
Wupatki, 28
Wylie, W. W., 97
Wylie Way Camp, 97
Wyoming, 23, 25, 33, 35-36, 72, 126

Y

Yaki Point, 88
Yale University, 76
Yavapai County, 29, 60
Yavapai Indians, 14, 29
Yavapai Lodge, 111
Yavapai Museum, 111
Yavapai Point, 92, 110
Yazzie, Ethelou, 123
Yellowstone, 38, 65, 77, 82, 97
Yevtushenko, Yevgeny, 118, 121
Yosemite, 65, 76, 85, 94
Young, Brigham, 27, 30
Young, Ewing, 25
Young, H. J., 47
Young, John W., 43
Yount, George C., 25
yucca, 9
Yuma, 60, 72
Yuman Indians, 11-12, 14, 20

Z

Zaphiris, Alexander G., 121, 123
Zion National Park, 97
Zuñi Indians, 17, 23, 25, 28, 30, 122